D1476808

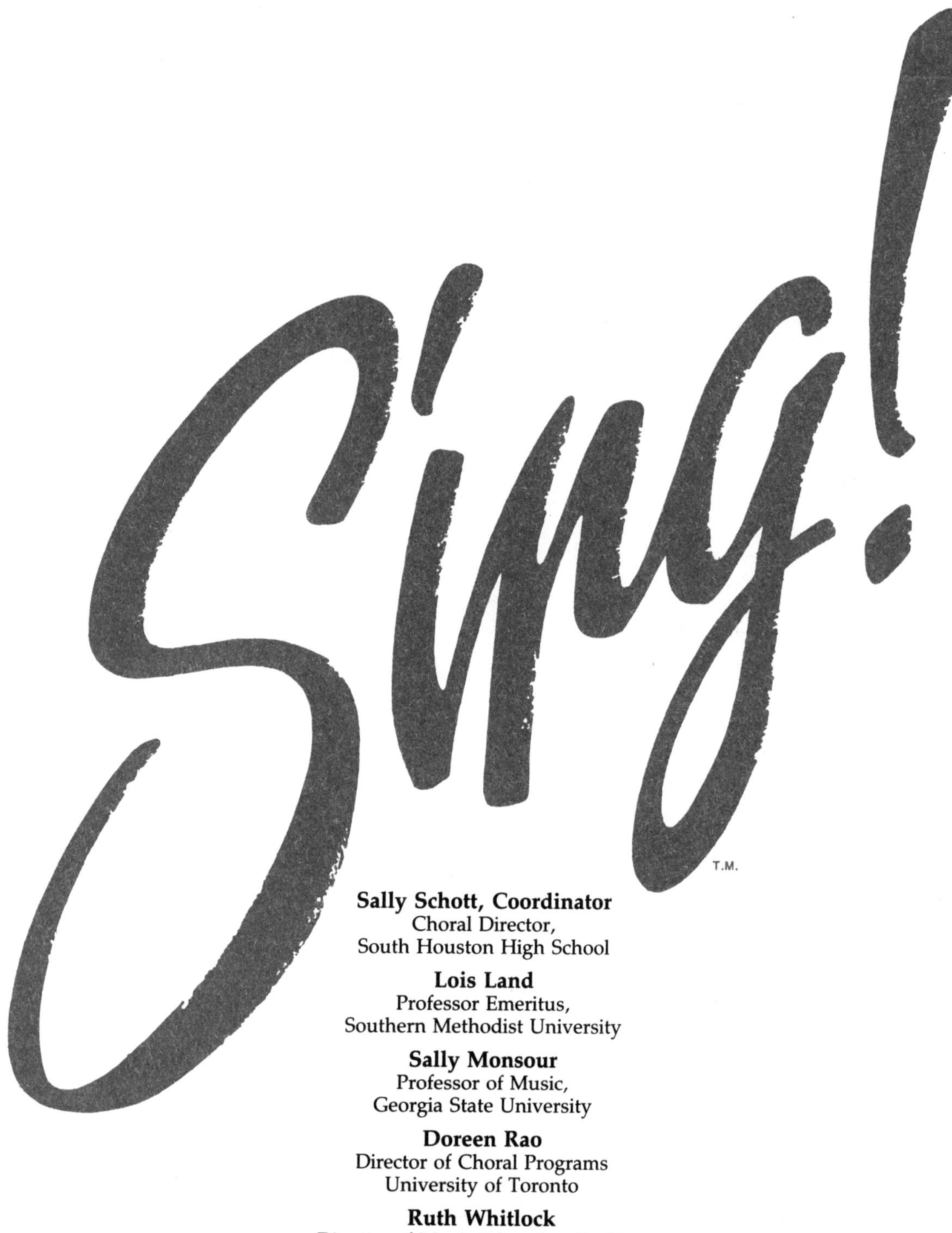

Sally Schott, Coordinator
Choral Director,
South Houston High School

Lois Land
Professor Emeritus,
Southern Methodist University

Sally Monsour
Professor of Music,
Georgia State University

Doreen Rao
Director of Choral Programs
University of Toronto

Ruth Whitlock
Director of Music Education Studies,
Texas Christian University

Edited by Charles Fowler

HINSHAW MUSIC TEXTBOOK DIVISION
Houston, Texas 77257

ISBN 0-937276-08-1

Special Contributors/Consultants
Roberta Marchese
Ray Robinson
John Rutter

Acknowledgements/Photographic Credits

Photographs, painting, and musical examples are reproduced with permission from the following sources: ALINARI/Art Resource, NY: pp. 336, 324, 333, 344, 351. Art Resource/Photo by Laimute E. Druskis, New York: pg. 354. BILDARCHIV FOTO MARBURG/Art Resource, NY: pp. 346, 342, 362. THE BRIDGEMAN ART LIBRARY/Art Resource, NY: pg. 337. Jim Caldwell, all rights reserved: pp. 368, 372. Culver Pictures: pp. 332, 334, 335, 353, 355, 356, 367. GIRAUDON/Art Resource, NY: pg. 330. Courtesy of Petrina J. Hughes, Bucks, U.K.: pg. 378. Interlocken Photo: pg. 22. Elliott Erwitt/Magnum Photos, Inc.: pg. 365. Ernst Haas/Magnum Photos, Inc.: pg. 377. David Hurn/Magnum Photos, Inc.: pg. 369. Courtesy of The Norman Luboff Choir: pg. 376. The Metropolitan Museum of Art, Fletcher Fund, 1956, all rights reserved: pg. 327. Metropolitan Opera Archives: pg. 357. Movie Star News: pg. 352. Collection, The Museum of Modern Art, New York: Pablo Picasso, THREE MUSICIANS, 1921, oil on canvas, 6′7″ × 7′3¾″. Mrs. Simon Guggenheim Fund: pg. 366. Netherlands Institute for Art History, Private Collection: pg. 358. Courtesy of the Norton Gallery and School of Art, West Palm Beach, FL: pg. 2. SCALA/Art Resource, NY: pp. 326, 340. Stephen C. Sumner: pg. 372. Martha Swope Photography, Inc.: pp. 360, 370. Thomas Jefferson Memorial Foundation: pg. 349. Copyright 1973, Walton Music Corporation, used by permission: pg. 363. Courtesy of Ward-Brodt Music Co., Madison, WI: pp. 378, 379, 380. Courtesy of The Welk Music Group, Nashville, TN: pg. 381.

Translations: Carey Stacy
Photographic Research: Clifford Poole
Music Autography: Helen Jenner

Book Design: Ken Dresser

CONTENTS

DETAILED CONTENTS

PART 1: THE ART OF SINGING 1

PART 2: MASTERING MUSICAL SYMBOLS 21

PART 4: SINGING THROUGH THE AGES 323

Overleaf ▶
"Ruby Green Singing" by American painter
James Chapin, Norton Gallery
and School of Art, West Palm Beach, Florida

PART 1

The Art of Singing

PART 1

The Art of Singing

Humans have been singing since the beginning of recorded history and probably earlier. Unless they are disabled, people are born with a sensibility to sound and with a sense of hearing. They are also born with the ability to feel and to express their emotions. Through your hearing mechanism—your ears—music reaches inside to stimulate your mind and your feelings. If you choose to respond to its stimulus, it will speak to your inner self.

Your capacities to hear and to respond to music can be improved. By studying music and practicing it, you can enhance your ability to understand music and to respond to it. You will expand your ability to grasp its message. That is what this book and this course in choral music is all about.

Singing is a special kind of pleasure. It is fun, but it is also challenging. And the more you learn about it, the more fun—the more rewarding and satisfying—it can be, not only for you but for your audiences.

In learning music, there is no substitute for practice. The exercises in this text should be repeated until they become easy and natural. With careful work and steady effort, you will see your own improvement. Your growing understanding and mastery should give you satisfaction. It has been said that practice is its own reward.

Chapter 1

Your Singing Voice

Singing is a special way of using your voice. It is different from speech, or laughing, or crying, or cheering, or sighing. Singing is a **musical** way of using your voice. When you *speak*, you use breath and words. When you *sing*, you also use breath and words, but you use them in *different* ways.

Actors use the *speaking voice* in at least two ways. In everyday conversation, the actor's voice can sound like anyone else's. On stage, the actor's voice has different qualities. It may sound darker, louder, or stronger. The "stage voice" is a special way of using the speaking voice for dramatic purposes. It carries the ideas of the play across the footlights to the audience.

Your speaking voice is an "everyday way" of communicating thoughts and feelings. Like the actor's stage voice, your *singing voice* is a musical way of creating the ideas of a song and carrying them to an audience. In speaking, you must breathe and form words that represent your thoughts. In singing, breath and words must form the musical ideas of the song—the pitch, the rhythm, the dynamics, and the color. Your *singing voice* sounds differently than your *speaking voice*. Your *singing voice* carries the musical idea from thought to physical expression.

When you speak, you are not always aware that you are breathing, and you may not be consciously aware of how the words sound. But your *singing voice* requires a different kind of breathing and a different use of words. Do you know why? There are two reasons: First, when you sing, the duration or length of the vowel sound is longer than in speaking. Your singing voice requires *more breath* in order to lengthen and sustain the vowel sounds. Second, the quality of your singing voice is louder and stronger than your speaking voice. For this reason, your singing voice requires more **breath**, more **energy**, more **concentration**, **coordination**, and **control**.

Ways of Using Your Voice

Speaking, sighing, crying, groaning, yawning, and yelling are just some of the many different ways you can use your voice. Singing is an enjoyable and artistic way of using it. Everyone has a singing voice, although many people have never learned to use it. In certain cultures, everybody sings (and dances!) from infancy to old age.

In our country, people use their singing voice in numbers of ways. They use it to sing jazz or opera as a solo artist, to sing pop or classical music in a vocal ensemble, or to sing in the folk style of their ethnic group. Listen carefully to some of these different types of vocal qualities and describe what you hear.

Some students can already sing clearly and tunefully because of their family traditions or their training. But most of us learn to use our singing voices in school, where we are taught by music teachers with special knowledge about the voice. It is important to remember that your *singing voice* is a very special instrument. With it, you can **explore** music, **experience** different styles of music, and **express** music to others. Your singing voice is like other kinds of musical instruments. It can bring you pleasure at the same time that it requires regular practice.

Vocalization

Knowing how to produce your singing voice will come from practicing and performing. Always begin practice with a short "warm-up" or *vocalization*. During this preparation or warm-up time, you may exercise alone or with your class to prepare your body and mind for singing.

There are four steps to prepare for singing. Each step is basic to developing healthy singing habits. The steps should be carefully practiced in the suggested order.

(1) Exercise

Exercising your body prepares the voice for singing, just as it helps an athlete prepare for the game. Exercise helps condition the muscles and the mind for singing. Practice the following exercises:

(a) Five long stretches up. Raise the hands high over the head as if reaching for the sky. Pull the entire body upward, pushing up from the toes to the finger tips.

(b) Five long stretches down. Bending over, touch the toes. The head should hang down, and the arms should be loose. The head, neck, and arms should feel loose and heavy. On a count of five, gradually unwind from the lower back keeping the head released down and the arms loose.

1(a)

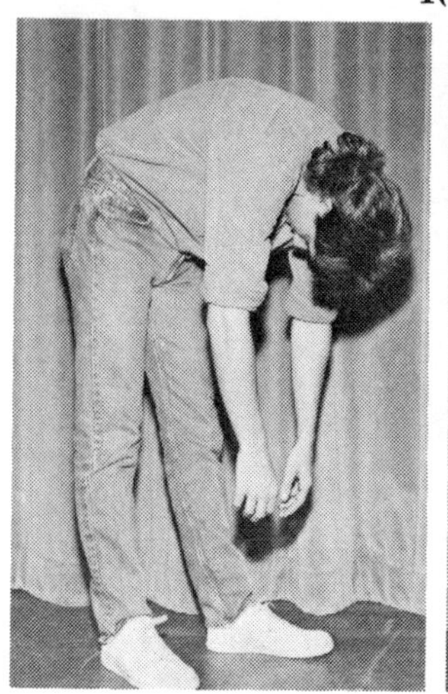

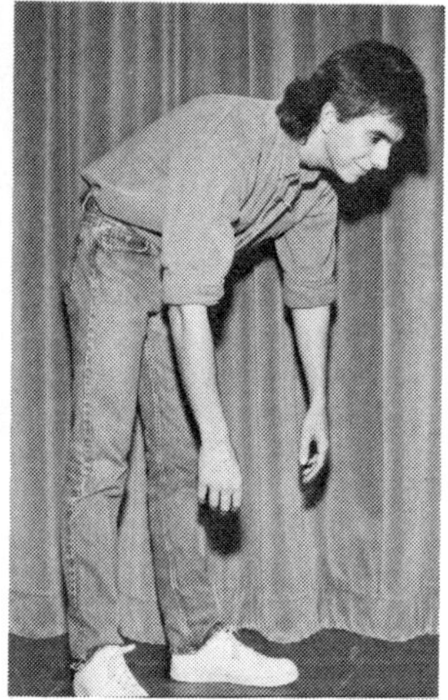

Correct 1(b) *Incorrect*

(c) **Rotate the shoulders forward in a circular motion five times**. Move them all the way around, slowly.

(d) Gently drop the head forward and rotate it in a circular motion to the right three times.

(e) Reverse the direction and rotate the head to the left three times. This exercise will rid you of possible tension in the neck area.

(f) Gently massage the face and jaw with the back of the hands. Do this *slowly*. This exercise will rid you of possible tension in the jaw and tongue.

(g) Rotate the shoulders backward in a circular motion five times. Rotate all the way around, slowly. On the fifth rotation, gently drop the shoulders back and down. This exercise positions the upper body into a singing posture.

1(f)

(2) Posture

Your body is your singing voice. The physical position of the body affects the way you breathe and the way you sound. The ability to produce a healthy singing tone depends on the physical position of the body. The way you look influences the way you sound. It is important to stand when singing. If you are sitting, sit in a standing position at the front edge of the chair with your feet flat and your back straight. Follow these simple rules:

(a) Keep your feet slightly apart. Keep your body facing forward and your weight evenly distributed. Knees may be slightly bent. Avoid a tight or "locked" position in the knees.

Correct

2(a)

Slumped

(b) Keep hands at the side. Do not fold your hands in front or back. Avoid any body tension due to pulling the body unnaturally forward or backward. A mental image of heavy hands will keep your hands hanging at your side.

(c) Keep the upper body high. Chest should be high, shoulders back. Raised shoulders should be avoided, as this will interrupt the air flow and restrict the tone.

2(c)

Correct

Slumped, rounded shoulders

(d) Keep head evenly and naturally aligned with the spinal column. Observe a child's natural head position. Avoid stretching or "reaching" for high notes, as this will interrupt air flow and restrict the tone.

2(d)

Incorrect, jutting jaw, raised shoulders

Good singing posture is the key to proper breathing and healthy tone quality.

(3) Breathing

Breathing is the most important part of healthy singing. Without proper breath management, your singing voice cannot function. When you breathe properly, all the important spaces in the throat open for singing. The result is a rich and *resonant* tone quality. To practice breathing properly, practice the following exercises:

(a) The "cold air sip." Form your lips for an *oo* vowel, as if sipping through a straw. Draw the air in slowly through the *oo* formation. Inhale slowly during the count of three. Exhale slowly over the count of five on a *ts* (hissing) sound. Gradually extend the exhalation over the count of ten.

Ex. 3

(a)

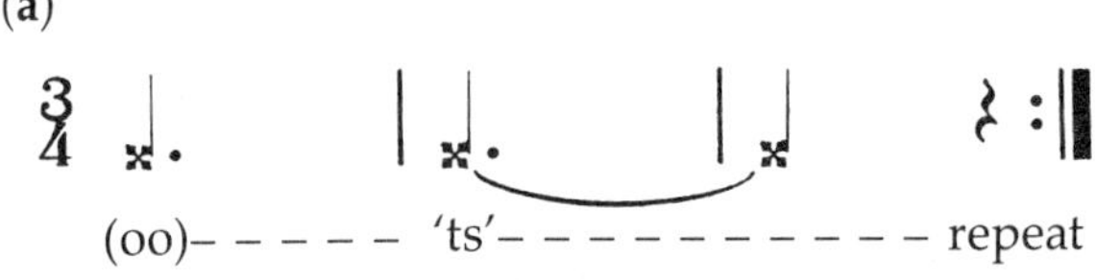

Form lips for an oo vowel

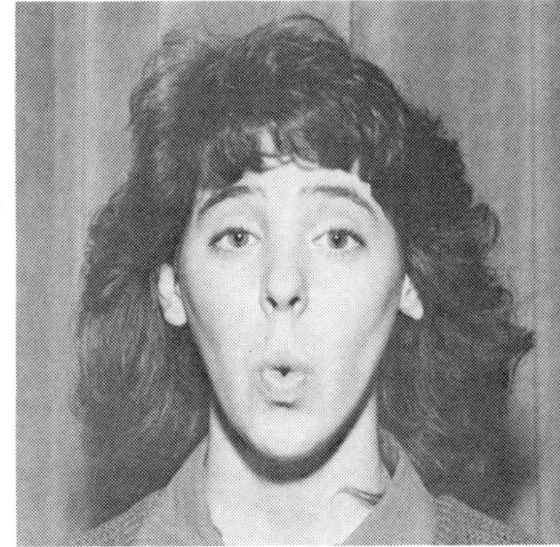

During exhalation, posture is *very* important. Keep shoulders back and upper body high. Your body should not collapse forward during exhalation.

(b) Short rhythmic staccato breathing. Practice the repeated patterns several times. This exercise will gradually strengthen the muscles used in breathing.

Ex. 3

(b)

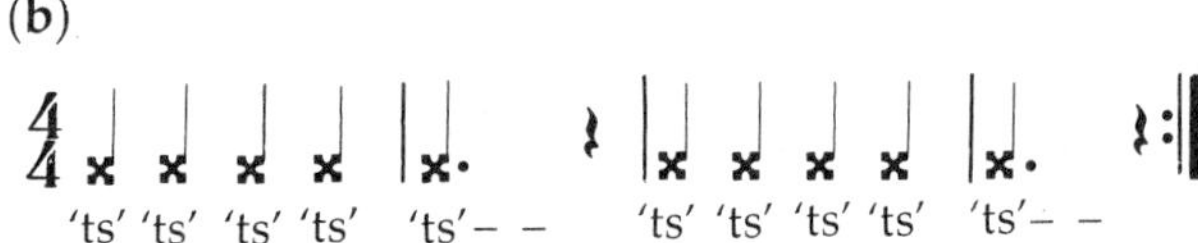

Repeat Exercise 3 (b) at different rates of fast and slow and with various levels of loud and soft.

(c) "Cleansing air breath." Through your nose, inhale all the way using full lung capacity. Release breath completely, ad lib.

(4) Tone

Sounds that are sung are *longer* and *stronger* than sounds that are spoken. Singing tone begins with breath. The vowel lengthens the pitch and colors the tone. Tone can be bright, like the *ee* in "me," or it can be dark, like the *oo* in "too." Choosing vowel colors for music is like choosing paint colors for a canvas. Each piece of music requires different vowel colors, depending on the text and the style of the music.

The proper singing of vowels requires practice. The following exercises will help you to learn how to sing vowels correctly:

(a) Speak the five primary singing vowels. Begin by speaking the vowels slowly, sustaining them without interruption by the diphthong. (A diphthong is a complex vowel sound that occurs in a word like "ride," in which the *ah* vowel continues into an *ee* vowel on the same syllable. The *ay* vowel in the exercise that follows ends in an *ee*. Do not let the *ee* interrupt the *ay*.)

Ex. 4

(a)

IPA Symbol[1]	*Phonetic Sound*	*Word Example*
[i]	*ee*	me
[e]	*ay*	ate
[ɑ]	*ah*	father
[o]	*o*	obey
[u]	*oo*	too

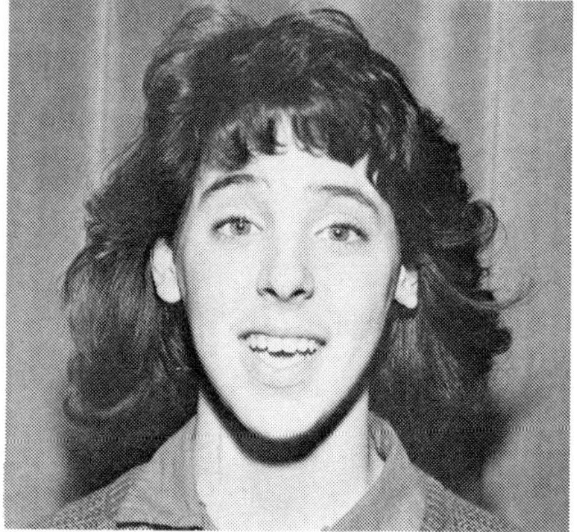

ee

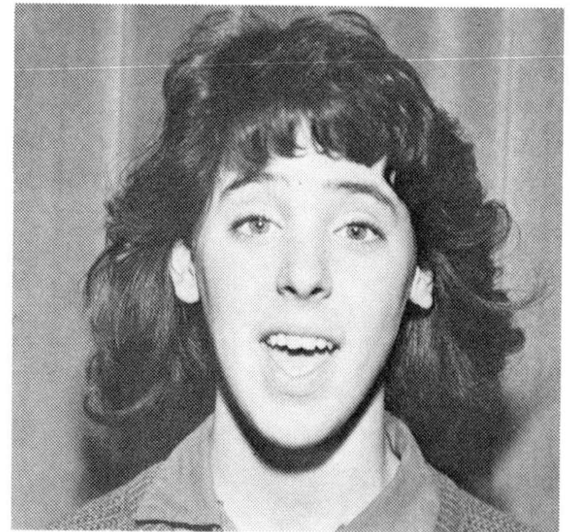

ay

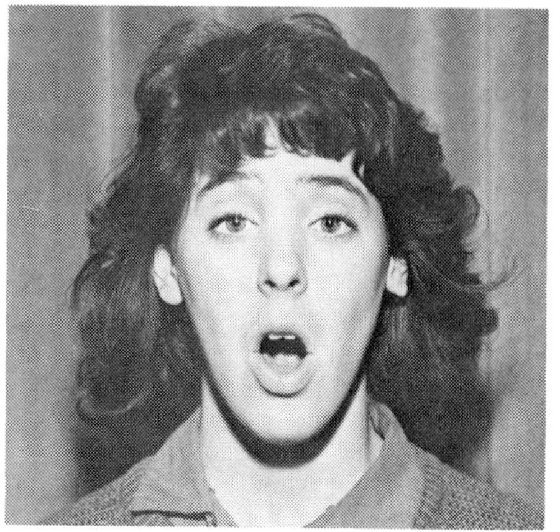

ah

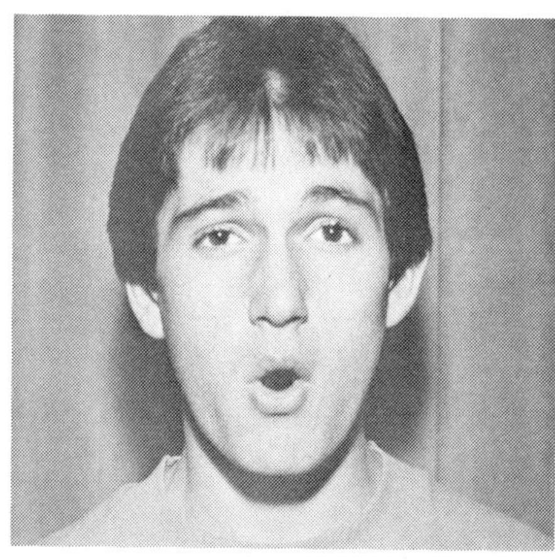

o

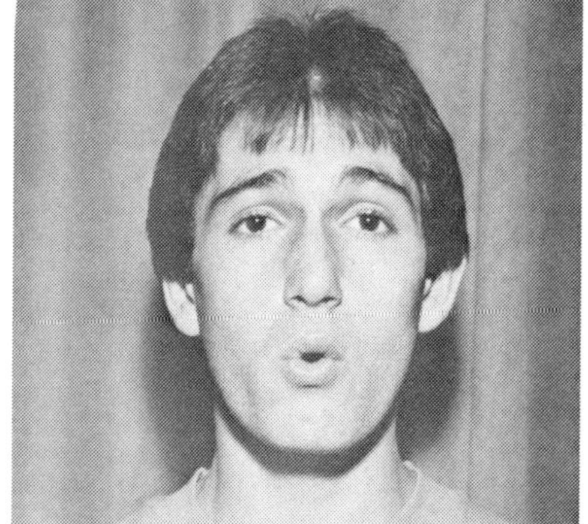

oo

[1]The International Phonetic Alphabet.

(b) Sip and sigh. Inhale through the "cold air sip" on the count of three. Release the air slowly and easily on an open *ah* vowel, descending in a slide from high to low. Maintain the same vowel sound throughout the descending line. Check your posture to insure that your chest and shoulders do not collapse forward as the pitch descends. Your upper body should remain high and poised.

Place the tip of your index finger gently on your lower jaw while you sustain the *ah* vowel through the descending line. This will keep the mouth *open* naturally, the tongue *forward*, and the vowel sound *even* while the pitch changes.

Ex. 4

(b, 1)

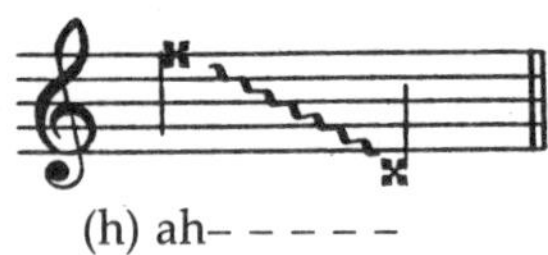

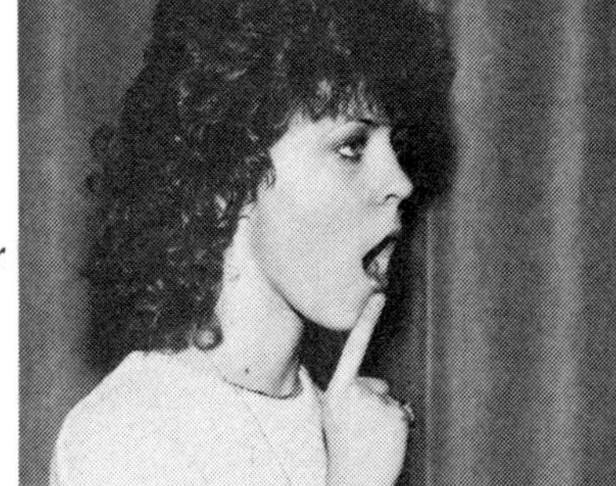

Tip of index finger on lower jaw

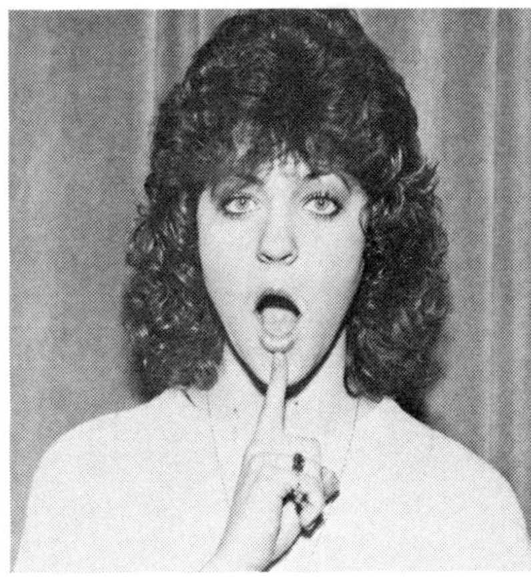

Mouth should be open, tongue forward

Exercise 4 (b, 2) repeats the same *sip and sigh* exercise on the *oo* vowel.

Ex. 4

(b, 2)

The sip and sigh exercise may be repeated on the "u" (oo).

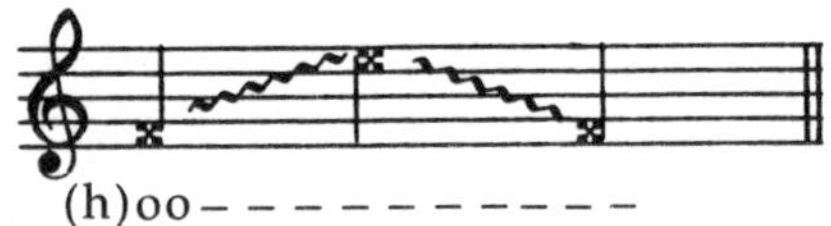

Exercise 4 (b, 3) will give you practice in singing the other basic vowels.

Ex. 4

(b,3)

(c) Unison *ni, ne, na, no, nu*. Practice the five basic vowels preceded by the consonant "n." The consonant places the vowel forward, making it easier for you to hear and to reproduce a pitch in tune. Sing these vowels in Exercise 4 (c) in unison, moving upwards. Sustain a pure vowel sound on each pitch.

Ex. 4

(c)

(d) Descending *oo*. Singing Exercise 4 (d) on *oo* will exercise your head voice, bringing the open *oo* space into the middle and lower ranges of your voice. As you inhale, you should have a sense of open space in your mouth and throat, as if there is an orange or grapefruit inside.

Ex. 4

(d)

(e) Ascending octave, slow, descending arpeggios. Exercise 4 (e) will help you sustain the basic vowels within a wide singing range. For comfort and evenness of tone, try the exercise with the hands gently placed on the face.

Ex. 4

(f) "Noah's Ark." In Exercise 4 (f), practice these vowels throughout the range of your voice that feels comfortable.

Ex. 4

No-ah, No-ah, No-ah, No-ah, No-ah, No-ah, No-ah's ark!

(Repeat exercise ascending chromatically. Do not sing higher than g2.)

Principles of Diction

Words have their own meaning apart from the music. The musical sounds also make a statement. Together, words and music can be a powerful means of expression. But in order for the text to convey its maximum meaning, it must be sung clearly, in tune, and with good sound.

The *text* or poetry in vocal music consists of vowels and consonants. To achieve resonant tone quality and good intonation, you must shape, support, and sustain the first element of the vowel—the pure vowel—for its *full* duration. The longer the duration of the pitch, the more breath support is required to sing a pure vowel. If the breath mechanism fails, or the shape of the vowel is too big or too small, or the final consonant is anticipated too soon, the vowel will deteriorate to a diphthong. It will close and the sound will be cut off. The music will stop! The added element of the diphthong can distort the desired pitch and make it sound out of tune.

The quality of the music itself determines how a piece should sound. Your teacher will guide you in making decisions about vowel color. As you learn a piece of music and analyze its style and what it is trying to convey, you will begin to understand what kind of vowel color is appropriate.

VOWELS

Until now, most of the study of your singing voice has concentrated on how to sing the five basic vowels—*ee, ay, ah, o,* and *oo.* Additional important vowels are listed in Exercise 5.

Ex. 5
Other Common Vowels in Singing

IPA Symbol	*English Word*
[æ]	hat, and
[ɔ]	tall, call
[ɛ]	wed, met
[I]	it, busy
[U]	pull, wolf
Neutral Vowels	
[ʌ]	up, of
[ə]	alone
Diphthongs	
[aI]	night
[eI]	day
[ou]	no
[au]	now
[j]	you

CONSONANTS

Consonant sounds are also important in singing. In choral music, they create clarity of diction and define rhythm. While vowels carry and sustain the sound, consonants adjust and move the sound from place to place. Consonants join pitches and separate them.

Some consonants can darken and pull the vowel back, while others can brighten and draw the vowel forward. For example, an "l" tends to pull the vowel back, while an "n" brings the vowel forward. Speak the consonants in Exercise 6, sustaining the sound while you analyze the sensations. Knowing how to produce the consonants and to give sufficient attention to them will help your audience understand the words you are singing.

Ex. 6
Consonants

Unvoiced (require air but not phonation)	*Voiced* (require phonation)
[t]	[d]
[f]	[v]
[p]	[b]
[k]	[g] (go)
[θ] (th)	[ð] (the)
[s]	z
[ʃ] (sh)	[ʒ] (fusion)
[tʃ] (ch)	[dʒ] (justice)
[hw] (wh)	[w] (well)
[h]	no partner
Unmatched	
[r] (right)	[n] (no)
[j] (hallelujah)	[ŋ] (singing)
[m] (man)	[l] (little)

RULES FOR SINGING 'R'

There are three general rules for vocalizing "r":

(1) **Neutralized**. Negate "r" or change it to a neutral vowel when it precedes a consonant, or when it is at the end of a word (heart, mercy, charm, Lord, ever).

(2) **Sung**. Sing the "r" in popular or folk styles. Always lengthen the vowel sound before the "r," and then get rid of it as quickly as possible. The "r" is sung (not negated!) when it is before a vowel (arise, dearest).

(3) **Flipped**. Flip or roll the 'r' in opera, sacred choral music, and when there are many voices singing together. The ability to flip or roll the "r" depends on the vocal register. It is easier to flip the "r" on a high pitch.

VOCABULARY

consonant	resonant	text
diphthong	singing voice	tone
intonation	staccato	vocalization
phonation		

Chapter 2

Singing in the Choir

Singing together makes you part of a very special group—a chorus. In choral singing, you use your voice together with others to create a musical statement that you could not make alone. Choral singing provides an opportunity to join with friends in contributing your best efforts toward a common goal—to understand music, to develop musical skills, to enjoy the social and musical benefits of choral performance, and to share your music with others.

Choral Technique

Just as singing alone requires vocal technique, singing together requires choral technique. Choral technique is the application of vocal technique to choral music. It involves three important activities: (1) your ability to understand the music, (2) your ability to make decisions about how the music should sound, and (3) your ability to produce music successfully through the singing voice.

Your ability to understand the music involves knowing how the composer uses the musical elements of timbre (tone quality), melody, rhythm, harmony, and dynamics to create an expressive musical form. Learning about the musical elements and how the composer organizes them into a musical form increases your ability to perform choral music well. If *you* understand the music, the chances are, the *audience* will, too.

Your ability to make decisions about how the music should sound requires careful listening and concentration on the music as it is being studied. Successful choral singing depends on the accuracy of pitch, rhythm, harmony, and dynamics. Your judgment is necessary. Without it, you will produce an out-of-tune, rhythmically sloppy performance. The more accurate you can make the performance, the better you will feel. As you learn to use your singing voice, and as you develop musical understanding, you will improve your ability to make decisions about how the music should sound.

Your ability to produce music successfully through the singing voice depends on vocal technique—good singing posture, conscientious breath management, healthy tone production, and clear vocal diction. Producing music with the singing voice means using your *intelligence* in judging the quality of the performance.

Choral technique enables you to understand, judge, and produce music. Although each piece of music is different, the goals of choral technique remain the same: to create beauty of tone quality, accuracy of pitch (intonation), rhythmic precision (exactness), balanced textures and timbres (evenness of sound between voices and between sections of voices, as well as dynamic variety), and blended harmonies. Expressive choral singing is the result.

A Way of Feeling Good

Choral technique prepares you to meet the challenges of many different musical styles, from early songs of the Renaissance to contemporary music of living composers. It will prepare you to perform the music authentically—just as the composer heard it when it was being written. Meeting the challenge of performing music with skill and understanding brings deep satisfaction and self confidence. It provides you with the opportunity to learn more about your own creative potential.

Most people want to do well and to improve. Improving your ability to understand and perform choral music depends upon improving your technique. When you do something well, you feel good about yourself, and you learn more about your own possibilities. Singing together is a way to feel good about yourself.

Developing Choral Technique

Choral technique depends on your ability to understand music. To begin with, you must identify the musical qualities that characterize the piece you are singing. You must learn to answer the following questions:

(1) What are the characteristic qualities of the piece?

- Is the *melody* step-wise, disjunct, wide in range, narrow in range, smooth, major, minor, modal, atonal?
- Is the *rhythm* short, long, accented, unaccented, regular, irregular?
- Is the *harmony* dissonant, consonant, tonal, atonal, chordal?
- Is the *texture* unison, homophonic, polyphonic, accompanied, unaccompanied?
- Are the *dynamics* loud, soft, constant, chang-

ing, stressed, accented?

- Is the *timbre* bright, dark?
- Is the *text* poetry, prose, nonsense, sacred, English, foreign language?

2. What are the characteristic relationships of the piece?

- Is there *repetition* (repeated, constant patterns that unify)?
- Is there *contrast* (different, changing patterns that alter)?

3. How are the qualities organized?

- Is the *tempo* fast, slow, moderate, constant, changing, altered?
- Is the *meter* duple, triple, compound, constant, changing?
- Is the *form* binary, ternary, variation, rondo, other?

4. How are the musical qualities, their relationships, and organization developed by the composer to create the expressive form?

- Can you identify the *vocal form*? (song, cantata, mass, oratorio, opera)
- Can you identify the *style*? (folk, classical, contemporary, avant-garde, jazz, vocal music of other cultures)

VOCABULARY

accompanied	duple	range
atonal	dynamics	rhythm
avant garde	folk	rondo
binary	form	step-wise
blend	harmony	ternary
cantata	homophonic	texture
choral technique	intonation	timbre
chordal	jazz	tonal
classical	mass	tone quality
consonant	melody	triple
contemporary	musical form	unaccompanied
contrast	opera	vocal technique
disjunct	oratorio	variation
dissonant	pitch	

The Application of Technique

Choral technique is the application of vocal skills and musical understanding to the music itself. Through active participation in choral singing, you will develop a deeper musical understanding. You will learn how technique contributes to the quality of performance.

The following guide describes choral technique from the perspective of the musical elements. First, each element is discussed, then a list of related choral techniques is provided. The terms *preparation* (preparing the body for singing through exercise, posture, and breathing), *phonation* (the shaping of vowel quality supported by the breath), and *articulation* (the consonants that control the length and definition of the sound) will be used to describe the related techniques for each of the musical elements.

1. TEXT

Text is the primary element of choral music. It is the element that makes choral music different from other musical forms. The meaning of the words and the sound of the text are keys to expressive choral singing. For maximum expressive effect, the text (words) must be projected so that they communicate with the listener. Projecting the text requires that special emphasis be given to the clarity and unity of vowels and consonants. The concept of *choral ensemble*—singing together musically—depends on the relationship of vowels and consonants as they shape the phrase and articulate the form.

Related Technique

The choral technique of communicating text requires an understanding and application of the principles of good diction to musical performance.

Preparation. Establish good singing posture. Maintain good body posture with a high upper torso. Stand or sit with a balanced and even body position. Prepare the breath for singing. Inhale purposefully at the beginning of every phrase. Maintain breath connection at all times.

Phonation. In choral music, vowels serve to sustain and to unify pitch. Choral blend and intonation depend on the unification and the quality of the vowel. Practice making clear and unified vowel sounds that give quality to the sound of the text and clarity to the words.

Articulation. Consonants serve to define rhythm and articulate text. Precision and definition in choral music depend on the production of consonants. Learn to articulate consonants together rhythmically, sustaining the clear vowel until the precise moment of the rhythmic and melodic change. Give added emphasis to the consonant where projecting the clarity of the text demands it.

2. MELODY

Melody in choral music is the arrangement of pitches as shaped by the element of text. Text is a literary form that has a rhythm and intonation apart from its musical function. In choral music, the sound of the text is lengthened and intensified by the musical arrangement of pitch in highs and lows. A horizontal succession of pitches creates melody. Some melodies have a wide range of pitch variation and rhythmic activity while others are limited in range and rhythmic movement. Melodies can be arranged in many forms and styles, from homophonic and unison music with one prominent melody, to imitative forms in polyphonic style with many melodies moving at different times. Whether single or multiple, the melodic vocal line carries the musical idea. To perform choral melody, the sound must be *prepared, sustained*, and *articulated*.

Related Techniques

The choral techniques involved in producing choral melody include the basic principles of vocal technique and vocal diction. These include:

Preparation. Refer to the vocal exercises and the principles of diction in Chapter 1. Remember that choral technique is the application of these skills and principles to all the musical elements.

Phonation. On the basis of good singing posture and breath preparation, shape the vowel indicated by the text. Support the length of the vowel on the breath. Keep the vowel forward and clear. Sustain the vowel throughout the duration of the pitch. Avoid premature diphthongs and early consonants. Work on unifying the color of your vowels to match throughout the ensemble.

Articulation. On the basis of good singing posture and breath preparation, articulate the beginning and ending consonants of important words in the text. Intensify the formation of the consonant to define the rhythmic character of the melody. Energize and support the consonants with the breath.

3. RHYTHM

Rhythm in choral music pertains to the organization of movement—the duration of the sound, the long and short, the fast and slow, and the stressed and unstressed. The expressive qualities of rhythm can be found in the contrasting relationship between the *constancy* of beat in regular rhythm and the *changing* beat in irregular movement—patterns getting faster (accelerando), slower (ritardando), resting (silence), or suddenly holding (fermata). The organization of rhythm in duple, triple, or changing meters provides other expressive qualities. Performing choral rhythms involves sustaining the respective rhythmic values and articulating the consonants of the text. When the rhythm is long, the vowel dominates; when the rhythm is short, the consonant dominates.

Related Techniques

Basic principles of vocal technique and vocal diction serve to *prepare, articulate*, and *intensify* the rhythmic qualities in choral music.

Preparation. Apply the same techniques for good singing posture, breathing, and maintaining breath as prescribed above for text and melody.

Articulation. In choral music, rhythmic definition and precision is directly related to the articulation of consonants. Careful score study determines the nature of the rhythm in relation to the consonants in the text. The clearer the beginning and ending consonants, the clearer the rhythmic precision. Consonants at the end of a word stop the sound. They define the meaning of the text. They determine the meaning of the rhythm. They introduce the continuation or the conclusion of the musical idea.

Intensification. Producing rhythm requires more than average amounts of energy. Unlike some foreign languages, consonants in English are generally unstressed and limp in nature. Articulating rhythm in choral music requires that the consonants be dramatized or exaggerated. Rhythmic definition depends on the intensification of consonants. Intensification requires frequent preparatory breaths, physical energy, and mental concentration.

4. HARMONY

Harmony in choral music suggests the horizontal and vertical organization of pitch—its thickness and thinness, consonance and dissonance, tonal and atonal qualities. Harmony is created by the simultaneous sounding of two or more voices. The expressive qualities of harmony are found in the relationship between consonance and dissonance. Dissonant or clashing harmony creates a sense of musical tension similar to the tensions of life. Consonant or compatible harmony creates a sense of calm and relaxation similar to secure and comfortable feelings in life.

Related Techniques

Producing harmony in choral music involves the unification of vowel color and the alteration of dynamics to create accurate intonation and blend. Blend in choral music is the evenness of weight, color, and intensity between voices. The choral techniques involved in producing harmony include the basic principles of vocal technique and vocal diction:

Preparation. Again, the same techniques for establishing good singing posture and breathing should be established.

Phonation. Each member of the choral ensemble is responsible for unifying the vowel to the same color. Sameness of vowel color in all voices creates good intonation. When vowels are focused and uniformly shaped, the intensity and frequency of pitch increases, and the harmony is heard clearly. When one voice within the ensemble is darker or heavier, the harmony will not be clear or in tune. The dynamics must also be even throughout the ensemble. The harmony will be heard more clearly when all voices conform to the same dynamic. When one voice is out of character, the harmony will not be heard clearly. The particular vowel color and the particular dynamic level are determined by the specific piece of music and the nature of its harmonic structure.

5. TEXTURE

Texture in choral music refers to the organization of the voices into *monophonic* (unison or single-line), *polyphonic* (more than one melodic line simultaneously), or *homophonic* (one melody with harmony) patterns of sound. Monophonic or unison texture usually includes an accompaniment that must be considered part of the musical character. In polyphonic or contrapuntal music, separate melodies are heard independently and together all at once. Most polyphony is somewhat imitative. Canons are an example of exact imitation. In homophonic texture, the melody is often prominent, and the harmony accompanies.

In choral music, texture is made more complex with the added element of text. In unison and homophonic textures, the vowels and consonants of the text must be carefully unified to achieve definition, exact intonation, and balanced harmonies. In polyphonic music, good vocal diction is essential for the clarity and definition of overlapping melodies. Although unison texture seems relatively simple, singing a single melody expressively and in tune requires a high degree of vocal skill. There is nowhere to hide! The thinner the texture, the harder the singer must work to unify vowels and energize consonants. When there are many voice parts, the temptation for the singer is to hide in the thick texture or the lush harmony.

Related Techniques

Choral techniques involved in producing texture include the basic principles of vocal technique and vocal diction:

Preparation. The same as above.

Phonation. Texture in choral music requires the careful balancing and blending of one or more melodies. Vowel unification is particularly essential in all choral textures. If one voice does not agree in color with the others, the clarity of the texture will be compromised. In homophonic organization, every vowel must be the same or the chord will not tune. Each member of the ensemble must be able to match other members in color and dynamic level.

Articulation. In polyphonic texture, definition and articulation are particularly important because of the complexity of the text due to overlapping of the voices. Consonants must be articulated. The thicker the texture, the more attention must be given to exact articulation or the result will be muddy and undefined.

6. DYNAMICS

Dynamics continually alter pitch and movement in music, forming a continuum of sounds from very loud (ff) to very soft (pp). Crescendo (getting louder) and decrescendo (getting softer) are ways that music continually changes. In Baroque choral music (dating from about 1600 to 1750), dynamic interpretation is left to the conductor because composers seldom specified particular dynamics in their scores. Dynamics at this time were "terraced." One level was generally maintained for each section of a work. In contrast, music of the Romantic and Modern periods contains clear indications for dynamics, and there is usually considerable shifting and variety.

Related Techniques

In choral music, dynamics are produced by the management of the breath and the control of the vowel. Choral technique involved in producing dynamics includes the basic principles of vocal technique and vocal diction:

Preparation. First and always, establish good singing posture and breathing. Altering the dynamic level in singing requires special attention to breath management. Making a change from loud to soft, or soft to loud requires *additional* breath support. *Breathe frequently*, making sure that the breath is continually connected to the sound. A soft dynamic level requires more breath support than loud singing. Changes in dynamic level require anticipation and preparation of the body and breath.

Phonation. In choral music, dynamic alteration requires special attention to vowel coloration. Soft singing is often lifeless and dull, unless you are careful to shape the color of the vowel and maintain the shape throughout the duration of the pitch. When the dynamics are soft, it is essential for the young singer to keep the vowels toward a bright, more "forward" position, otherwise the sound will be entirely lost. In loud singing, the vowel tends to spread or splatter unless the singer controls the breath and sustains the shape of the vowel throughout the duration of the pitch. It is important to remember that brighter, more "forward" vowels will sound louder. The same vowels, produced in the head voice and supported by the breath will maintain their vitality in soft singing. Darker vowels, placed back in the throat will be out of tune, inaudible and unhealthy. Experiment with these choral techniques. The key to dynamic control in choral music is the relationship of breath to vowel color.

7. TIMBRE

Timbre or tone color in choral music is the quality of sound produced by the singing voice—bright or dark, high and low, thin or full. The tone color of the singing voice is entirely different than the speaking voice. The range of the speaking tone is limited to under an octave, while the potential of the singing range extends to nearly two octaves! The speaking voice is generally lower than the singing voice. It has less color variation and less vibrations. The singing voice has more intensity, greater color variation, and longer durations of sound. This comparison suggests that the singing voice has unusual expressive power. This power is produced by the creative use of tone color.

Related Techniques

The production of a particular tone color depends on the innate quality of each singing voice, and the

VOCABULARY

accelerando	energize	projecting
articulation	fermata	ritardando
Baroque	forward	rhythmic precision
canon	imitative forms	Romantic
changing meters	intensify	sustain
choral ensemble	Modern	technique
crescendo	musical elements	terraced dynamics
decrescendo	octave	text
diction	phonation	unison
duration	preparation	vibrations

nature of the text in relation to the expressive qualities of the music. Producing timbre in choral music requires the coordination of basic vocal techniques with the principles of vocal diction.

Preparation. As above.

Phonation. On the basis of good singing posture and breath preparation, shape the vowel indicated by the text. Support the length of the vowel on the breath. Each vowel creates a different color. The color must reflect the nature of the text. When the pitch is high, the vowel color must be more open in quality. When the pitch is low, the vowel color should be brighter and as far forward as possible.

Chapter 3

Expressing Yourself

Fine musical performance goes beyond just singing all the notes correctly. Expressive—meaningful—musical performance requires more.

You and Music

As a music student and choral performer, you are a living link between the great music of the past and the music of today. The notes and other musical markings that are printed on a sheet of paper are only a representation of music. They have to be transformed into sound to become actual music. That is where you as a musical performer play an important role. Through your singing, you make that music come alive again. You bring it into today's world.

Music is a kind of time machine that transports our minds and hearts back through the ages. It can help us to think and to feel the way people did centuries ago. Through music we can experience other peoples and their cultures. For these reasons, music is often called a "universal language." It is capable of erasing language and cultural barriers and putting us in direct touch with other times and other peoples. In these ways, the study of music gives you opportunities to understand your musical heritage and the peoples and cultures of the world that preceded you.

Your Singing Voice

Your voice is your personal musical instrument, very closely tied to your own knowledge and emotions. Using your voice to sing provides you with a way to communicate what you know and how you feel. As you study ways to develop your own singing voice, you will increase your ability to understand and to communicate the ideas and the moods found in music. Some music will speak about your many individual emotions and thoughts—pop songs, folk songs, love songs, humorous songs. Other music will speak about spiritual and ceremonial matters and celebration—hymns and other church music, patriotic and school songs, and songs for holidays and special occasions. Through your voice, you can participate in some of the world's greatest intellectual, cultural, and artistic achievements.

Your singing will also permit you to know the joy that comes from joining together with others to create something you can all be proud of. It will give you a means to share these accomplishments with others. In performance, music connects our private and our public selves. It brings people together to share their feelings, their spirit, their wonders. In this way, it enhances the quality of life. The study of music can give you a sense of personal and group pride, yet it provides one of the rare occasions in life when work is fun, and the skills that you learn can be enjoyed for a lifetime.

Expressiveness

What music "says" or conveys is often dependent upon the way it is presented. If a piece of music is about war, it may be sung harshly or, perhaps, mournfully. If it is about friendship and understanding, it may be sung warmly and enthusiastically. If it is about celebration, it might best be rendered energetically and joyously. How we sing a piece has much to do with the message that is conveyed.

Performances of the same work by different groups differ enormously. What makes one thrilling, and another boring? The extra "ingredient" that attracts attention and arouses feeling in the listener is *expressiveness*. In order to communicate the message of a work to an audience, singers must give thoughtful attention to the expressiveness required by the music and the text.

To help singers communicate the desired emotion, composers include expressive markings in the musical score. These markings guide the performers to a better understanding of what the composer intended to "say." Performers try to meet these demands by a process of *interpretation*. By reading the composer's expressive markings, we try to judge what the composer wanted performers to do in order to achieve the impact desired.

Dynamics

One of the ways in which music can be made more expressive is by varying the intensity or volume of sound—the *dynamics*. To make a dramatic effect, for example, singers can make the sound suddenly louder. Often, however, dynamic changes are subtle, moving very gradually from soft to loud or loud to soft.

But what is loud? What is soft? These terms are

only relative. They require judgment. Singing that seems loud in your rehearsal room may by heard as soft in a large auditorium. Your knowledge of the expressive markings in your songs and your familiarity with the environment in which you will perform will help you to respond to factors that will make your performance effective. Your director will help you interpret these markings to make your performance convey the meaning of the text.

Dynamic Markings

Because Italian composers were probably the first to have marked dynamics in their music, the Italian language has been used ever since by composers to indicate how their music should be performed. These Italian dynamic markings are shown in Exercises 1, 2, and 3. Using a single tone or the first line of a song you are learning, practice performing these different levels of sound and how to make gradual transitions between them.

Ex. 1
Gradations of Dynamic Change

SOFT		
pp	*pianissimo*	very soft
p	*piano*	soft
mp	*mezzo piano*	moderately soft

LOUD		
mf	*mezzo forte*	moderately loud
f	*forte*	loud
ff	*fortissimo*	very loud

GRADUAL CHANGES		
cresc. or	*crescendo*	gradually louder
decres. or	*decrescendo*	gradually softer
dim. or	*diminuendo*	gradually softer

Ex. 2
The Total Dynamic Spectrum

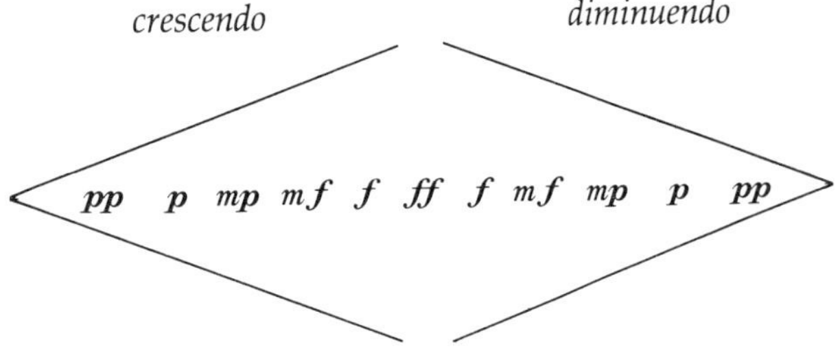

Ex. 3
Other Dynamic Marks

sf or *sfz*	*sforzato* or *sforzando*	a sudden, strong, forced accent
fp	*forte piano*	loud, immediately soft
subito	*subito*	suddenly

Music moves through time. In this sense, it is like the arts of dance and theatre. It has to be re-created. In contrast, a painting can be viewed all at one time. Its message is fixed. The colors remain the same. In music, the notation on the printed score is only the beginning. Musical markings are indications. They are not exact. The actual performance, therefore, depends upon the interpretation of those markings by the conductor and performers. Because the element of human judgment must come into play, a musical composition changes with each performance.

Tempo

Another important factor in the interpretation of music is the tempo or speed of the music. Try singing some familiar songs at various tempos. Note how a song with a serious text sung at an excessively fast tempo loses its character and tends to become funny, even disrespectful. In like manner, a lilting, happy song sung too slowly becomes dull and morbid. Achieving a proper tempo is of great importance in making music express what it is meant to convey. Again, as performers, we try to judge what tempo best suits the composer's intention.

Metronomic Markings

In order to be precise in showing their desired tempos, contemporary composers often place metronomic markings at the beginning of their pieces. The *metronome* is an instrument that indicates exact tempo. It is all based on the number of beats per minute. A quarter note ♩ = 60 means 60 quarter notes per minute or one each second. Try clapping beats at this tempo. A quarter note ♩ = 120 means 120 quarter notes per minute or two quarter notes per second (twice as fast as before). Some bands march at this tempo. Some examples of metronomic markings:

M.M. ♩ = 80 M. 𝅗𝅥 = 60
M.M. ♩ = c.80 ♩ = 120

(about or approximately 80; c. stands for "circa")

Tempo Markings

Like dynamic changes, tempos may change suddenly or gradually. As with dynamics, composers generally use Italian terms to indicate desirable tempos. Since the differences in tempo are often very small, even subtle, it is usually helpful to *think* the first few measures before starting to sing a piece.

Study the Italian tempo indications in Exercise 4. They are the terms most frequently used in music. Try singing the first line of a familiar piece in the various tempos and discuss the expressive effect.

Ex. 4
Terms for Tempo

SLOW	*largo*	very slow
	larghetto	slightly faster
	lento	slow
	adagio	slow
MODERATE	*andante*	walking speed
	andantino	slightly faster
	moderato	moderate speed
FAST	*allegro*	fast, happy
	allegretto	moderately fast
VERY FAST	*vivace*	lively
	presto	very quick
	prestissimo	fastest speed

Other Musical Terms

Composers use a variety of terms to indicate how their music is to be performed. Example 6 shows some of the other Italian terms that are used to indicate mood and/or expressiveness. Example 7 lists technical terms that serve to make the published score more clear and concise. These terms are used in the music in this book, and you will find them in other music as well.

Performance

Understanding the meaning of these terms when they appear in your musical scores, and understanding how to apply these directions vocally, will make your performances more expressive. Expressiveness marks the difference between "ho-hum" and "WOWEE!" musical performances.

As a singer, it is your job to transmit the full meaning of the music to the listener. Effective musical communication requires skill *and* knowledge. Performance is the sum total of what has been accumulated through the study, practice, and application of skills. It combines your musical knowledge, your interpretive understanding, and your expressive ability. It is a challenge. You and your choral director have to figure out how to make the music speak its message, and then you have to try to do it. In the process, you will learn to express yourself, and this is one of the greatest rewards any student can know.

Ex. 5
Other Terms for Tempo

accel.	*accelerando*	gradually faster
rit.	*ritardando*	gradually slower
rall.	*rallentando*	gradually slower

a tempo	return to the previous tempo
tempo I	return to the original tempo
rubato	make the tempo flexible, alternating slight accelerandos and ritardandos
con moto	with motion
più	more, as in *più lento*, more slowly
meno	less, as *meno mosso*, less motion
poco	little
poco à poco	little by little, as *poco à poco* accel.
un poco	a little, as *un poco rall.*
molto	much
ma non troppo	but not too much

Ex. 6
Descriptive Terms

agitato	agitated
allargando	becoming slower, usually with an implied crescendo
attacca	attack what follows without pause
brio or *con brio*	with spirit
calmo or *calmato*	calmly
delicato	delicately
dolce	sweetly
gracioso or *con grazia*	gracefully
grandioso	majestically
legato	connected
marcato	heavy accent
molto	very
sostenuto	sustained
staccato, stacc. or a dot over or under a note	short, detached

Technical Terms

ad lib. or *ad libitum*	at the pleasure of the performer, freely	*obb.* or *obbligato*	an added melodic part
coda ⊕	an added ending	*8va*	placed above or below a note or notes to indicate an octave higher or lower
D.C. or *da capo*	repeat from the beginning	♩‿♩ or slur	curved line connecting notes of different pitch, indicating legato
D.S. or *dal segno*	repeat from the sign	*sotto voce*	in a half voice
div. or *divisi*	divided vocal parts	*ten.* or *tenuto*	placed over a note to indicate a hold of shorter duration than a fermata
𝄐 or *fermata*	placed over a note to indicate a hold	*tutti*	all, the entire ensemble
fine or *al fine*	the end, or to the end	unis. or unison	performing the same melody together
1. 2. or first and second ending	endings of a piece or a section		
gliss. or *glissando*	sliding up or down a scale		

VOCABULARY

dynamics
dynamic markings
expressiveness
interpretation
metronome
metronomic
tempo
tempo markings
markings

Overleaf ▶
The Interlochen Arts Academy (high school) Choir
Interlochen, Michigan

PART 2

Mastering Musical Symbols

PART 2

Mastering Musical Symbols

Why should you learn to read the symbols of music? There is no question that you can enjoy music without knowing anything about musical notation, just as you can speak and communicate with other people without knowing how to read and write. But just as being able to read and write permits you to explore whole worlds of different literature and ideas and to broaden the ways that you can express yourself, so, too, does your ability to read music open you to whole new worlds of musical expression and understanding.

Like verbal, mathematical, and scientific symbols, the symbols of music are the means people have invented to express, to record, to store, and to recall their ideas, in this case, their musical thoughts. Knowing how to read musical symbols opens up the doors to understanding and becoming acquainted with all of the musical ideas that have been set down in the past and in the present. And understanding musical symbols permits us to write down, share, and save our own musical thoughts and ideas.

A singer or instrumentalist who cannot read music is limited to learning new music by repetition (rote) or by ear. In contrast, those who can read music can learn a wider range of music, can learn it faster, and can master more difficult music. You will also better understand the music that you hear. But, more important, being able to read music, gives you independence. It enables you to learn music *on your own*.

The explanations and the exercises that follow will teach you how to read music. They take you one step at a time. Try to understand each step before you go on to the next. You'll be surprised at how fast you can come to understand these musical marks and turn them into the sounds they represent.

Chapter 4

Feeling Rhythm

Rhythm and music—the two go hand in hand. Much of the excitement of music is due to rhythm, one of the basic building blocks of all music. It is the *pulse* or the *beat* of music that makes us want to move to it—to tap, clap, sway, or dance. Like your own steady heart beat, the one-two, one-two pulse of the marching band gives the music a life of its own. Because it is such an important element of music, choral music included, rhythm should be studied and understood.

Developing a feeling for and an understanding of rhythm will make you a better musician. The explanations and the exercises that follow are designed to sharpen your rhythmic sense. With practice, they will enable you to sight read rhythmic notation and perform it accurately.

Feeling Beat

Underlying most music is a steady beat. The examples in **Exercise** 1 will help you to feel this pulse and internalize it. Perform these with loose, bold movements. Saying "beat," "beat," "beat," etc., aloud or silently, will help keep this inner pulse strong—and even. Remember, in such rhythmic "keeping time," you are dividing time into equal parts, much as a clock does with its second hand.

Ex. 1

First Pattern

	BEAT	BEAT	BEAT	BEAT
(a)	Tap (desk)	Clap	Tap	Clap
(b)	Pat (thighs)	Clap (overhead)	Pat	Clap
(c)	Tap (shoulders)	Snap (hands raised)	Tap	Snap
(d)	Sway (right)	Clap	Sway (left)	Clap
(e)	Heel	Toe	Heel	Toe

Second Pattern

	BEAT	BEAT	BEAT
(a)	Pat	Clap	Clap
(b)	Tap (desk)	Snap	Snap
(c)	Sway (right)	Clap (hands raised center)	Sway (left)
(d)	Tap (head)	Tap (shoulders)	Clap
(e)	Raise arms	Pat	Bend

The Beat Note

In print, how is this steady beat shown? Each piece of music designates a particular kind of note or rest for the beat. The one most often used in choral music is the *quarter note* or the *quarter rest* . These indicate, respectively, sound and silence of equal length. Other notes and rests that may be assigned one beat are: the *half note* and the *half rest* ; and the *eighth note* and the *eighth rest* .

Practice the patterns in Exercise 2 to learn to change the basic beat from quarter, to half, to eighth. To perform the patterns, (1) *tap* (or clap, pat, etc.) on each note, and (2) *lift* the hand in a palm-up or -out gesture for each rest, while you (3) *say* "beat" or "rest." Keep the speed of the beat—the *tempo*—steady. Even though the rest is silent, make certain you feel its pulse value.

Ex. 2

First Pattern

(a)

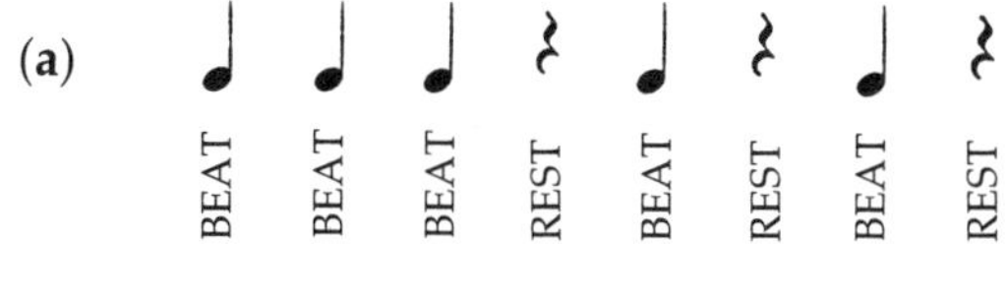

(b)

B B B R B R B R

(c)

Second Pattern

(a)

(b)

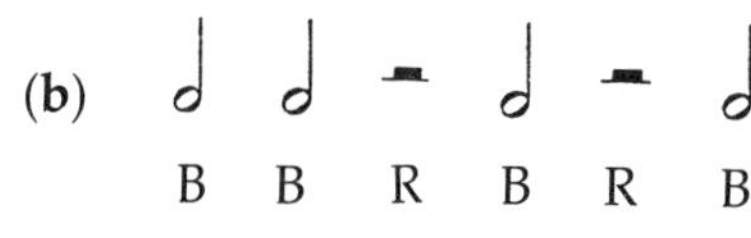

(c)

B B R B R B

VOCABULARY

beat	half rest	quarter rest
eighth note	patschen (pat)	rhythm
eighth rest	pulse	tempo
half note	quarter note	

Grouping Beats

It is natural to want to organize the steady beats into groups of 2's and 3's. These groupings are basic to all music. To feel the natural groups of two and three beats, perform the patterns in Exercise 3 using steps 1, 2, and 3 (*tap, lift,* and *say*) as in Exercise 2. To mark the groupings, emphasize the notes with the *accent mark* , making them stronger and louder. Note the use of the word *simile* to indicate the continuing of the pattern in the same way or "in like manner."

Ex. 3

First Pattern

(a)

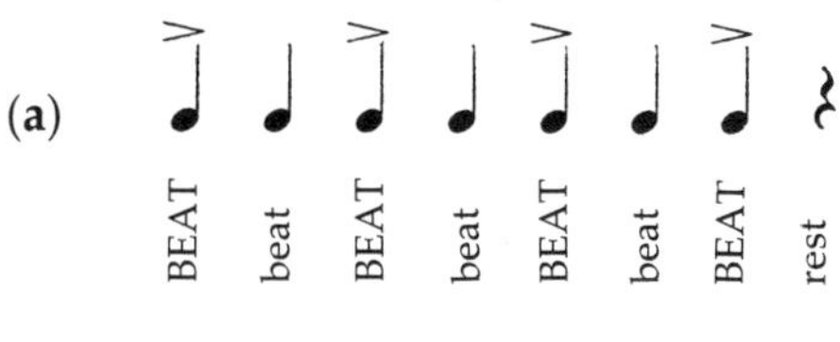

(b)

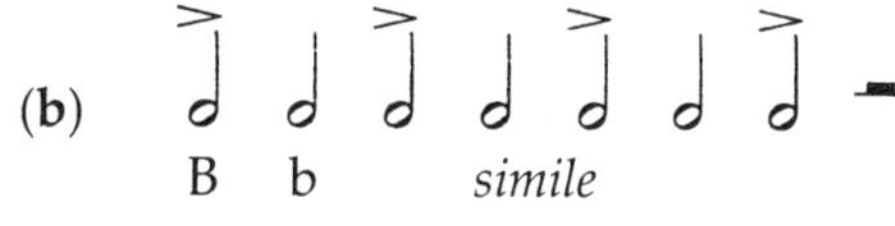

(c)

Second Pattern

(a)

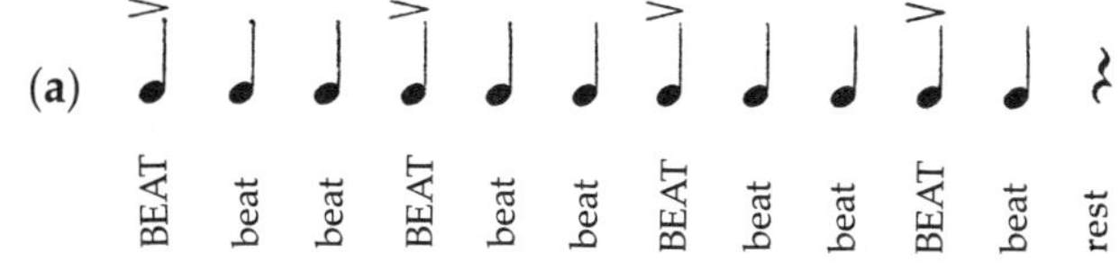

(b)

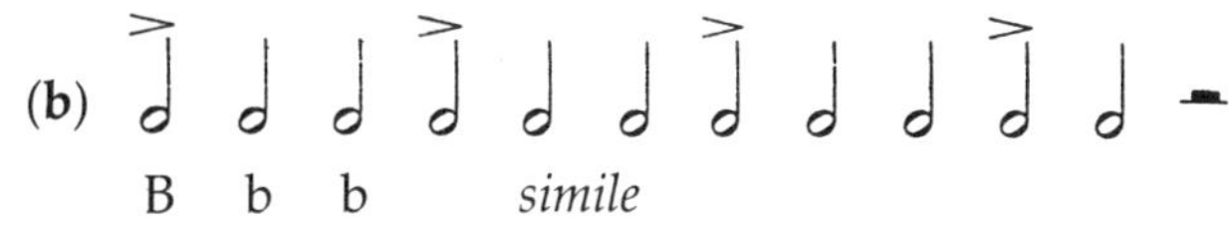

(c)

Vertical lines called *bar lines* are added to organize the basic beats into groups. Each of these groups consists of a set number of beats, or segments of time, and is called a *measure*. Perform Exercise 4 using the same three steps as before. Accent the first beat of each measure.

Ex. 4

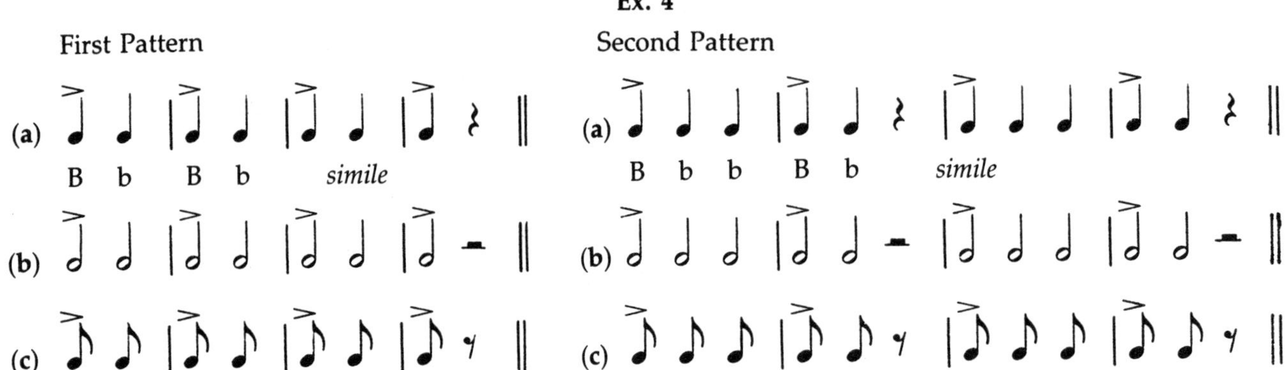

Meter Signature

The organization of the rhythm is indicated at the beginning of each piece of music by two numbers called the *meter signature*. The upper number indicates the number of beats in each measure. The lower number shows the kind of note that receives one beat. In Exercise 5, practice counting the beats in each measure. For instance, in $\frac{2}{4}$ or $\frac{2}{2}$ you will count 1 2. In $\frac{3}{4}$, $\frac{3}{2}$, or $\frac{3}{8}$, you will count 1 2 3. Note that the accent always falls on the first beat.

Ex. 5

Duple Meter

(a) 2 beats in each measure — ♩ = 1 beat — 2 ($\frac{2}{4}$)
1 2 1 2 1 2 1 (2)

(b) 2 beats in each measure — 𝅗𝅥 = 1 beat — 2 ($\frac{2}{2}$)
1 2 1 2 1 2 1 (2)

Triple Meter

(a) 3 beats in each measure — ♩ = 1 beat — 3 ($\frac{3}{4}$)
1 2 3 1 2 3 1 2 3 1 2 (3)

(b) 3 beats in each measure — 𝅗𝅥 = 1 beat — 3 ($\frac{3}{2}$)
1 2 3 1 2 3 1 2 3 1 2 (3)

(c) 3 beats in each measure — ♪ = 1 beat — 3 $\frac{3}{8}$
1 2 3 1 2 3 1 2 3 1 2 (3)

Measures can contain more than two or three beats. Some examples of four-beat measures are shown in Exercise 6. As you perform them (*tap* or *pat*, *lift*, and *say*), continue to accent the natural groups of 2's as indicated, but give the first beat in each measure the strongest accent.

Ex. 6

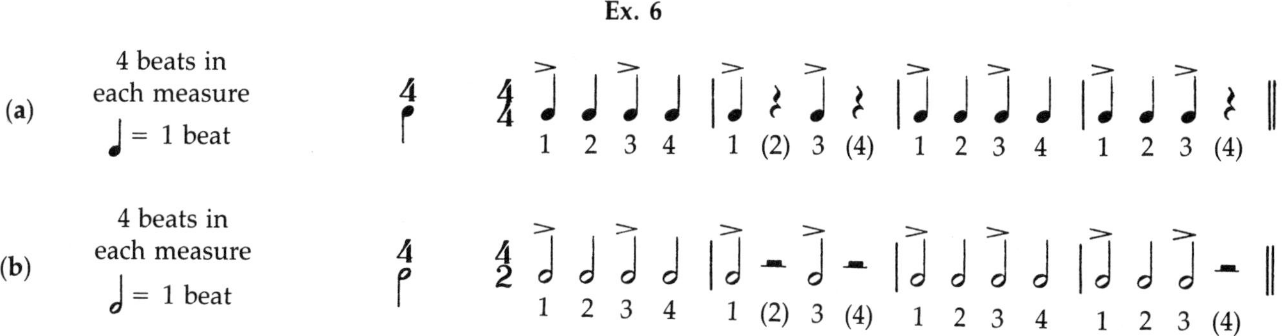

As you study the songs in this book you will find alternate ways of writing $\frac{4}{4}$ and $\frac{2}{2}$:

$\frac{4}{4}$ is often written **C** (Common time) $\frac{2}{2}$ may be written **¢** (Cut time)

Conducting

Another way to learn to "keep the beat" is to conduct. By learning to conduct, you will also respond better to your director's conducting and improve your performance. Two- and three- beat conducting patterns are shown in Exercise 7 (a) and (b). Practice these patterns with the left or right hand as you count 1, 2 or 1, 2, 3. Note the strong *down* direction of beat 1. Exaggerate that movement to feel the accented first beat of each measure.

Ex. 7

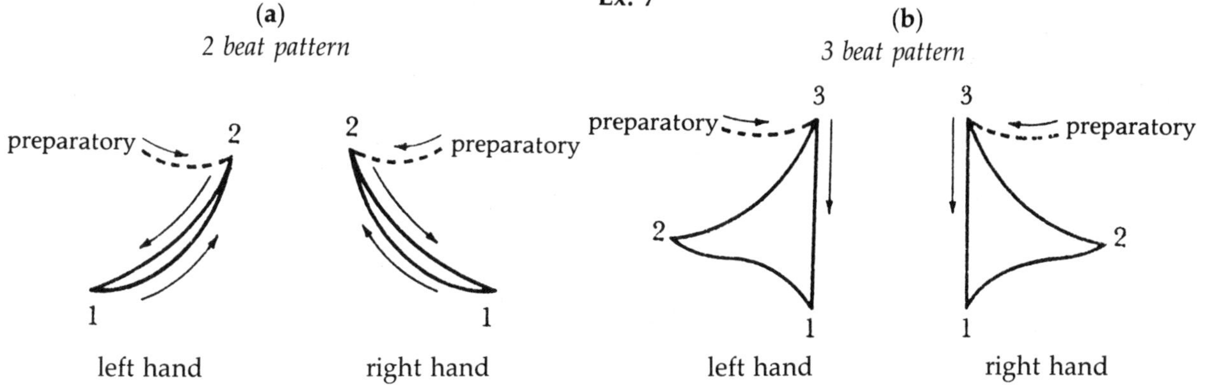

The conducting pattern for the four-beat measure is shown in Exercise 7 (c). Continue to emphasize the downward motion of each first beat, called the *downbeat*. Count to 4 as you conduct. Follow the downbeat motion with a bounce or rebound of the arm.

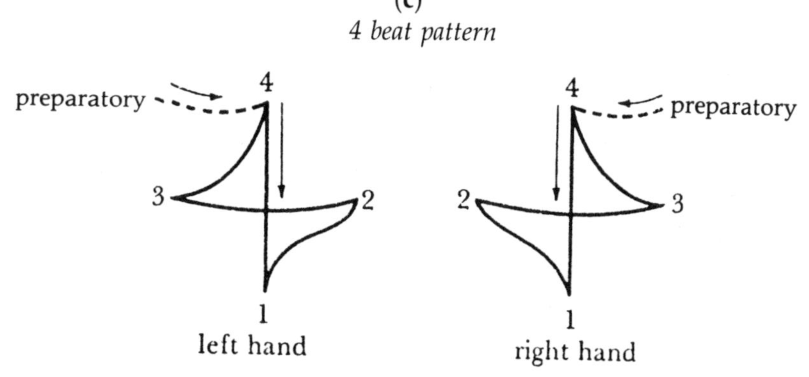

Duration

While the basic beat continues, often relentlessly, various other rhythms may overlay this steady undercurrent. To hear this variety, speak or sing the songs in Exercise 8. Notice that some syllables and words are held longer than others as indicated by the lines under the words.

Ex. 8

Jin - gle bells, jin - gle bells,

Down in the val - ley,

To show these different lengths of sound and silence, different kinds of notes and rests are used. Notes indicate the *duration* or length of sounds. Rests indicate the *duration* or length of silences. The quarter ♩, half 𝅗𝅥, and eighth ♪ notes that serve as basic beats also serve another function. Through their relation to each other, they indicate different lengths of time. If, for example, the quarter note ♩ is one beat in length, than the half note 𝅗𝅥 is twice as long, or two beats, and the eighth note, ♪ one-half beat. These different note values relate to each other like fractions in math. The same is true for quarter 𝄽, half 𝄼, and eighth 𝄾 rests, except that they indicate different lengths of silence.

Two other kinds of notes and rests give even more variety to the possible length and shortness of sound and silence. The *whole note* 𝅝 or *whole rest* 𝄻 is twice as long as a half note 𝅗𝅥 or half rest 𝄼, and the *sixteenth note* 𝅘𝅥𝅯 or *sixteenth rest* 𝄿 is one-half the length of the eighth note ♪ or eighth rest .

VOCABULARY

accent	down beat	simile
accent mark	duple meter	sixteenth note
barline	duration	whole note
common time	measure	whole rest
cut time	meter signature	

To read the various notes and rests, you must first recognize their differences. Here are some guidelines:

Ex. 9

(**a**) The parts of the note are the *head*, *stem*, *flag*, and *beam*.

(**b**) A note with a stem can be written with the stem up or down.

(c) Two or more eighth and/or sixteenth notes can be connected.

Exercise 10 shows how the various note values relate to each other in duration. Each of the rows—a, b, c, d, and e—covers the same amount of time. Note that it takes 16 sixteenth notes to equal the same amount of time as one whole note.

Ex. 10

*Relative Duration**

(a)

(b)

(c)

(d)

(e)

Counting Systems

As you begin to learn one of the following rhythmic reading systems, remember to internalize the feeling for beat that you have been practicing. Continue to use movement—especially patting, tapping, and conducting—to reinforce this feeling for the steady pulse. The use of a system will help you to become more skilled in reading music. Regular practice is important. A few minutes of daily practice is more valuable than one hour weekly.

System I*

This system is based on counting the basic beats. Subdivisions of the basic beat use spoken or chanted syllables: ta (tah) te (teh) la (lah); li (lee). Practice chanting the syllables in Exercise 11 while you count the steady beat (1, 2 or 1, 2, 3 or 1, 2, 3, 4) evenly.

*Used by permission of Cloys Webb.

*McHose, Allen Irvine and Ruth Northrup Tibbs. *Sight Singing Manual.* (Third Edition.) (Place of publication: Appleton-Century-Crofts, Inc., 1957).

Ex. 11

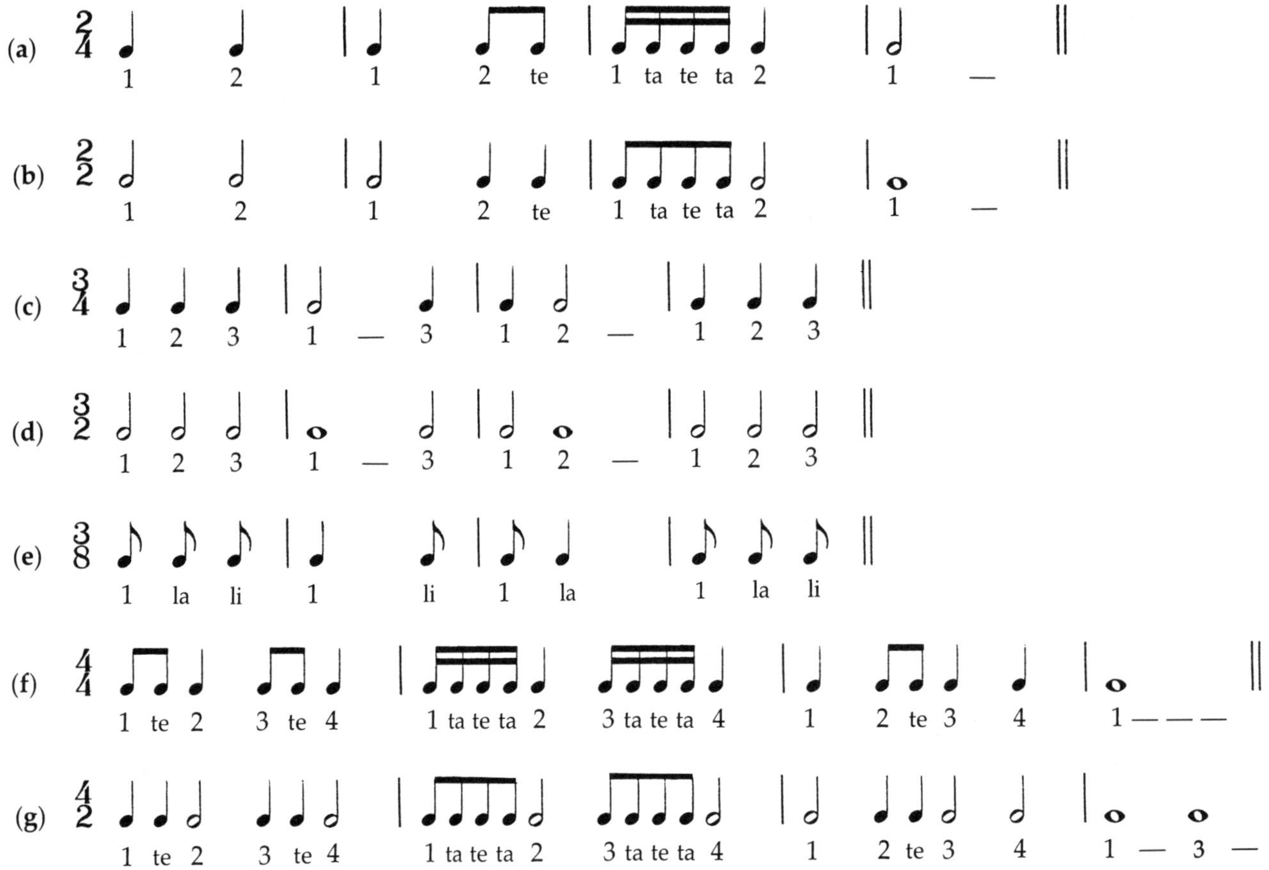

(a) 2/4 1 2 1 2 te 1 ta te ta 2 1 —

(b) 2/2 1 2 1 2 te 1 ta te ta 2 1 —

(c) 3/4 1 2 3 1 — 3 1 2 — 1 2 3

(d) 3/2 1 2 3 1 — 3 1 2 — 1 2 3

(e) 3/8 1 la li 1 li 1 la 1 la li

(f) 4/4 1 te 2 3 te 4 1 ta te ta 2 3 ta te ta 4 1 2 te 3 4 1 — — —

(g) 4/2 1 te 2 3 te 4 1 ta te ta 2 3 ta te ta 4 1 2 te 3 4 1 — 3 —

System II*

In this system, the basic beat is called the *macro beat,* macro meaning "long." The macro beat is always represented by du. Subdivisions of the macro beat are called *micro beats,* micro meaning "small." The chanted syllables are: du-doo; de-deh; di-dee; da-dah; and ta-tah. Duple micro beats are named du-de. Triple micro beats are du da di. Practice chanting the syllables in Exercise 12 while you keep the macro beat du steady.

Ex. 12

*Gordon, Edwin E. *Learning Sequences in Music.* (Chicago: G. I. A. Publications, 1984).

(e)

3/8
du da di du ta da ta di ta du da — du — di

(f)

3/4
du da di du ta da ta di ta du ta de ta da di ta de ta du — di

(g)

4/4
du de du du de du du ta de ta du du ta de ta du du du de du — du — — —

(h)

4/2
du de du du de du du ta de ta du du ta de ta du du du de du — du — du —

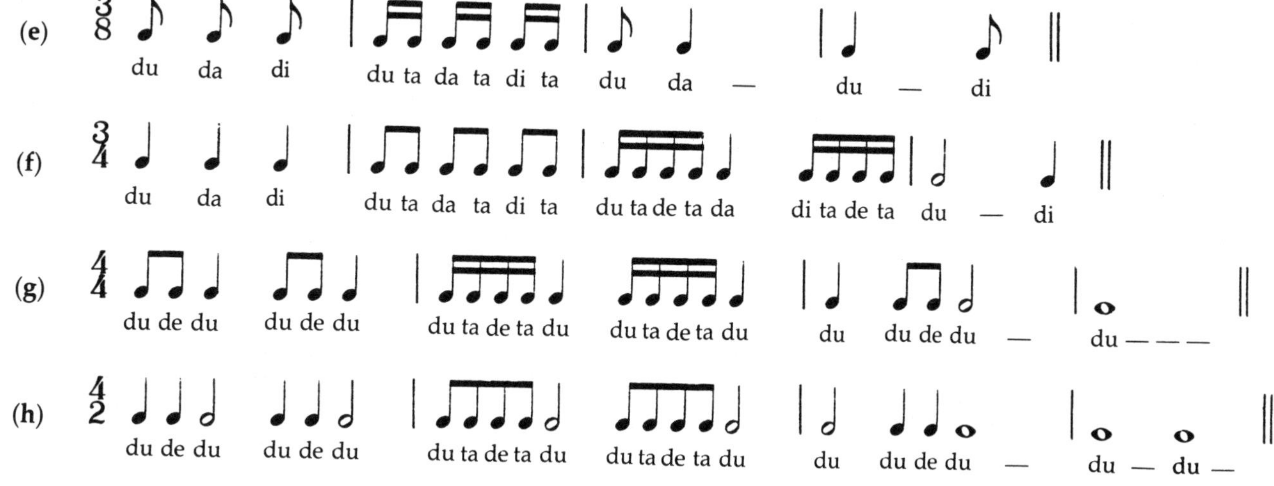

Exercise 13 provides an opportunity to practice your chosen system. As you perform the exercises, pat or tap the basic beat while you speak the rhythmic syllables. Repeat the exercise using conducting patterns while you chant. Remember to accent the first beat of each measure.

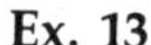

Ex. 13

(a)

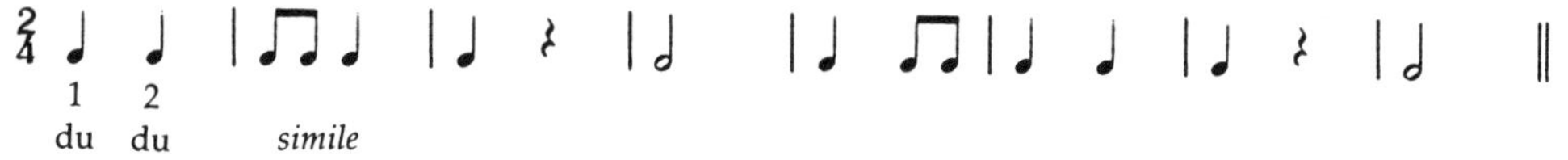

2/4
1 2
du du
simile

(b)

2/4
1 2 te
du du de
simile

(c)

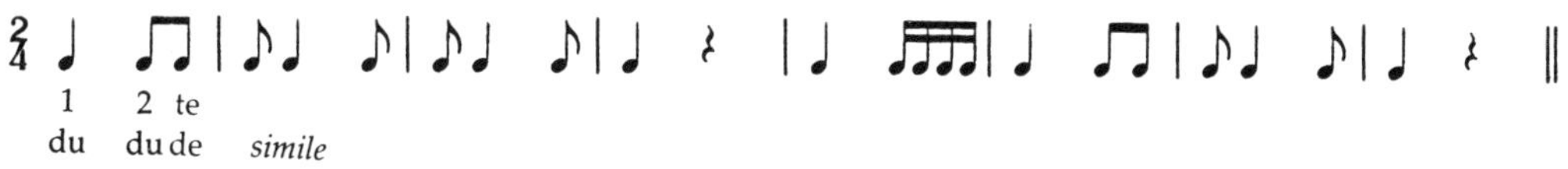

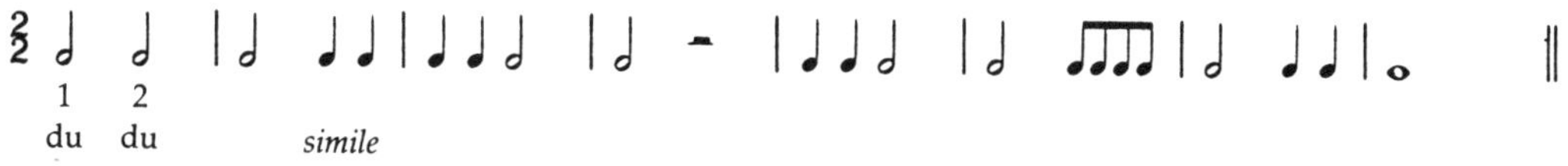

2/2
1 2
du du
simile

(d)

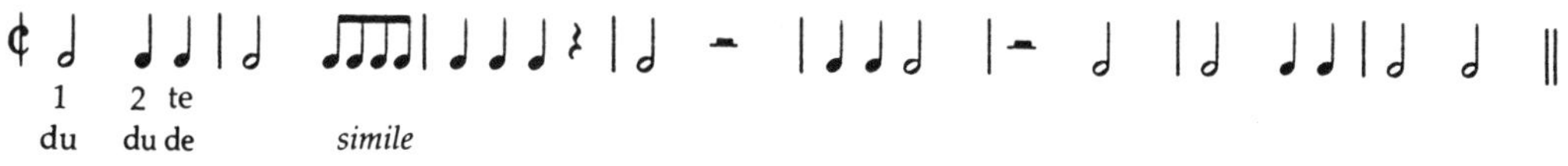

1 2 te
du du de
simile

(e)

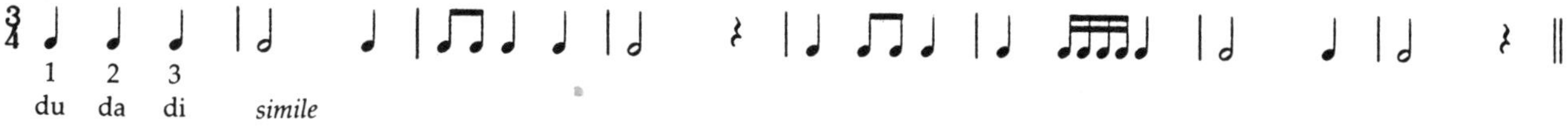

3/4
1 2 3
du da di
simile

(f)

3/4
1 2 te 3
du da ta di
simile

(g)

3/2
1 2 te 3
du da ta di
simile

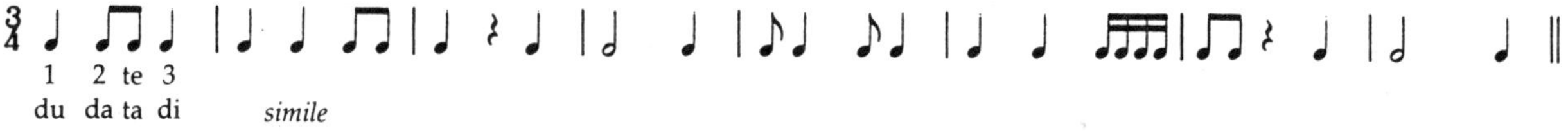

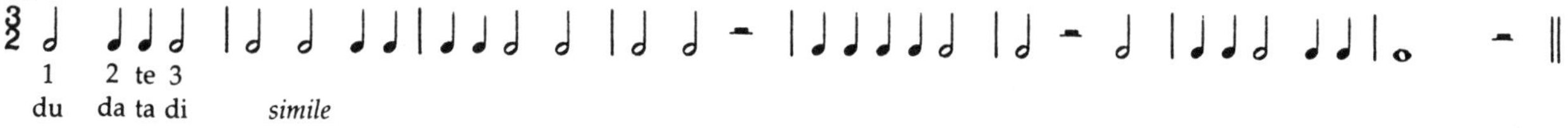

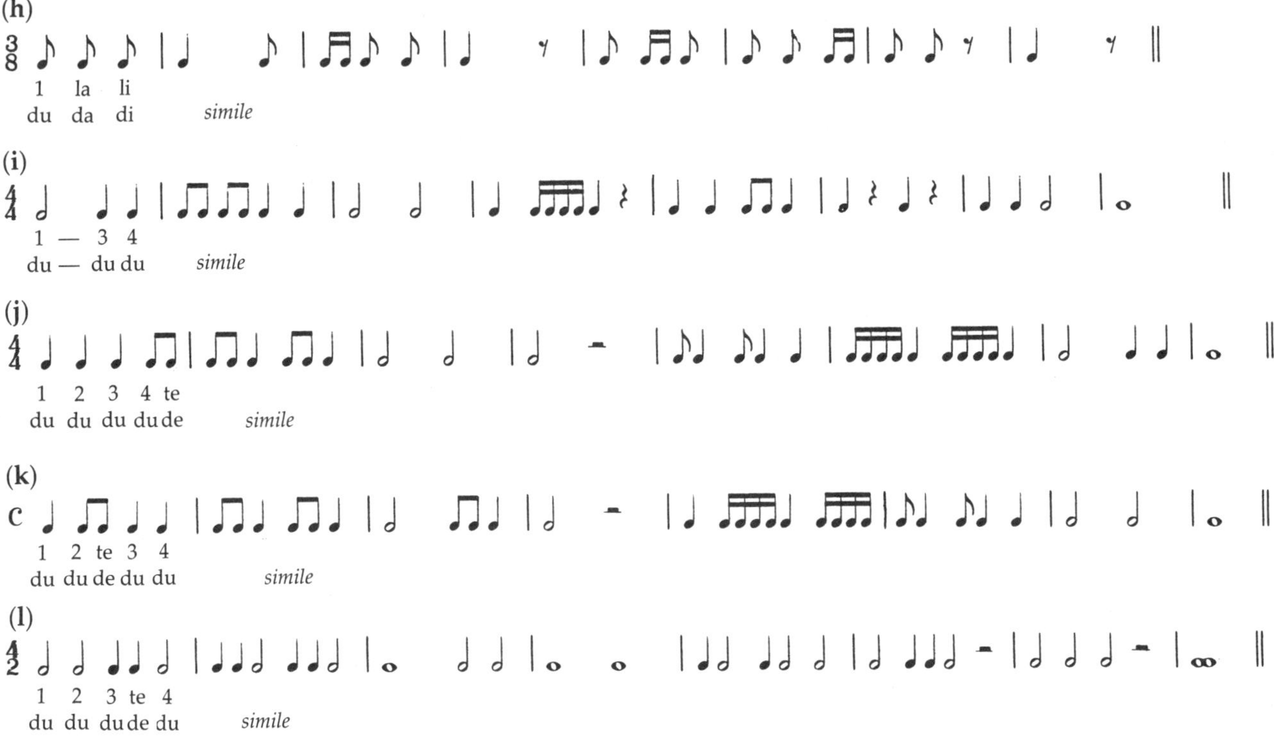

Dotted Notes and Tied Notes

Two ways of extending duration are (1) by placing a *dot* after a note or rest and (2) by using the *tie,* a curved line between two or more notes or rests. Example 14 shows the use of the dotted half note in meter.

Ex. 14

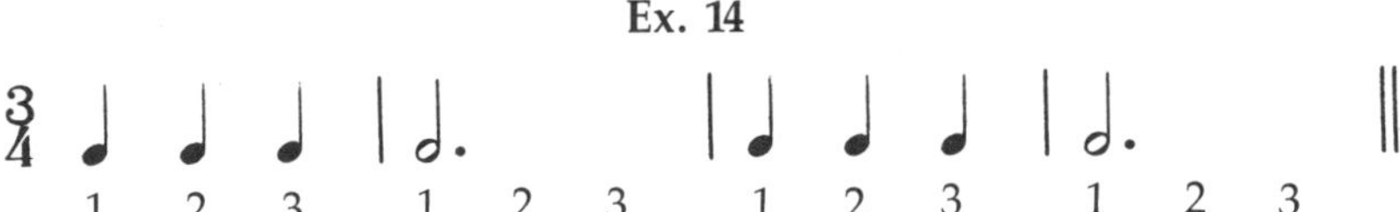

Whenever a dot is added to a note, the same mathematical rule is applied: the duration of the note is extended by one-half. Exercise 15 shows the method of counting the beats in a measure with a dotted note. Practice using your rhythmic syllables.

Ex. 15

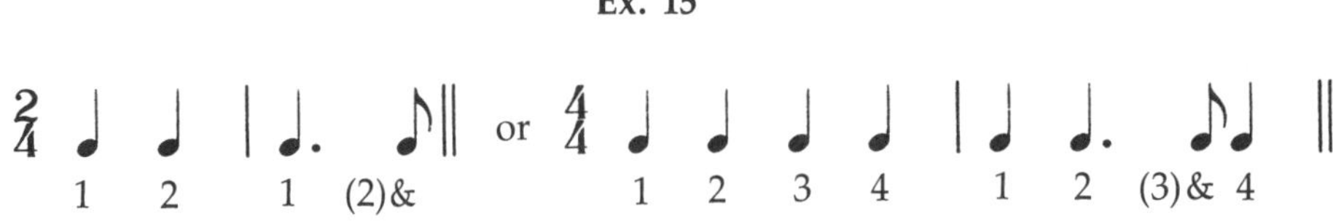

Exercise 16 shows how duration is extended by the use of a tie. The tied note is not sounded. Instead, its value or length is added to the preceding note.

Ex. 16

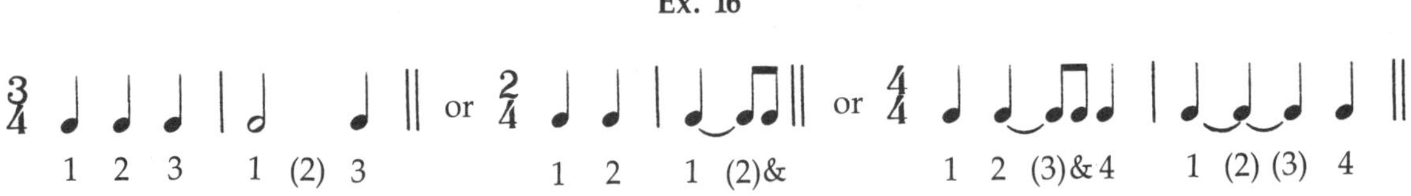

Use the rhythmic reading system of your choice as you practice Exercise 17. Tap, then conduct, the steady beat while you chant the syllables and accent the first beat of each measure.

Ex. 17

(a) 2/4
1 2 1 — 1 — te 1 —
du du du — du — de du —

(b) 2/2
1 2 1 — 1 — te 1 —
du du du — du — de du —

(c) 3/4
1 2 3 1 — 3 1 — te 3 1 — —
du da di du — di du — ta di du — —

(d) 4/4
1 2 3 4 te
du du du du de *simile*

(e) 2/4
1 2
du du *simile*

(f) 3/4
1 2 te 3
du da ta di *simile*

(g) ¢
1 2
du du *simile*

(h) 4/4
1 2 3 — te
du du du — de *simile*

(i) C
1 — 3 te 4 te
du — du de du de *simile*

(j) 3/2
1 2 te 3
du da ta di *simile*

(k) ¢
1 2 —
du du — *simile*

(l) C
1 — te 3 — te
du — de du — de *simile*

6/8 Meter

There are many other meter signatures. One that is often found in choral music is 6/8. Exercise 18 shows the note value relationships in this meter signature.

Ex. 18

6 beats in each measure
♪ = 1 beat

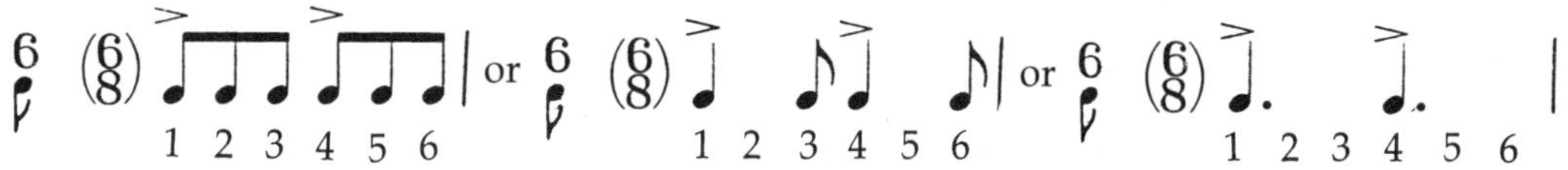

6/8 (6/8) 1 2 3 4 5 6 or 6/8 (6/8) 1 2 3 4 5 6 or 6/8 (6/8) 1 2 3 4 5 6

Although 6/8 meter indicates that there are six beats in each measure and that an eighth note receives one beat, the natural grouping of notes in 2's and 3's again occurs. Exercise 19 shows how these groupings occur at the same time in 6/8 meter. The two strong, or macro, beats are heard within the two groups of three weak, or micro, beats.

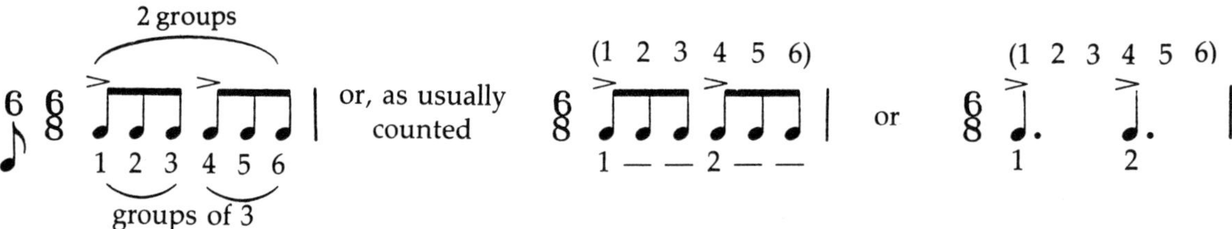

6/4 Meter

Exercise 20 shows how the same feeling of 2's and 3's occurs in 6/4 meter.

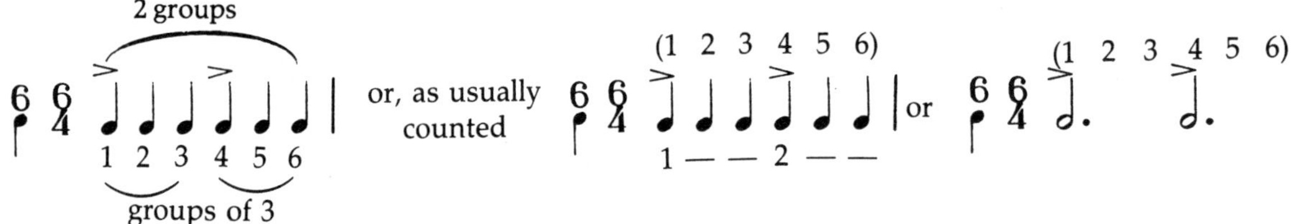

Because the feeling of two strong accents, rather than six beats, generally predominates in 6/8 and 6/4 meters, the conducting pattern for two beats in usually used. Typical rhythmic patterns in these meters are given in Exercise 21.

Occasionally, the groups in 6/8 and 6/4 are changed by accent to alter the rhythmic effect, as shown in Exercise 22. Tap or clap examples A and B to experience the feeling of the shift from 3 to 2 and 2 to 3. Repeat the exercises as you conduct, using the pattern for two and three as appropriate.

Ex. 22

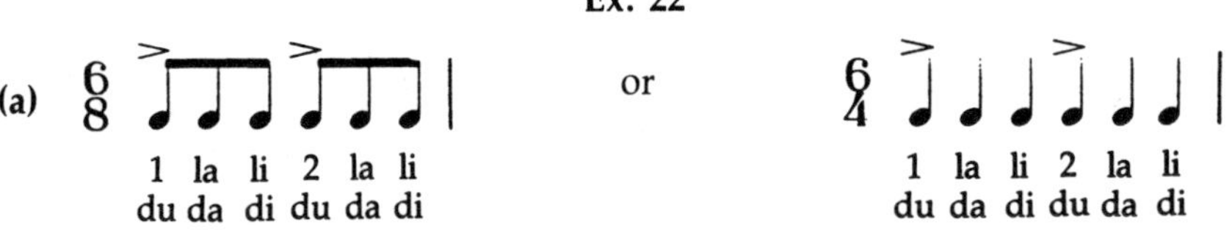

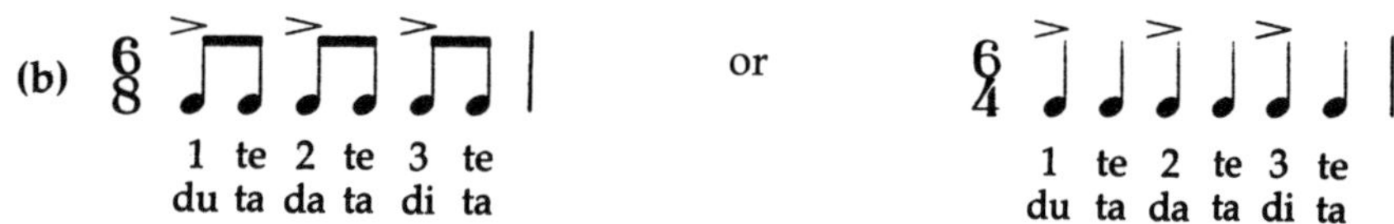

In Exercise 23, use your rhythmic reading system to practice reading 6/8 meter.

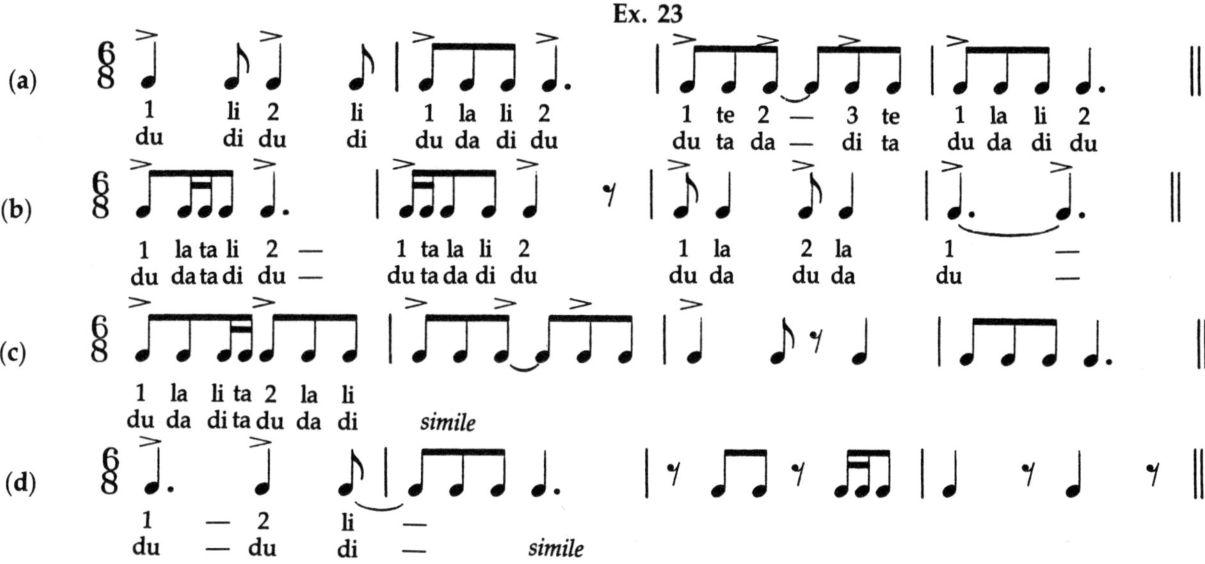

Triplets and Duplets

Three notes grouped together by a curved line or a bracket with the number 3, or simply identified by the number 3, is called a *triplet*. The triplet is to be performed in the same time as two of the same kind of notes. See Exercise 24.

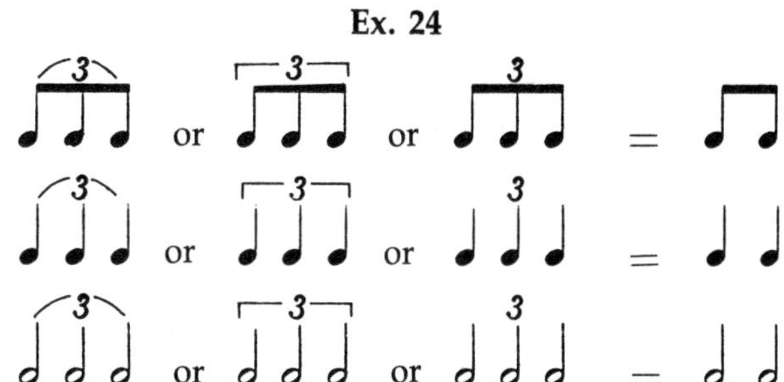

Using your rhythmic reading system, practice reading the triplets in Exercise 25.

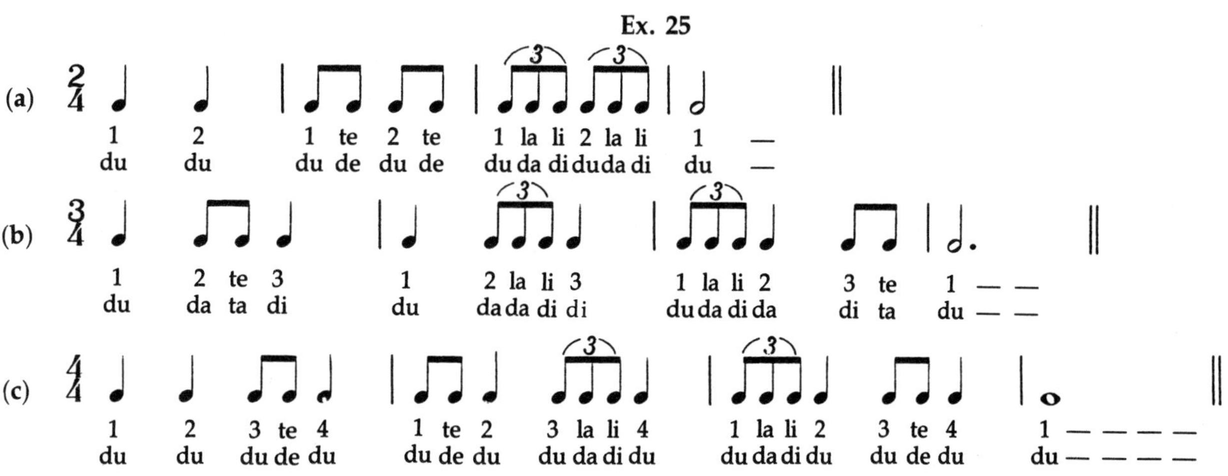

Similarly, the duplet is shown by a curved line ⌒, a bracket ⌐¬, or with just the number 2. It indicates that a group of two notes is to be performed in the same time as three of the same kind of notes. See Exercise 26.

Ex. 26

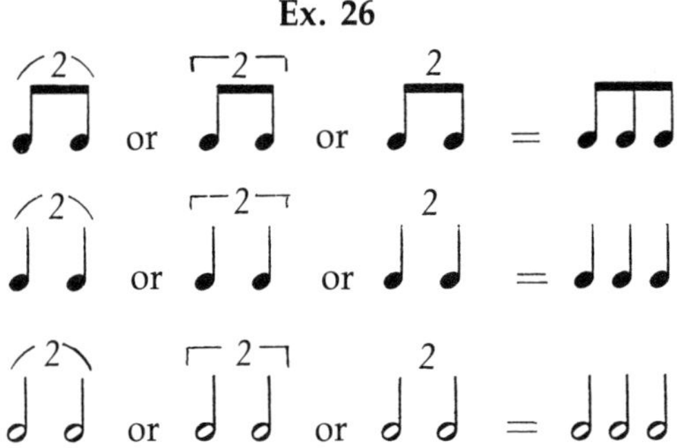

Syncopation

To this point, you have practiced musical examples in which the accent occurred naturally on the first beat of each measure. In fact, you may have come to *expect* an accent on the first beat. To create a special rhythmic effect, however, composers frequently place the accent on an *unexpected* beat or on the subdivision of a beat. This displacement, or shifting, of the normal accent is called *syncopation*. It is what gives music a jazzy or "catchy" feeling.

Exercise 27 shows several ways in which composers create syncopation. Practice performing these with your reading system.

Ex. 27

(a) Holding through a strong beat with a tie.

(a) 4/4 — or 3/4

1 2 3 4 — 2 — 4   1 2 3 — 2 3
du du du du — du — du   du da di — da di

(b) Holding through the subdivision of a beat with a tie.

(b) 3/4 — or 2/4

1 2 3 te — te 2 3   1 2 — te 2
du da di ta — ta da di   du du — de du

(c) Placing a rest on the strong beat.

(c) 4/4 — or 3/4

2 4   2 3 te
du du   da di ta

(d) Placing an accent on a weak beat.

(d) 4/4 — or 2/4

1 2 3 4   1 2 1 2
du du du du   du du du du

(e) Following a note of shorter duration with one of longer duration.

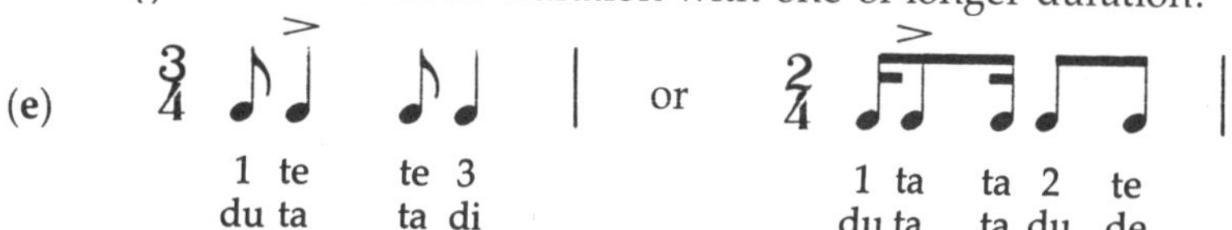

Exercise 28 contains a variety of syncopated patterns for further practice.

Ex. 28

Mixed Meters

While most choral music maintains one basic meter throughout, some choral pieces change meter once or twice or frequently. In such *changing, shifting, mixed,* or *multimeter* works, the feeling for the basic beat usually remains constant. Study and perform the examples in Exercise 29.

Ex. 29

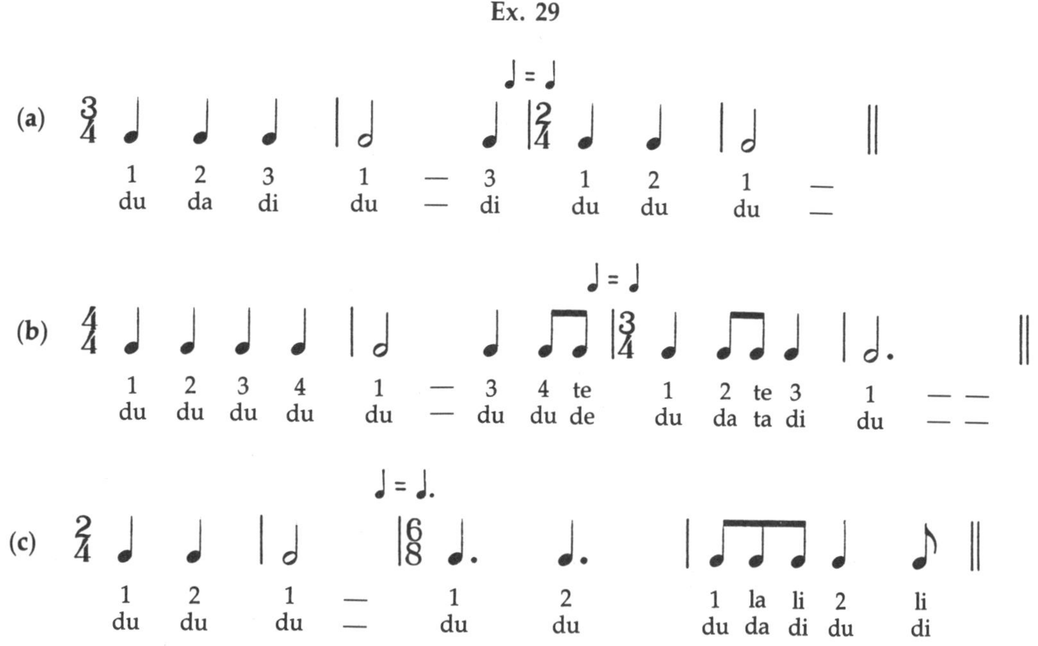

Upbeat

While the exercises you have been practicing have begun on the first beat of the measure, music can begin on any beat. Exercise 30 shows how the text of two well known songs requires an unaccented beat or *upbeat* ahead of the accented word. The rhythmic accents of a text must match the rhythmic accents of the music. The remaining counts of the first incomplete measure will be found in the last measure of the piece.

Ex. 30

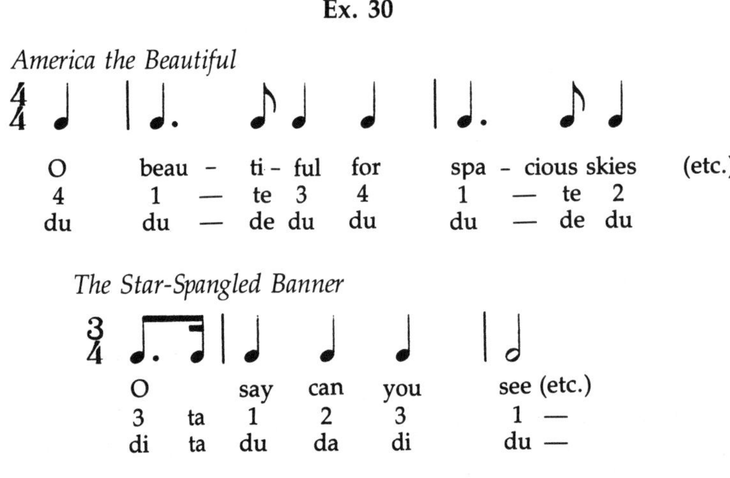

Practice the upbeat, or upbeats, in Exercise 31 using your system for rhythmic reading.

Ex. 31

In conducting, you will need to use a gesture to indicate the upbeat. To conduct the upbeat, use the basic conducting pattern for the meter but begin with the preceding beat as a preparation. To practice conducting the upbeat, repeat Exercise 31.

VOCABULARY

beam	micro beat	stem
changing meter	mixed meter	syncopation
flag	multimeter	tie
head	note	triplet
macro beat	shifting meter	upbeat

Rhythmic Challenges

You have now studied many of the rhythmic patterns included in the songs in this book. As you practice these exercises use the exaggerated movements—tap, pat, conduct—as you chant the rhythmic syllables.

Perform Excercise 32 in various ways: (1) one person/group on the upper line, another person/group on the lower line; exchange parts; (2) all use both hands, the right hand tapping the upper line, the left hand the lower; (3) speak the top line, move to the lower line; exchange parts.

Ex. 32

(a)

(b)

(c) 2/4

(d) 2/2

(e) 4/4

(f) 4/2

(g) 4/8

(h) 

(i)

(j)

In Exercise 33, speak the rhythmic syllables as you pat or tap the beat. Repeat the exercise, speaking the rhythmic syllables and conducting the appropriate beat pattern.

Ex. 33

(a)

(b)

(c)

(d)

(e)

(f)

(g)

(h)

(i)

(j)

(k)

(l)

To perform the rhythms in Exercise 34, follow the procedures suggested in Exercise 33. As the exercise is repeated, exchange parts.

Ex. 34

(a) I
II

(b) I
II

(c) I
II

(d) I
II

(e) I
II

(f) I
II
III

(g) I
II
III

(h) I
II
III

(i) I
II
III

(j) I
II
III

(k) I
II
III

Chapter 5

Understanding Pitch

Like the alphabet and words, a page of music is a code. Learning to understand that code, like learning to read this page of text, takes a bit of effort. For those who know little about them, musical symbols may appear mysterious and look difficult, but they are relatively simple.

Singing and speaking are learned in much the same way. You may not remember your early attempts at learning to speak. You first heard sounds that you copied by imitation. You practiced making sounds, then speaking words, then putting words together into sentences. Only after you had acquired a vocabulary of many words and could express many ideas were you ready to learn to read and to write the language. You first learned the sound, then the symbol.

The same process is true in learning to sing. First you heard musical sounds. You imitated these sounds and finally were able to sing simple songs that someone taught you. Growing up, you heard many pitch patterns and rhythm patterns. When musical ideas "made sense" to you, you were ready to learn to read and write music. As you have grown up, you have become familiar with many rhythm and pitch patterns.

This chapter outlines the process of learning to hear, then read, musical patterns. It will teach you to hear music inside your head as well as read it from the page. You have been studying rhythm, that element of notation that indicates how music moves in time. This chapter focuses your attention on the highness or lowness of the sound—how the actual tone or pitch is indicated in print. Pitch is another of the basic elements of music.

Tonal Patterns

The number of tonal or pitch patterns that you have stored inside your brain might surprise you. They probably number in the thousands. The musical patterns you have acquired have prepared you to read music. Test yourself. Think the first three pitches of "Three Blind Mice." Now sing the three pitches aloud. Notice that these pitches go in a downward direction:

Three ——
Blind ——
Mice ——

Thinking pitches is the first step in the process of **reading** pitches. In fact, practicing exercises mentally is just as valuable as singing them aloud. Olympic diver Greg Louganis says "Whether I was singing or dancing or diving, I've been doing mental rehearsals since I was three years old. Through any given competition, I will do a dive about 40 times in my head before I ever get on the board, and I'll do it to music. Then, when I'm on the board, I just relax and stop thinking about anything, and at that point the dive becomes a reflex."[1]

Mental rehearsal will help music reading to become a reflex, too. To start, try recalling the simple patterns in Exercise 1, first in your head, then by singing them aloud. Notice the direction of the pitches:

Ex. 1

Jingle Bells	3 notes	—— —— ——
Yankee Doodle	4 notes	—— —— —— ——
God Bless America	6 notes	—— —— —— —— —— ——

[1]Quoted in Elaine Rogers, "Perfect 10," *American Way*, June 10, 1986.

America the Beautiful	4 notes
Star Spangled Banner	6 notes

Note that a pitch can move in only one of three ways. It can **remain the same** (as in "Jingle Bells"); it can **go up** (as in "Yankee Doodle"); or it can **go down** (as in "Three Blind Mice").

Hand Signs, Solfege, and Numbers

For almost a thousand years, singers have used *hand signs* (also called "hand signals") to indicate pitches. The value of hand signs is that they connect pitches to something we can see. Hand signs show the direction of pitch movement and the distance between pitches. This distance between two pitches is called an *interval.*

Another system, also centuries old, that helps singers to sing intervals is *solfege,* the use of DO, RE, MI, etc. Instead of solfege, some singers prefer to call pitches by *number* names—1, 2, 3, etc. Using a combination of hand signs and solfege (or numbers) has helped many singers learn to read music.

Hand Signs*

DO (Doh)	(1)
TI (Tee)	(7)
LA (Lah)	(6)
SO (Soh)	(5)
FA (Fah)	(4)
MI (Mee)	(3)
RE (Reh)	(2)
DO (Doh)	(1)

*Developed by John Curwen and Sarah Glover in the nineteenth century.

In order to get the maximum benefit from the hand signs, make an obvious difference in the physical placement of the hand. Low DO(1) should be about waist level, RE(2) a little higher, MI(3) mid chest, etc. Be energetic with the signing movements. This will help you feel the distance and direction of the intervals.

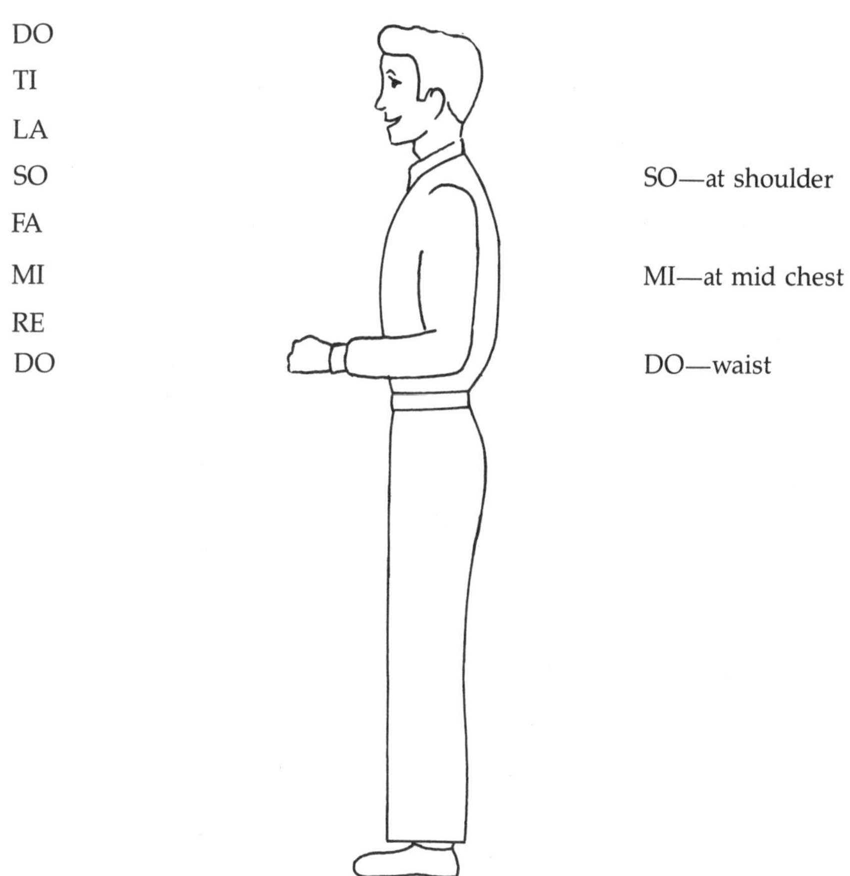

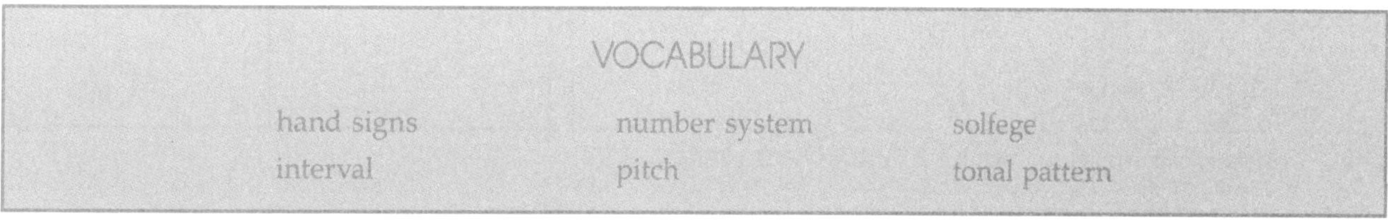

VOCABULARY

hand signs	number system	solfege
interval	pitch	tonal pattern

In Exercises 2 through 7, sing the tonal patterns with solfege, numbers, and hand signs.

Ex. 2

Combinations of DO(1) MI(3) and SO(5):

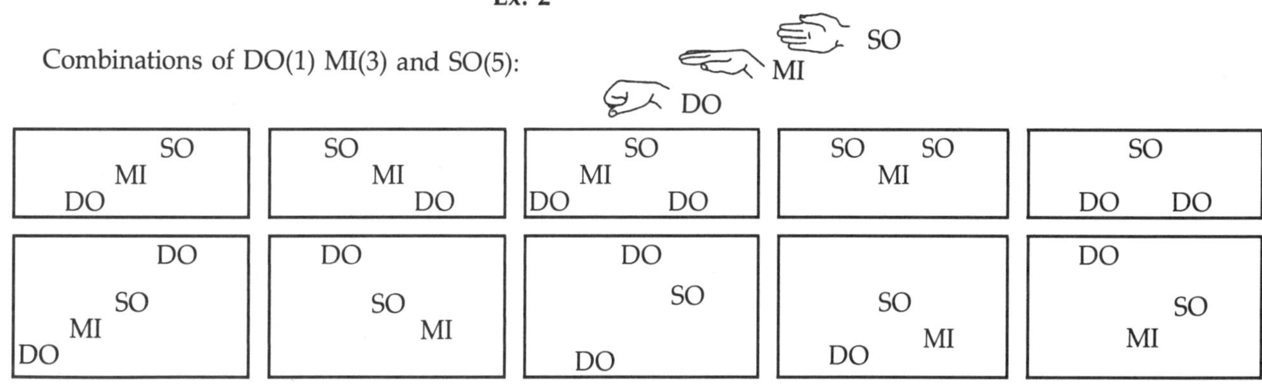

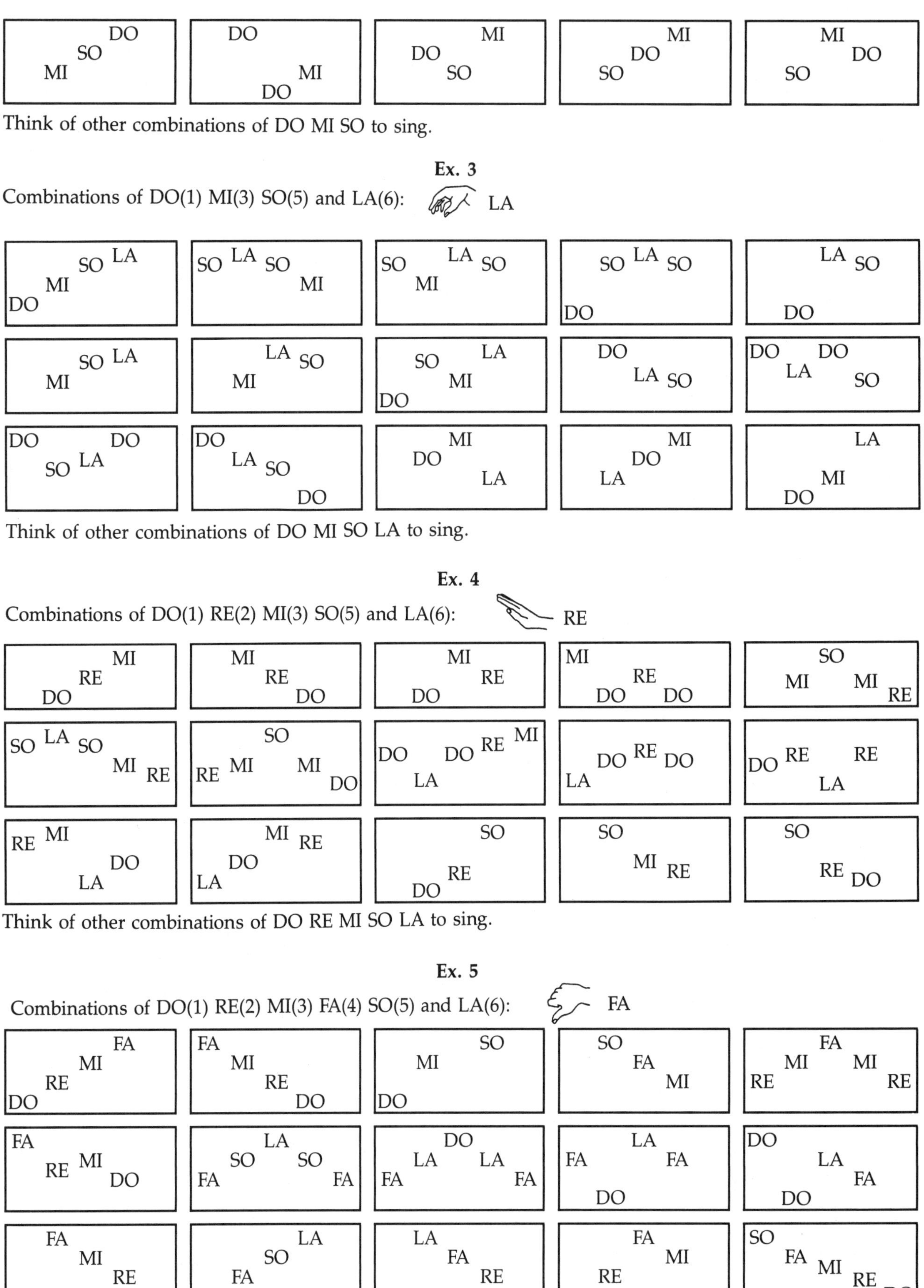
MI SO DO
DO MI DO
DO SO MI
SO DO MI
SO MI DO
Think of other combinations of DO MI SO to sing.
Ex. 3
Combinations of DO(1) MI(3) SO(5) and LA(6):
LA
DO MI SO LA
SO LA SO MI
SO MI LA SO
SO DO LA SO
DO LA SO
MI SO LA
MI LA SO
SO DO LA MI
DO LA SO
DO LA DO SO
DO SO LA DO
DO LA SO DO
DO MI LA
LA DO MI
DO MI LA
Think of other combinations of DO MI SO LA to sing.
Ex. 4
Combinations of DO(1) RE(2) MI(3) SO(5) and LA(6):
RE
DO RE MI
MI RE DO
DO MI RE
MI DO RE DO
MI SO MI RE
SO LA SO MI RE
RE MI SO MI DO
DO LA DO RE MI
LA DO RE DO
DO RE LA RE
RE MI LA DO
LA DO MI RE
DO RE SO
SO MI RE
SO RE DO
Think of other combinations of DO RE MI SO LA to sing.
Ex. 5
Combinations of DO(1) RE(2) MI(3) FA(4) SO(5) and LA(6):
FA
DO RE MI FA
FA MI RE DO
DO MI SO
SO FA MI
RE MI FA MI RE
FA RE MI DO
FA SO LA SO FA
FA LA DO LA FA
FA DO LA FA
DO DO LA FA
FA MI RE
RE FA SO LA
LA FA RE
RE FA MI
SO FA MI RE DO
Think of other combinations of DO RE MI FA SO LA to sing.

Ex. 6

Combinations of DO(1) RE(2) MI(3) FA(4) SO(5) LA(6) and TI(7):

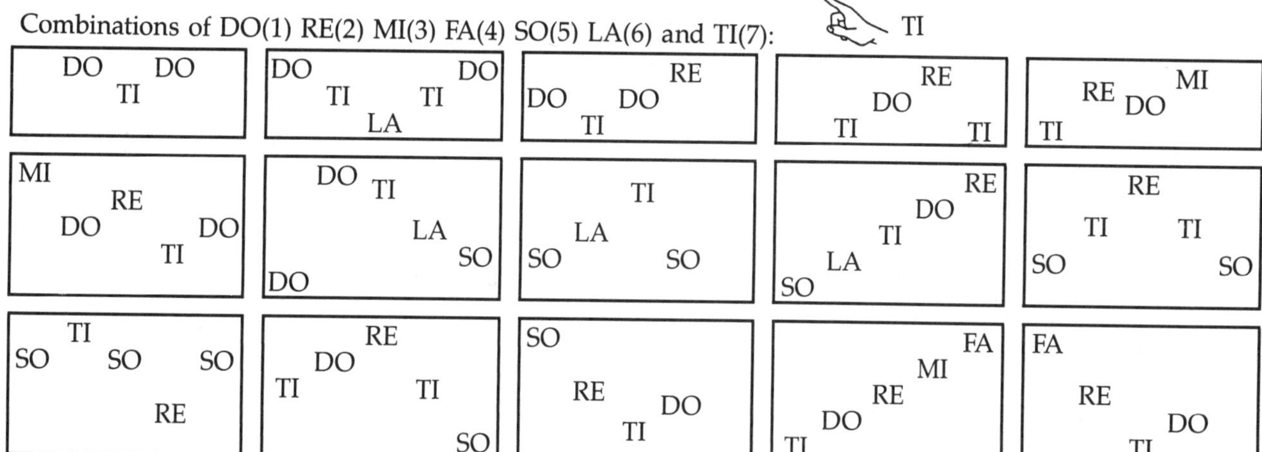

Think of other combinations of DO RE MI FA SO LA TI to sing.

Charts

Another aid to connecting eyes and ears to certain pitches is the solfege or number chart in Exercise 7. Singing the syllables as you refer to the chart is one way of "reading" music. Practice singing tonal patterns as your director points to the chart.

Ex. 7

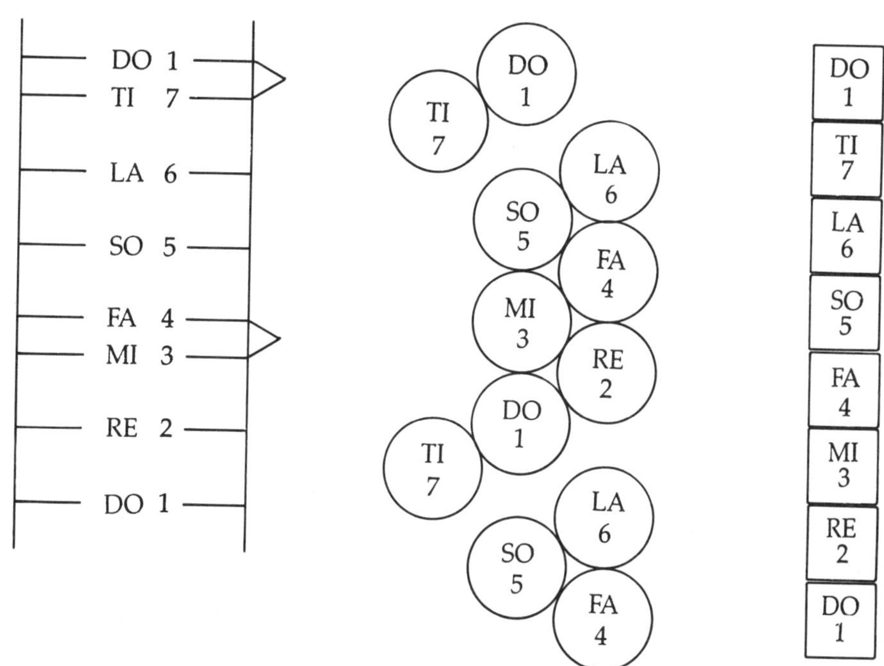

The Staff

The basic system of notation was invented in the Middle Ages. By the year 500 A.D., there were so many chants and hymns in use in the early Christian churches that people had difficulty remembering the many tunes. They needed a way to write these melodies down. At first, the problem was solved by placing little marks above the words to remind the singers when to sing higher or lower or stay on the same pitch. Example 8 (a) shows how such a reminder might be helpful:

Ex. 8

(a) Hot Cross Buns, Hot Cross Buns, One a penny, two a penny, Hot Cross Buns

The development of the music "staff" of lines began with Guido of Arezzo (see page 328). These lines and the spaces between them are like a ladder that indicates the highness or lowness of sounds—the "pitch" that is to be played or sung. At first one line was used as in Exercise 8 (b):

(b)

Hot Cross Buns, Hot Cross Buns, One a penny, two a penny, Hot Cross Buns

Gradually, more lines were added as they were needed for songs with a wider range of pitches. These pitches were indicated by notes that were placed on the four-line staff, as you can see in Exercise 8 (c).

(c)

Are you sleeping, Are you sleeping, Brother John, Brother John,

Morning bells are ringing, Morning bells are ringing, Ding Ding Dong, Ding Ding Dong.

Different numbers of lines were used. At one time, some musicians used an eleven-line staff:

Having so many lines is just as confusing as having no lines. Today, the most common staff has five lines and four spaces:

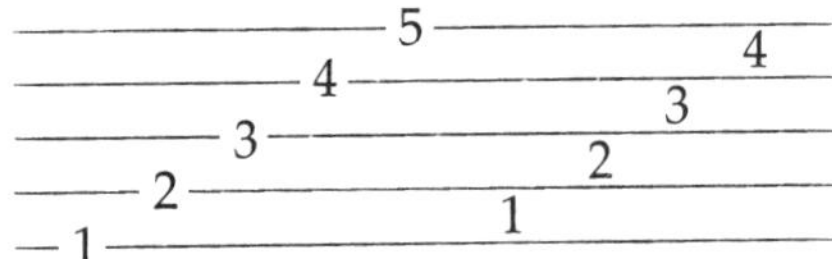

Note that lines and spaces are numbered from the bottom to the top.

Clefs

By itself, a staff is not complete. The only help it provides is to indicate pitch direction: the same, up, or down. In order to name the pitches, the staff must have a *clef*. The clefs used today for singers are the *treble* or *G clef* ("treble" means high) and the *bass* or *F clef* ("bass" means low). The treble (G) clef is used for soprano, alto, and sometimes, tenor voices:

The bottom part of the clef circles around—and names—the second line as G. G

After you know where G is, it is easy to determine the other pitch names because they are alphabetical. Pitch names are the same as the first seven letters of the alphabet: A B C D E F G. When you get to G and want to go higher, start over again with A.

Ex. 9

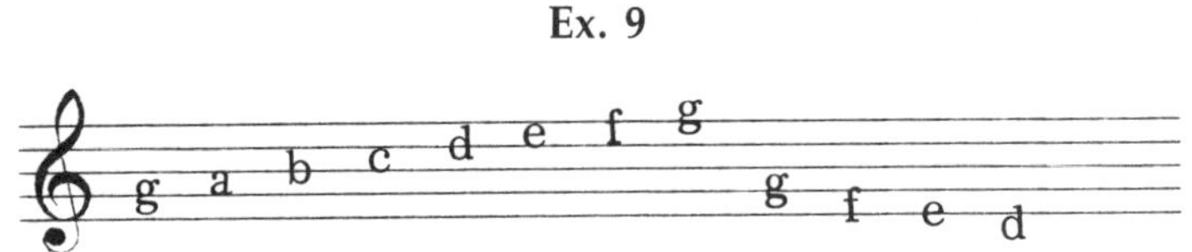

If a higher or lower pitch than can be shown on the staff is needed, the composer extends the staff by added *ledger lines*:

Ex. 10

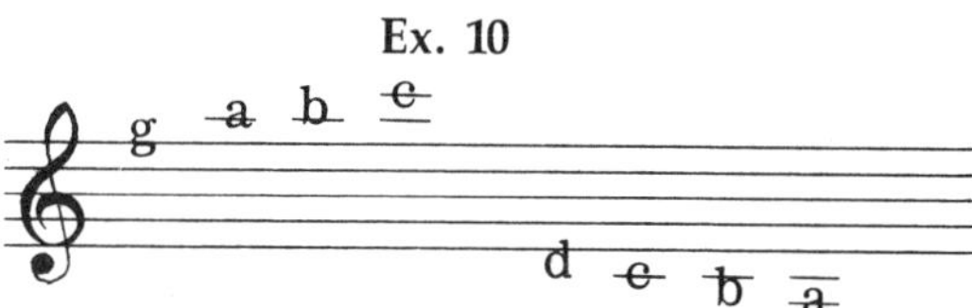

The bass (F) clef is used by baritone, bass, and sometimes tenor voices. When placed on the staff, the bass or F clef names the fourth line as F. Just as with the treble (G) clef, once you know the name of one pitch, you know all the others.

Ex. 11

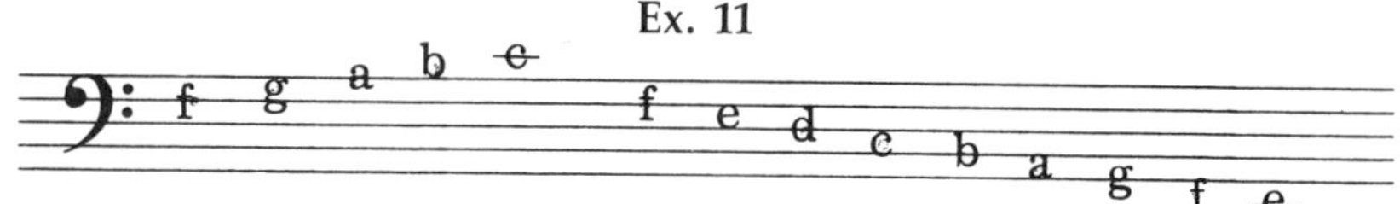

When two staves are placed together, with the treble clef on top and the bass clef below, as shown in Example 12, they form the *grand staff*. The grand staff can show the highest and lowest sounds that can be produced by human voices. The note on the ledger line between the staves is *middle C*.

Ex. 12

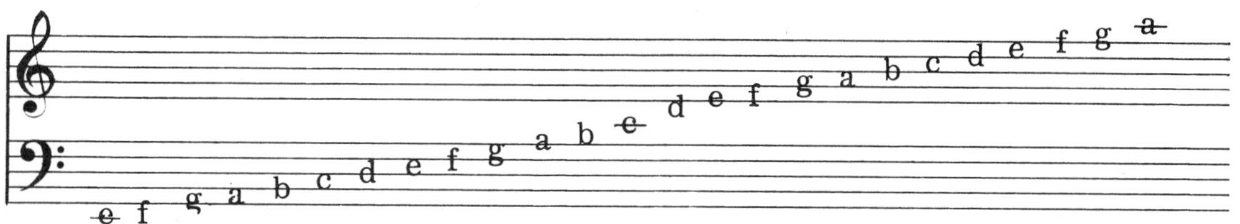

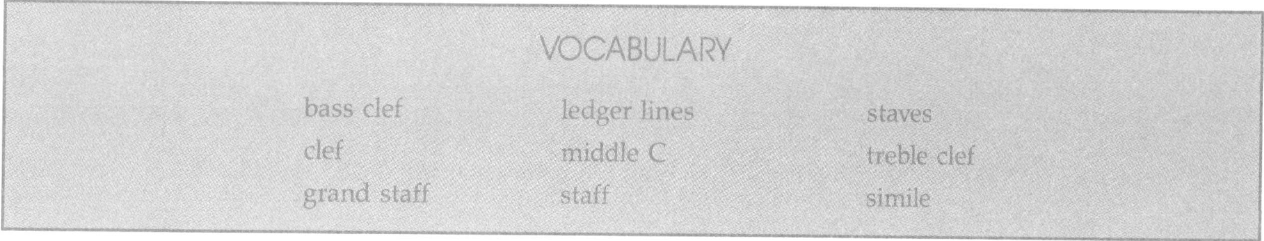

VOCABULARY

bass clef	ledger lines	staves
clef	middle C	treble clef
grand staff	staff	simile

The Choral Score

As Example 13 shows, choral scores usually use different staves to indicate the different sections of the choir. Music written for sopranos, altos, tenors, and basses, will have four staves, plus two for the piano accompaniment.

Ex. 13

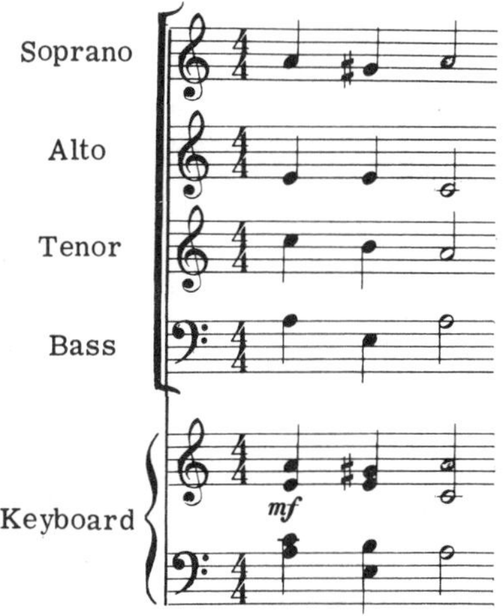

While tenor voices usually use the same treble (G) clef as sopranos and altos, they sing the pitches eight tones—or one *octave*—lower.

Now use Exercises 14 through 17 to practice reading the notes with solfege, numbers, and hand signs. The syllables and numbers for the first pattern are given. Identify the syllables and numbers in the other patterns.

Ex. 14

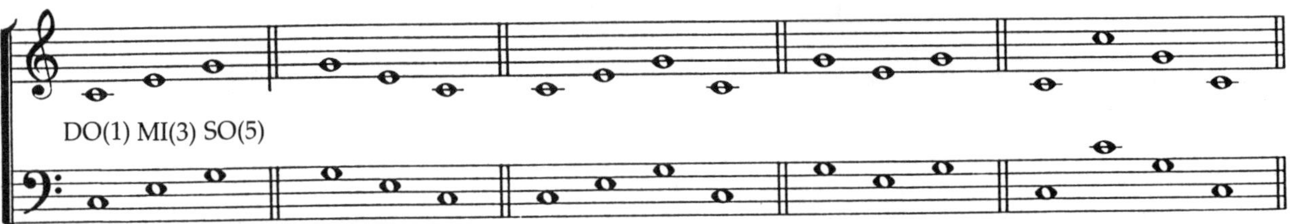

Movable DO

We probably all remember a time when we sang "Happy Birthday" or "The Star Spangled Banner" and the tune turned out to be so high that we could hardly reach the upper pitches. Just as you can choose to sing a familiar song high or sing it low, melodies can be pitched at any level. What is important is that the relationship between the pitches remains the same proportionally. If the intervals are exactly the same, the tune will sound the same whether it is played high or low. In the same manner, DO can be moved lower or higher. Exercise 15 raises DO from middle C up to F. Sing the patterns using syllables, numbers, and hand signs.

Ex. 15

Exercise 16 raises DO to G. Practice singing the patterns again.

Ex. 16

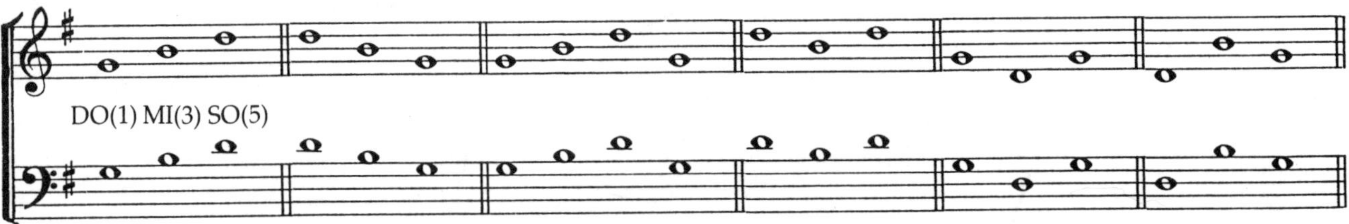

Exercise 17 lowers DO to D. Practice the same way.

Ex. 17

Look at the first tonal pattern of Exercises 14, 15, 16, and 17. Did you notice that if DO(1) is on a line, then MI(3) and SO (5) are also on lines? Likewise, if DO is on a space, then MI and SO are also on spaces. Repeat Exercises 14 through 17 several times singing pitch names, syllables, and numbers.

Intervals

As already defined, an interval is the distance between two pitches. Solfege and numbers are ways to help you learn to **hear**, **think**, and **sing** intervals correctly. Hand signs help you **to see** and **to feel** the distance between pitches. Syllable and number charts are visual reminders of intervals, and notes on the staff are visual representations. Exercise 18 illustrates the intervals formed by DO(1) and the other syllables or numbers. Practice singing these intervals.

Ex. 18

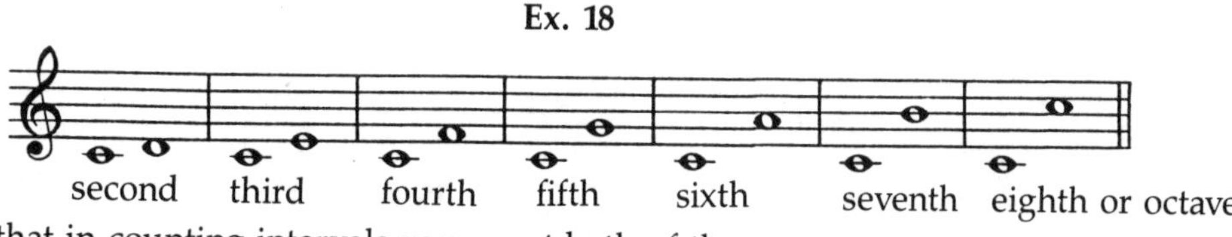

Notice that in counting intervals you count both of the outer notes.

Visual Recognition

On the staff, a *second* moves from a space to line or line to space:

When you sing DO up to RE or MI down to RE, you are singing a second.

On the staff, a *third* moves from space to next space or line to next line:

When you sing DO up to MI or SO down to MI, you are singing a third.

In counting intervals you count each line or space with a note on it, plus the lines and spaces in between. Practice counting, writing, and singing fourths, fifths, sixths, sevenths, and octaves. Try to begin to recognize these intervals by sight and by sound.

Half and Whole Steps

While the intervals between lines and spaces on the staff *look* the same, they are not all exactly the same distance apart. Similarly, the tones A B C D E F G appear to be separated equally from each other, but they are not. The keyboard can help you to see and to hear this difference.

Note that black keys are grouped in twos and threes. The white note immediately to the left of any pair of two black keys is C. Starting with C and moving up (to the right), the white keys are named alphabetically:

Ex. 19

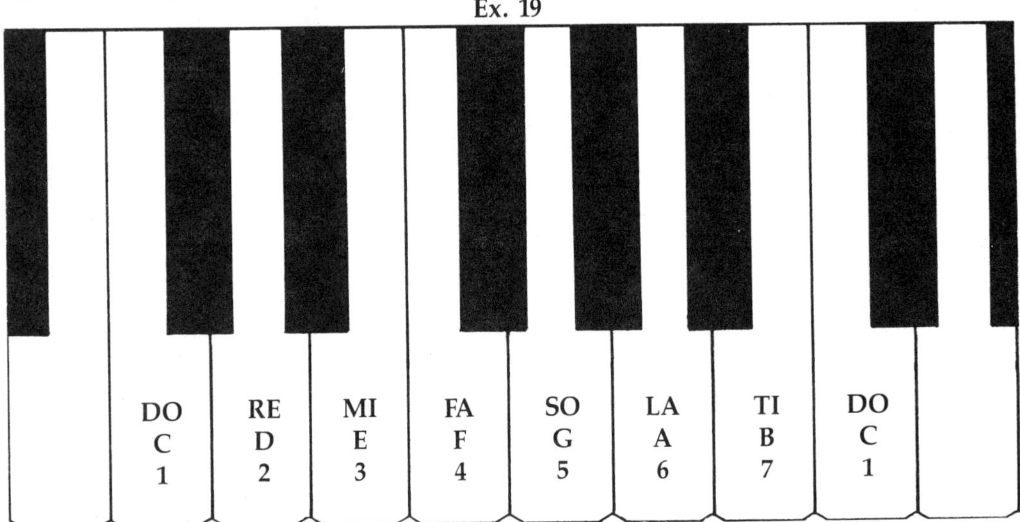

Sing C to C in Exercise 19 using letter names, numbers, and syllables (DO to DO). Can you detect the closeness between E and F (MI and FA) as well as B and C (TI and DO)? There is no black key between E and F, nor B and C. These are half steps. By comparison, there is a black key between C and D, D and E, F and G, G and A, and A and B. These are whole steps. Sing and compare these intervals to see if you can hear the difference between half and whole steps.

From any key on the piano to the very next key (black or white) is a half step. Two half steps make a whole step. Whole steps skip a key. Practice singing a half step up from any pitch your teacher gives you. A whole step up. Practice singing a half step down from any pitch. A whole step down.

Major Scale

A *scale* is a pattern of successive pitches. In Exercise 19, the tones C to C form a *major scale*. As you sing and play this scale, listen for the pattern of whole and half steps. Note that the lower four tones have the pattern: whole, whole, one-half; and the upper four tones have the same pattern: whole, whole, one-half:

C		D		E		F		G		A		B		C
	whole		whole		one-half		whole		whole		whole		one-half	

There is a whole step between the two groups of four tones so that the pattern of a major scale in whole and half steps is: 1 1 1/2 1 1 1 1/2

DO		RE		MI		FA		SO		LA		TI		DO
1		2		3		4		5		6		7		1
	1		1		1/2		1		1		1		1/2	

Note the half steps between MI and FA (3 and 4) and TI and DO (7 and 1).

Just as melodies and tone patterns can be sung higher or lower, the pattern of the major scale can be moved around and started anywhere on the keyboard. Example 20 shows how this pattern of whole and half steps can be made if we start the major scale on G:

Ex. 20

DO	RE	MI	FA	SO	LA	TI	DO
1	2	3	4	5	6	7	1
G	A	B	C	D	E	F♯	G

1 1 1/2 1 1 1 1/2

Using syllables, numbers , or a neutral syllable, sing the pattern of the major scale starting on G: Whole step, whole step, half-step, whole step, whole step, whole step, half-step. The pattern works on the white keys until E to F (LA to TI or 6 to 7). This is a half step, but the pattern calls for a whole step. Change F to F♯ (sharp), the black key to the right of F, which **raises** the pitch one-half step. This makes a whole step between E and F♯ (LA to TI or 6 and 7) and the necessary half-step between F♯ and G (TI and DO or 7 and 1).

Example 21 shows how the G major scale looks on the staff. Sing the scale from the staff while you observe its relationship to the keyboard:

Ex. 21

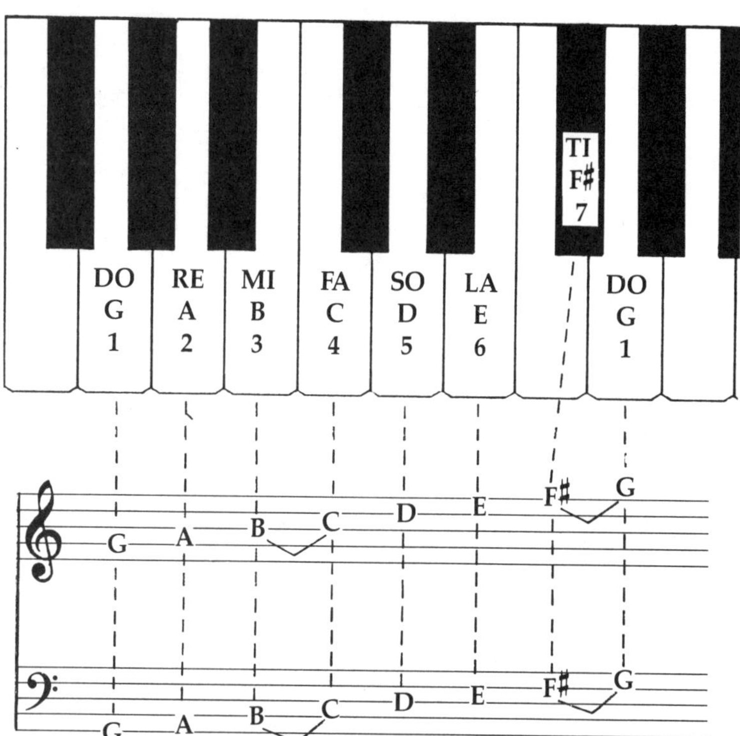

Key Signatures

In written music, the sharp on F in the key of G is moved to the beginning of the music. This is called the *key signature*. The sharp tells the singer that F's in this piece are to be sung F♯.

Key signature for G major:

Sing the G scale **with** and **without** the F♯. A composer can cancel a sharp (♯) by inserting a *natural sign* (♮) in front of the note.

Exercise 22 builds a major scale pattern beginning on D. Observe that the pattern calls for two sharps—F♯ and C♯.

Ex. 22

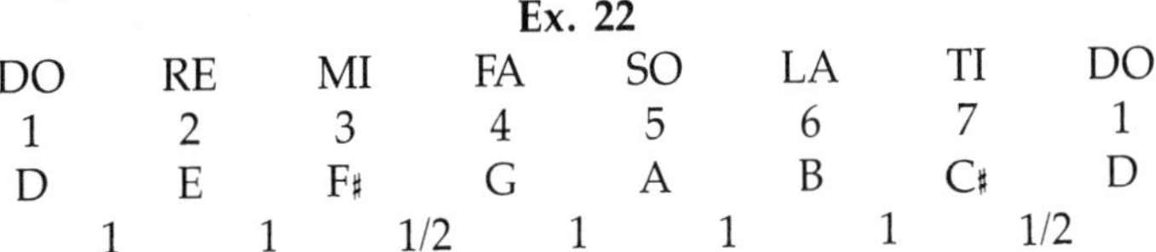

DO	RE	MI	FA	SO	LA	TI	DO
1	2	3	4	5	6	7	1
D	E	F♯	G	A	B	C♯	D

1 1 1/2 1 1 1 1/2

Key signature for D major.

Sing the D scale using syllables, numbers, and hand signs while you observe the look of the scale on the staff and its relation to the keyboard.

In G major, the **final** (and only) sharp is F♯ which is TI or 7. In D major, the **final** sharp is C♯ which also is TI or 7. So, the rule for determining the name of major keys with sharps is to call the final sharp TI or 7 and go up a half step to find DO or 1 which is the key name. Exercise 23 shows how this rule works.

Ex. 23

Exercise 24 builds a major scale beginning on F. Sing or listen to this scale and note that the pattern calls for a half step between A and the next tone (between MI and FA or 3 and 4). That next tone must be B flat. A *flat* (♭) is a symbol that **lowers** the pitch one-half step.

Ex. 24

DO	RE	MI	FA	SO	LA	TI	DO
1	2	3	4	5	6	7	1
F	G	A	B♭	C	D	E	F

1 1 1/2 1 1 1 1/2

Key signature for F major.

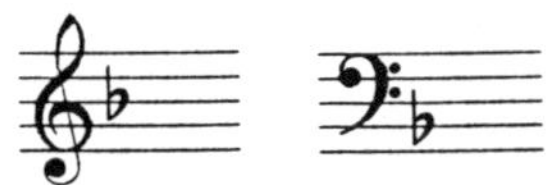

Exercise 25 builds a major scale beginning on B♭. Sing the scale and observe the relationship between the half and whole steps on the keyboard with the printed notation. Starting the major scale pattern on B♭ required the use of an Eb to create the half-step between MI and FA or 3 and 4.

Ex. 25

DO	RE	MI	FA	SO	LA	TI	DO
1	2	3	4	5	6	7	1
B♭	C	D	E♭	F	G	A	B♭

1 1 1/2 1 1 1 1/2

Key signature for B♭ major.

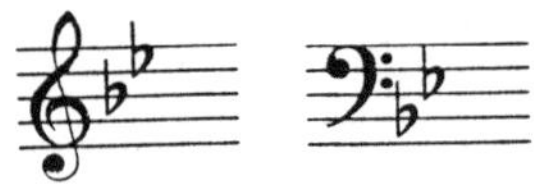

Notice that in F major, the **final** (and only) flat is B♭ which is FA or 4. In B♭ major, the **final** flat is E♭ which is FA or 4. So, the rule for determining the name of major keys with flats is to call the last flat FA or 4 and count down to DO or 1 to find the key name. Exercise 26 shows how this rule works.

Ex. 26

Another method for identifying the name of major keys with flats is to find the **next to last** flat in the key signature. That flat is the key name.

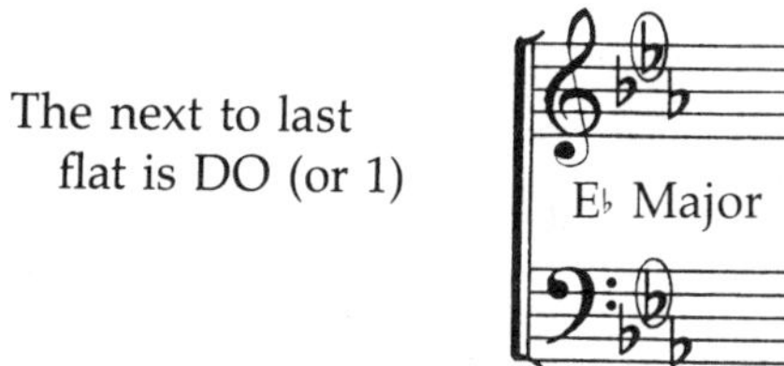

VOCABULARY

flat	major scale	scale
half step	natural	sharp
keyboard	octave	whole step
key signature		

Minor Scale

You have been studying the major scale and major key signatures. There are many other scales, and one of the most common is the *minor scale*. In major keys, DO is like a musical magnet that pulls us back to it. When the musical *tonality* is major, DO is home base, home tone, or *tonic*.

While DO is tonic in major keys, **LA is tonic in minor**. Minor scales begin and end on LA(6). LA is the musical magnet in minor keys. In Exercise 26, practice singing the minor scale from LA to LA (or 6 to 6) with hand signs. Sing a major scale from DO to DO for comparison. These tonalities sound different because they have different patterns of whole and half steps. Notice that the pattern of whole and half steps in minor is whole step, half step, whole step, whole step, half step, whole step, whole step.

Ex. 27

LA	TI	DO	RE	MI	FA	SO	LA
6	7	1	2	3	4	5	6
E	F♯	G	A	B	C	D	E

1   1/2   1   1   1/2   1   1

Each major scale has a **relative** (related) minor scale which is found by moving from DO to LA. Each key signature represents both a major and a minor key. The key signature with one sharp is G major: However, since every major has a relative minor, this may also be e minor, as in Exercise 27.

How do you tell, then, by looking at the key signature, whether the piece of music is in major or minor? You can't tell by the key signature alone. One way to determine if a piece is in major or minor is to look at how the song ends, since most pieces end on the **tonic** or DO(1) in major, or the **tonic** or LA (6) in minor.

Some relative major and minor key signatures:

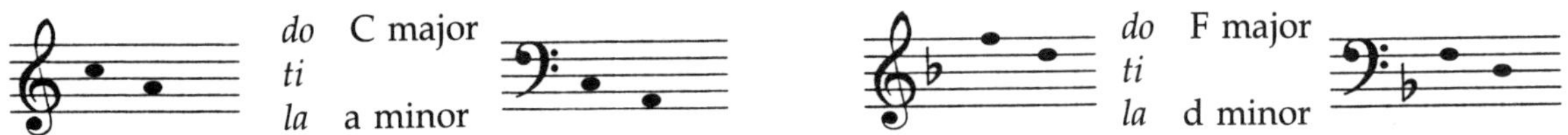

The minor scale shown in Exercise 27 is the *natural minor* scale. It uses the same key signature and exactly the same pitches as its relative major scale of G major. Similarly, C major and a minor use exactly the same pitches:

C major uses: C D E F G A B C
a minor uses: A B C D E F G A

You will practice learning to read in minor keys using some of the songs in this book. Practice using syllables and/or numbers and hand signs to become familiar with the tonal patterns of the minor scale.

Accidentals and Chromatics

As a scale is shifted to begin on various tones, you have seen that sharps (♯) and flats (♭) are needed to create the major and minor scale patterns. Sometimes composers want to introduce pitches outside the normal scale tones. This creates variety and interest. Composers may raise a scale pitch by adding a sharp, lower a scale pitch by adding a flat, or cancel a sharp or a flat in the scale by adding a natural sign (♮). When sharps, flats, and natural signs are used to alter the pitches in a scale, they are called *accidentals* or *chromatic* tones.

One commonly used chromatic tone (or accidental) is the raised 7th degree in the *harmonic minor* scale. Compare the e natural minor scale in Exercise 27 with the e harmonic minor scale in Exercise 28. Sing these and listen to the difference.

Ex. 28

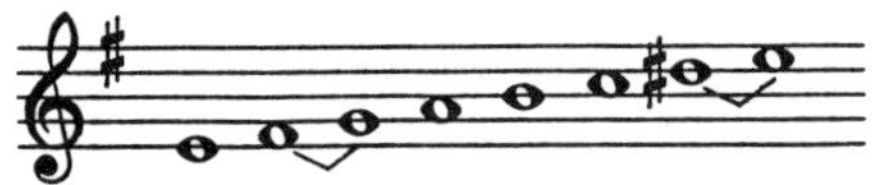

Exercise 29 shows the sharp chromatics on the keyboard. When you sing and play all 12 different tones from C to C, you have sung the *chromatic scale* or *twelve-tone scale*. This scale is made up entirely of half steps. Like the major and minor scales, the twelve-tone scale is also used to create music.

Ex. 29

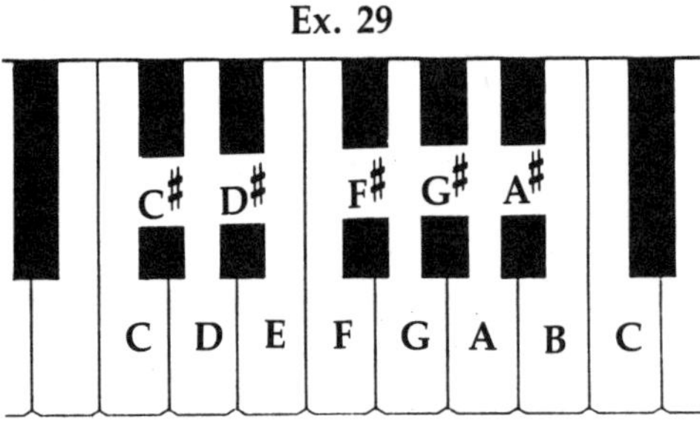

Chromatic tones also have solfege syllables. For sharps, all syllables end with I (an EE sound). (There are no special chromatic names to use with the number system.) Practice singing up the sharp chromatic scale with solfege syllables from the chart in Exercise 30.

Ex. 30

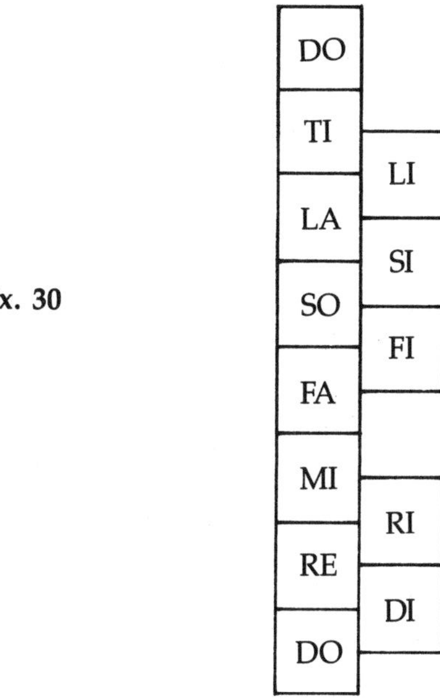

Example 31 shows the flat chromatics on the keyboard. Note that each of the black tones has a flat name and a sharp name. For example, C♯ and D♭ are actually the same pitch. They are *enharmonic tones.*

Ex. 31

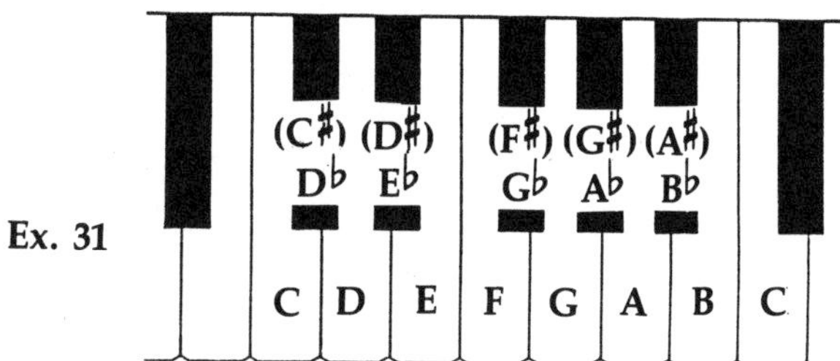

Flat chromatics also have solfege syllables. For flats, syllables end in E (an EH sound), except for the syllable for RE-flat which is RA (RAH). Practice singing down the flat chromatic scale using the syllables in the chart in Exercise 32.

Ex. 32

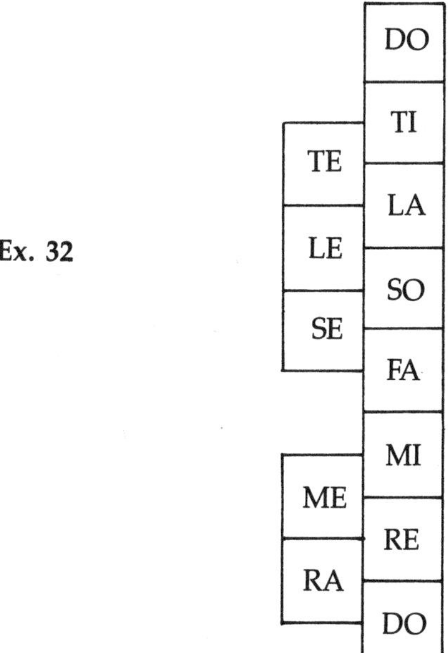

Example 33 shows the chromatic solfege chart complete. Use the chart to practice singing the chromatic scale up using sharp names and down using flat names.

Ex. 33

	DO	
	TI	
TE		LI
	LA	
LE		SI
	SO	
SE		FI
	FA	
	MI	
ME		RI
	RE	
RA		DI
	DO	
	TI	
TE		LI
	LA	
LE		SI
	SO	

There are hand signs for chromatic tones. The signs used most often are:

Exercise 34 includes accidentals. Sing these using syllables and hand signs in the most comfortable octave.

Ex. 34

Major keys

Key of F Major

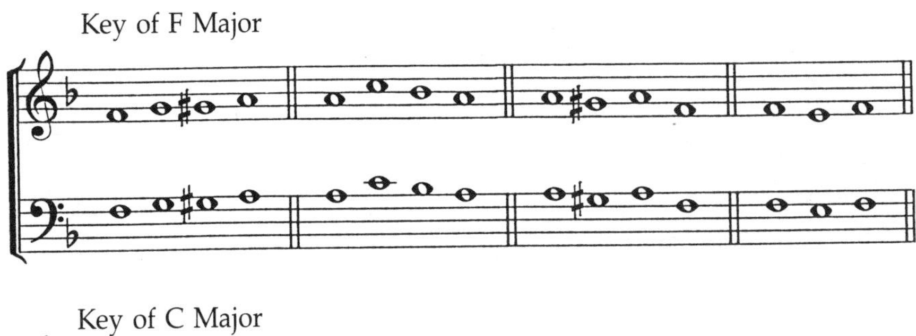

Key of C Major

Harmonic minor keys

Key of a minor

Key of e minor

VOCABULARY

accidental	harmonic minor	tonic
chromatic	minor scale	tonality
chromatic scale	natural minor	twelve-tone scale
enharmonic tone	relative minor	

Chapter 6

Reading Melody

You have learned how to tap and chant rhythms from musical notation, and you have learned to translate musical notation into pitches. You have read the symbols for rhythm and pitch separately. You are now ready to combine the reading of rhythm and pitch in the reading of melody.

Consider that each note has two functions:

(1) *To indicate rhythm.* (This function is shown by the type of note; for example, a quarter note receives one beat in meter.)

(2) *To indicate pitch.* (This function is shown by the placement of the note on the staff; for example, a note placed on the second line of a staff with a G clef signifies the pitch G.)

It will still be helpful to you to separate rhythm and pitch as you study notation and mentally prepare to sing music. At first, you may want to think the rhythm through and then the pitch before you put them together.

Reading Procedure

For the best results in reading melody, use the following procedure:

(1) Establish the basic beat by conducting or patting your leg or desk. Speak the rhythm using your preferred counting system. Once you are secure about the rhythm go on to the next steps.

(2) Locate DO(1), then silently read the syllables or numbers while you **think** the sounds. Use the hand signs to help you hear the pitches.

(3) Re-establish the beat. **Speak** the solfege syllables or numbers in the correct rhythm.

(4) Determine if the song (or exercise) is in a major or minor key. Sound the key name on a piano or other instrument. For songs in major, sing DO(1) MI(3) SO(5) MI(3) DO(1) *SO(5)* DO(1), and for songs in minor, sing LA(6) DO(1) MI(3) DO(1) LA(6) *MI(3)* LA(6) to establish the feeling for the tonality or key.

(5) Sing the syllables or numbers as you continue moving to the beat.

(6) Review any pitches you missed by hand signing and/or looking at the solfege or number chart while you sing those intervals.

(7) Repeat steps 4 and 5 when you feel secure about all the intervals.

Practice using the above procedure in reading the melodies in the following exercises. Be deliberate about the steps, and they will soon become habit.

Tonic Triad Melodies in Major

The melodies in Exercise 1 are based on the tonic triad in major keys. Baritones and basses should read from the bass clef. Tenors read from the treble clef but sing an octave lower (with the baritones and basses). Altos and sopranos read from the treble clef at actual pitch. Practice reading these melodies until you can read both the rhythm and melody easily.

Ex. 1

(c)

(d)

(e)

(f)

(g)

(h)

Tonic Triad Melodies in Minor

The melodies in Exercise 2 are based on the tonic triad in minor keys. Practice reading these with the reading procedure specified above.

Ex. 2

(a)

(b)

(c)

(d)

(e)

(f)

(g)

Chordal and Scalewise Melodies in Major

The melodies in Exercise 3 are based on simple chordal outlines and patterns that move upward or downward by step in the major scale. Again, use the reading procedure to practice these.

Ex. 3

(a)

(b)
(c)
(d)
(e)
(f)
(g)
(h)
(i)

Chordal and Scalewise Melodies in Minor

The melodies in Exercise 4 are based on simple chordal outlines and patterns that move upwards or downwards by step in the minor scale. Practice these using the reading procedure.

Ex. 4

(a)

(b)

(c)

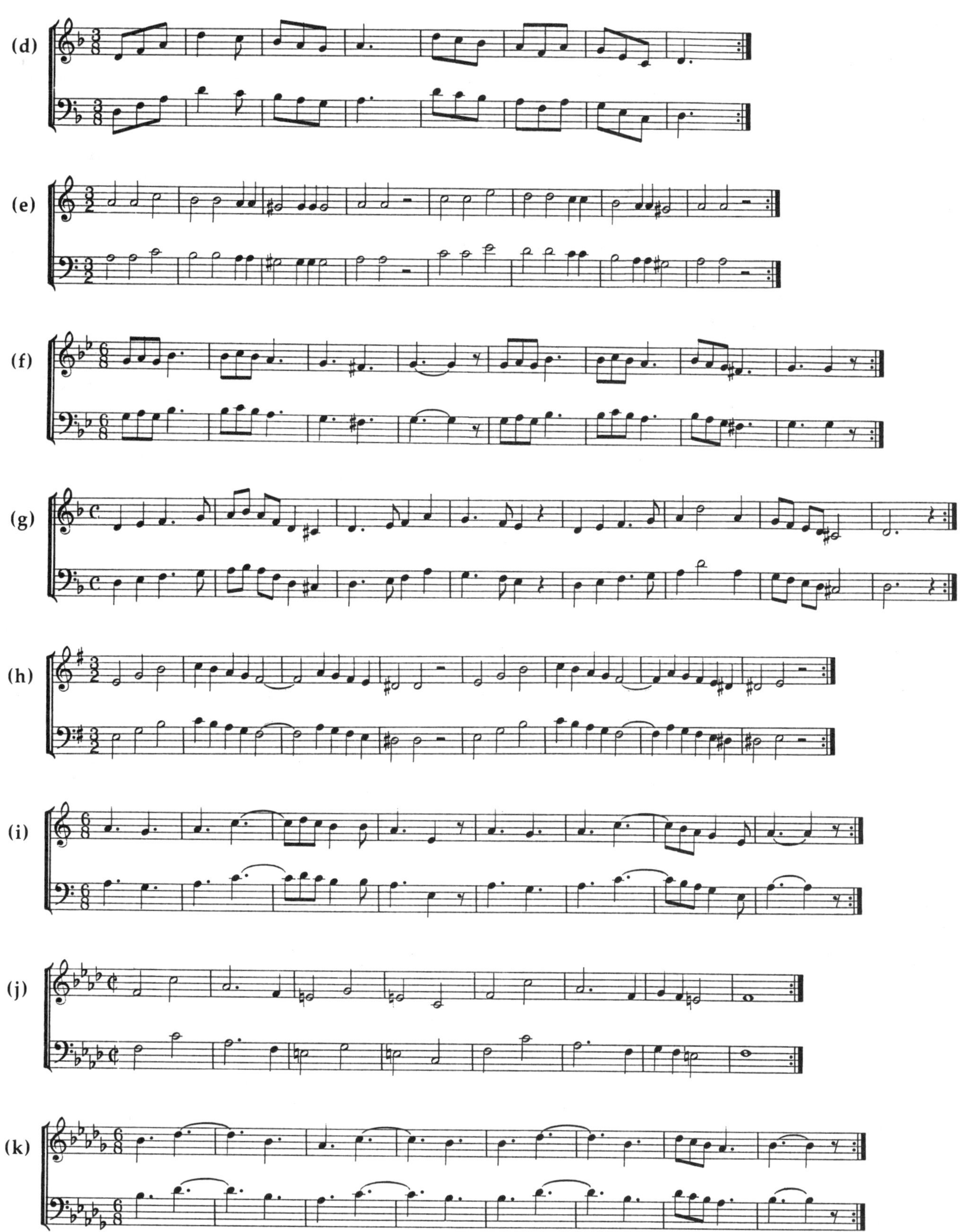
(d)
(e)
(f)
(g)
(h)
(i)
(j)
(k)

Melodies in Major and Minor

Practice reading the melodies in Exercise 5 using the reading procedure.

Ex. 5

(h)
(i)
(j)
(k)
(l)
(m)
(n)
(o)
3

Chordal Melodies in Major

The melodies in Exercise 6 are based on simple chords in major keys. Practice these using the reading procedure.

Ex. 6

Chordal Melodies in Minor

The melodies in Exercise 7 are based on simple chords in minor keys. Practice these using the reading procedure.

Ex. 7

(a)

(b)

(c)

(d)

(e)

CHAPTER 7

Singing in Harmony

You have now studied pitch and sung many tonal patterns. You have practiced singing melodies. Pitches can be sung one after another by one person as a *solo* or by many people in *unison*. When we combine two or more melodies and sing them together, we are singing in *harmony*. In order to sing harmony, a choir divides into two or more parts.

Triads and Chords

Harmony is a combination of vertical pitches that are sounded together. Each one of these vertical combinations of pitches is called a *chord*. The following examples illustrate the difference between the horizontal succession of pitches (melody) and the vertical arrangement of pitches (harmony or chords).

1. *Melody*:

2. *Harmony*:

(a) Chord for treble voices

SO 5 soprano
MI 3 soprano
DO 1 alto

(b) Chord for mixed voices

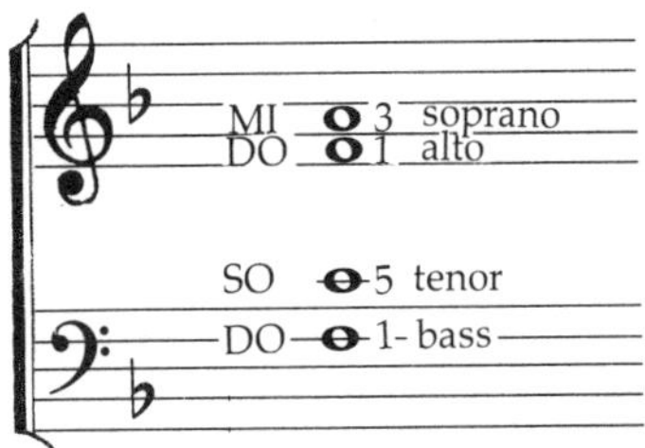

A succession of chords forms a "harmonic pattern" in the same way that a series of pitches forms a "tonal pattern." The songs in this book most frequently use chords called *triads*. Triads consist of three tones arranged in thirds. As the illustration shows, a triad may be formed above each degree of the scale:

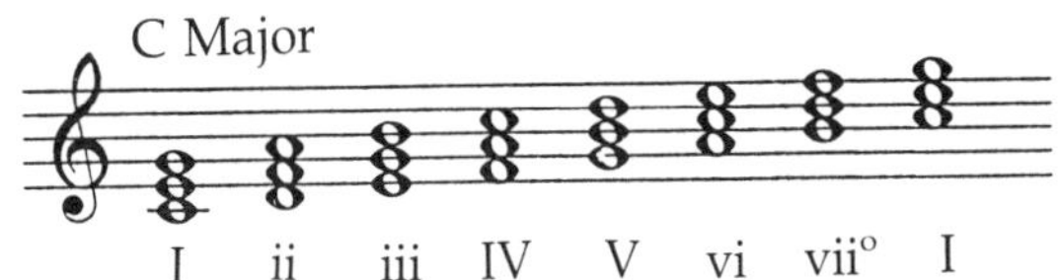

Notice that instead of solfege or Arabic number names, triads are named with Roman numerals. Large Roman numerals tell you that the triad is a major triad. Small Roman numerals tell you that the triad is a minor triad. The difference has to do with the size of the third. The major triad has a major third (2 whole steps) on the bottom and a minor third (1½ steps) on the top. In the minor triad the arrangement is reversed, with the minor third on the bottom and the major third on the top. A diminished triad, indicated by o, consist of two minor thirds. A triad of two major thirds is called augmented and indicated by +.

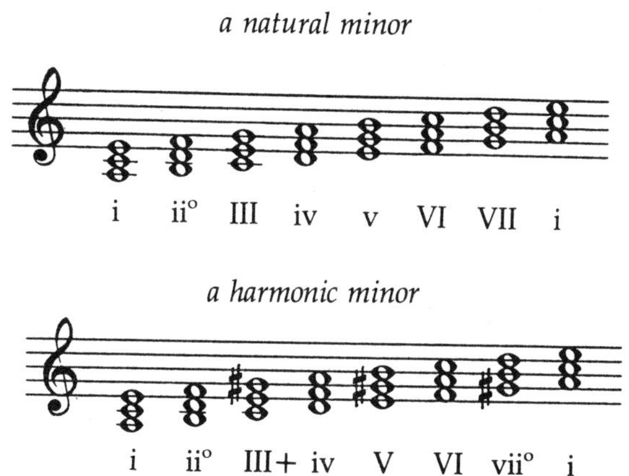

Cadences

The three most important triads are built on the first, fourth, and fifth tones of the scale. In major keys these are built on DO(1), FA(4), and SO(5) and are called the I, IV, and V chords. In minor keys these three triads are built on LA(6), RE(2), and MI(3). These are called the i, iv, and v (or V) chords. The V chord becomes major through use of the harmonic minor scale:

These three chords can be performed in an order that creates a harmonic pattern called a cadence, which usually occurs at the end of a piece or a section. Like a comma or a period in a sentence, it makes a point of rest. Learning to sing cadences will help you discover the feeling for tonality that is so important in reading and performing most music.

Part Singing

Most of your choir songs are written to be sung in parts. Each part—soprano, alto, tenor, and bass—is singing a familiar tonal pattern such as DO(1) SO(5) DO(1) or MI(3) RE(2) MI(3). The combination of these tonal patterns creats harmony.

Prepare for singing harmony by practicing cadences. Follow the steps outlined below, and **use hand signs for all steps**.

4-part, SATB choir	*2- or 3-part choir (SA, SSA, TB, TTB, TBB):*
All sing line 1, then line 2, then line 3, and then line 4.	
Bass sings line 4 alone. Add tenor on line 3, then alto on line 2, then soprano on line 1.	Choose two or three lines from the 4-part cadences. All sing line 1, then line 2, and then line 3.

Cadences in Major and Minor Keys

Sing the cadence in Exercise 1 in the keys of F, G, A♭, and A.

Ex. 1*

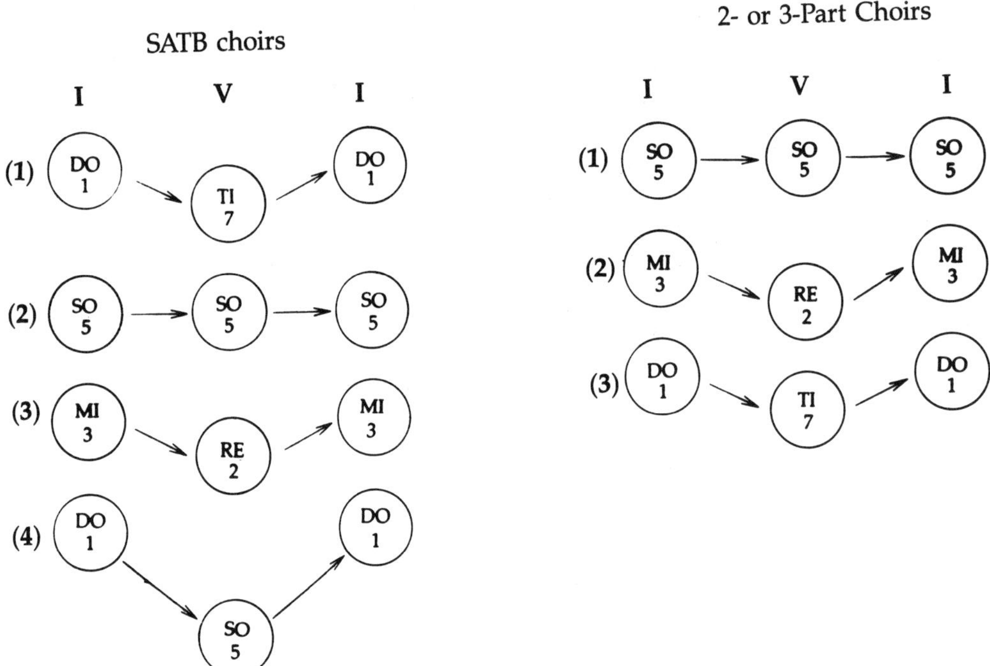

Sing the cadence in Exercise 2 in the keys of F, G, A♭, and A.

Ex. 2

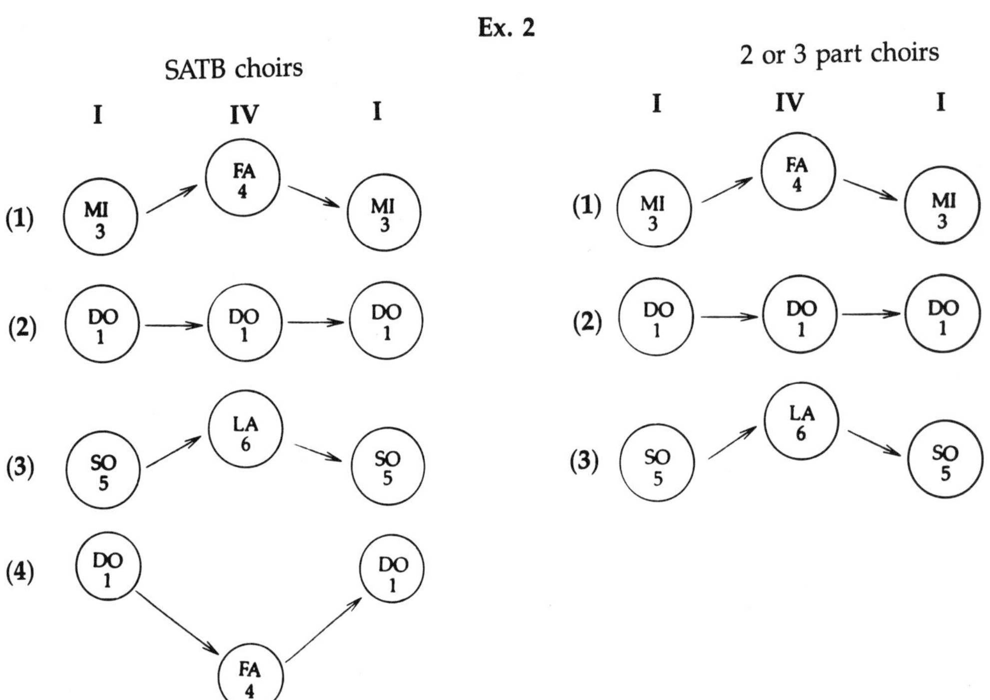

*These graphs of cadences are used with the permission of Cloys Webb, Music Supervisor and Choral Director, Perryton, Texas.

Sing the cadence in Exercise 3 in the keys of D, E♭, E, F, A♭, and A.

Ex. 3

SATB Choirs

	I	vi	I
(1)	MI 3	MI 3	MI 3
(2)	DO 1	DO 1	DO 1
(3)	SO 5	LA 6	SO 5
(4)	DO 1	LA 6	DO 1

2- or 3-Part Choir

	I	vi	I
(1)	MI 3	MI 3	MI
(2)	DO 1	DO 1	DO 1
(3)	SO 5	LA 6	SO 5

With the remaining cadences, choirs of two and three parts choose 2 or 3 lines to sing. Find the lines that sound best together.

Sing the cadence in Exercise 4 in the keys of F, G, A♭, and A.

Ex. 4

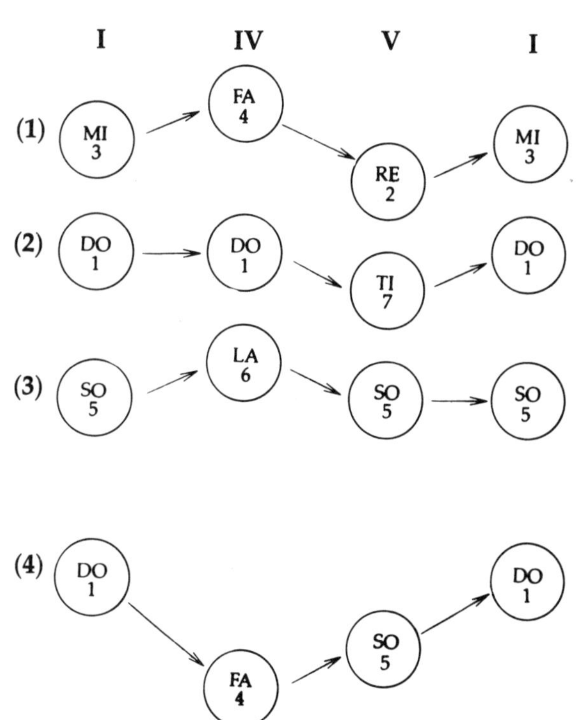

Sing the cadence in Exercise 5 in the keys of e, f, g, and a.

Ex. 5

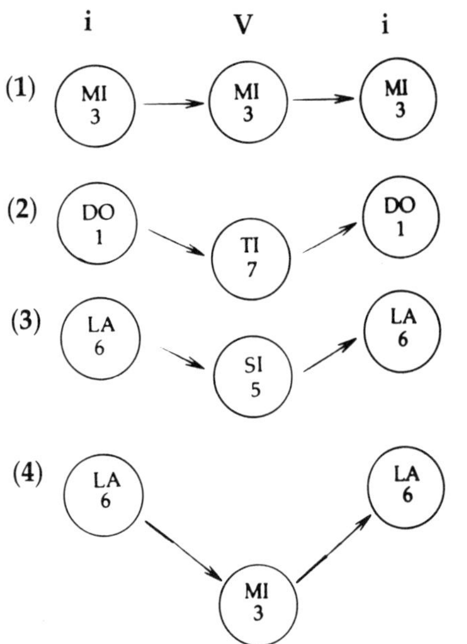

Sing the cadence in Exercise 6 in the keys of f, g, a, and b.

Ex. 6

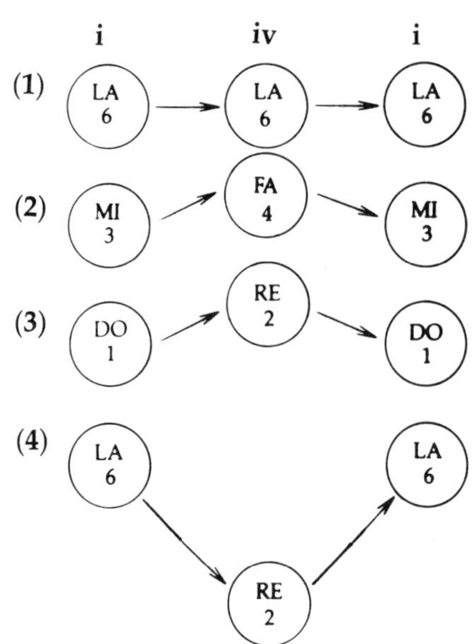

Sing the cadence in Exercise 7 in the keys of f, g, a, and b.

Ex. 7

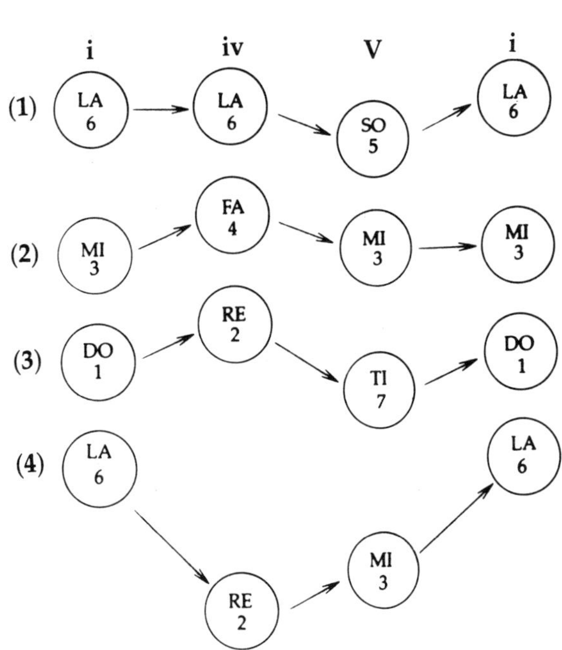

Sing the cadence in Exercise 8 in the keys of f, g, a, and b.

Ex. 8

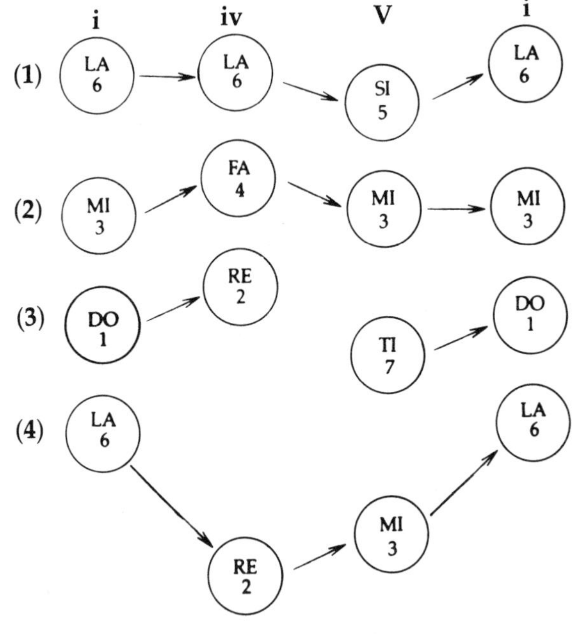

Sing the cadence in Exercise 9 in the keys of f, g, a, and b.

Ex. 9

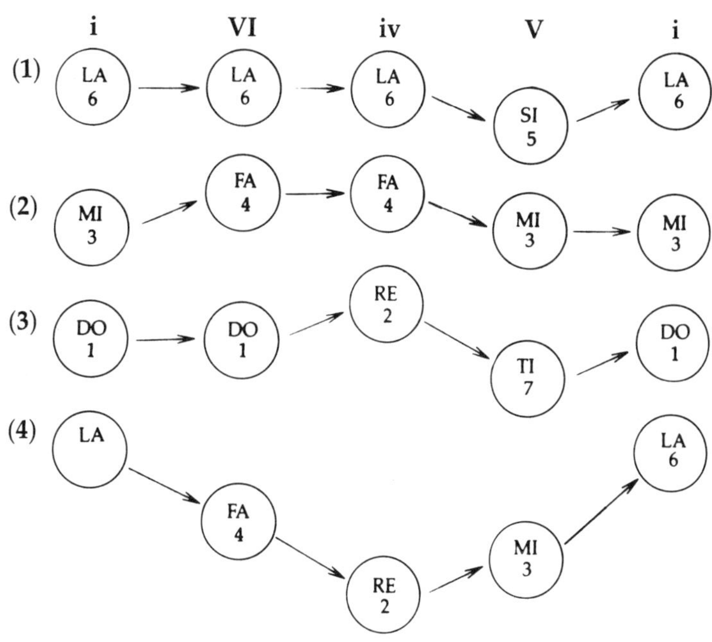

Sing the cadence in Exercise 10 in the keys of E♭, E, F, G, A♭, and A.

Ex. 10

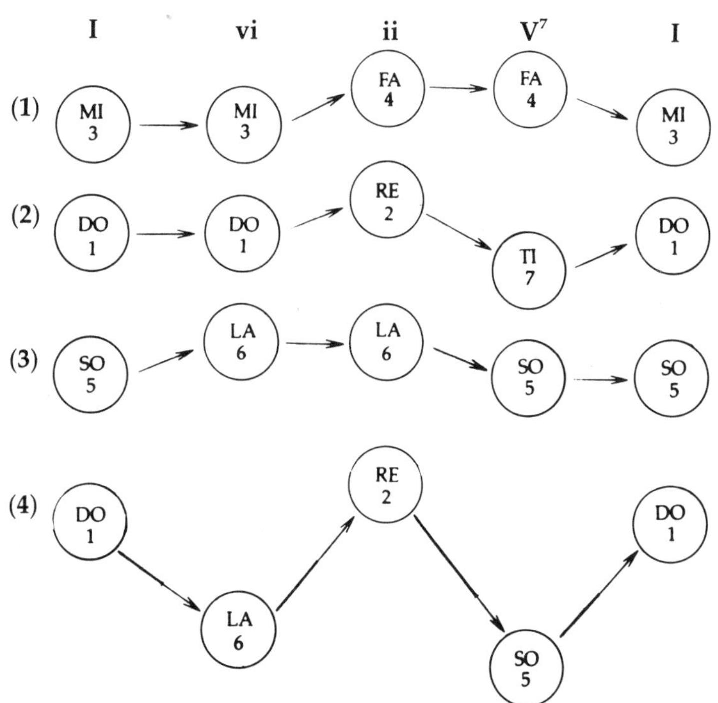

Sing the cadence in Exercise 11 in the keys of E♭, E, F, G, A♭, and A.

Ex. 11

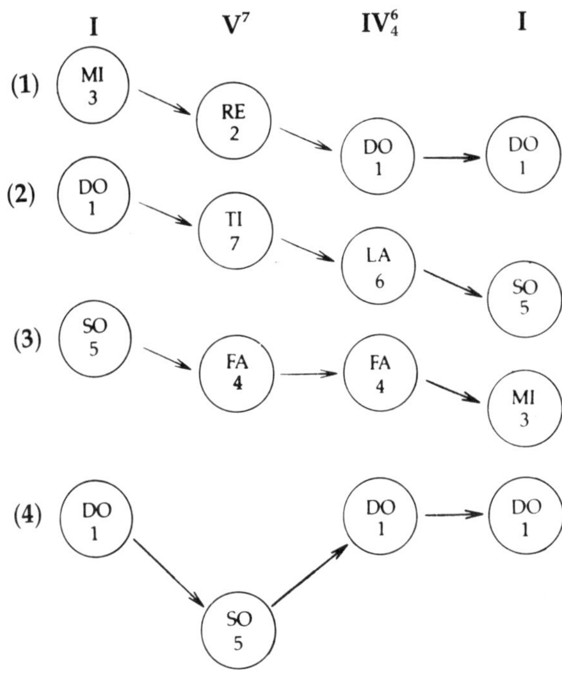

Chords Combined with Rhythm

The patterns in Exercises 12 through 16 can be sung in two, three, four, or even more parts. To practice singing harmony with the rhythm indicated, follow these steps:

(1) the entire choir sings each of the lines 1, 2, 3, and 4 in unison, keeping a steady beat.

(2) the entire choir divides into parts to sing harmony, always keeping a steady beat.

Suggestions for practicing harmony:

	1	2	3	4
Line 1	Soprano (S)	B	T	A
Line 2	Alto (A)	S	B	T
Line 3	Tenor (T)	A	S	B
Line 4	Bass (B)	T	A	S

This permits each part to sing each line.

(3) Practice the eighth-note lines in Exercise 13 in unison, then in parts. Switch parts as suggested above.

(4) In Exercises 14, 15, and 16, do not attempt to sing the sixteenth notes and triplets quickly. Begin slowly, keeping a steady beat. After all the linesare mastered, you may wish to sing the excercises at a faster tempo.

(5) After all the lines in Exercises 12 through 16 are learned, experiment with combining rhythms; for example, line one of Exercise 12 with line 2 of Exercise 13, or line 4 of Exercise 12 with lines 1 and 2 of Exercise 16.

Ex. 12

Quarter Notes

(1)	Do	Re	Mi	Fa	Fa	Mi	Re	Do
	I	V_7	I	IV	IV	I	V_7	I
(2)	Do	Ti	Do	$\underline{\text{La}}$	$\underline{\text{La}}$	Do	$\underline{\text{Ti}}$	La
(3)	Mi	Fa	So	$\underline{\text{La}}$	$\underline{\text{La}}$	So	Fa	Mi
(4)	Do	$\underline{\text{So}}$	Do	$\underline{\text{Fa}}$	$\underline{\text{Fa}}$	Do	$\underline{\text{So}}$	Do

Ex. 13

Eighth Notes

(1) D M R F M S F   L F S M F R D

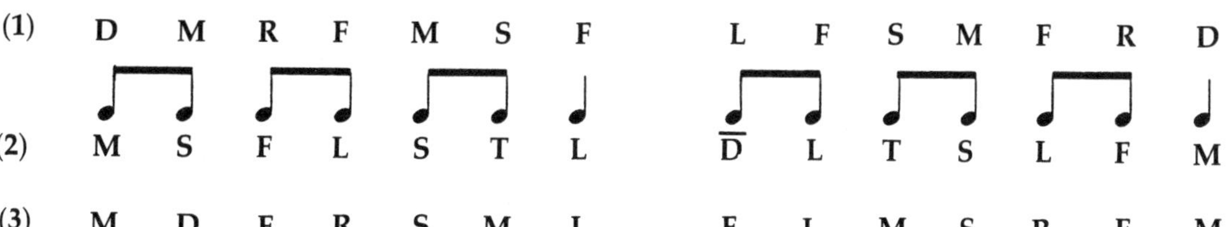

(2) M S F L S T L $\overline{\text{D}}$ L T S L F M

(3) M D F R S M L   F L M S R F M

Ex. 14

Sixteenth Notes

(1) D R M D R M F R M F S M F S L   L S F L S F M S F M R   D

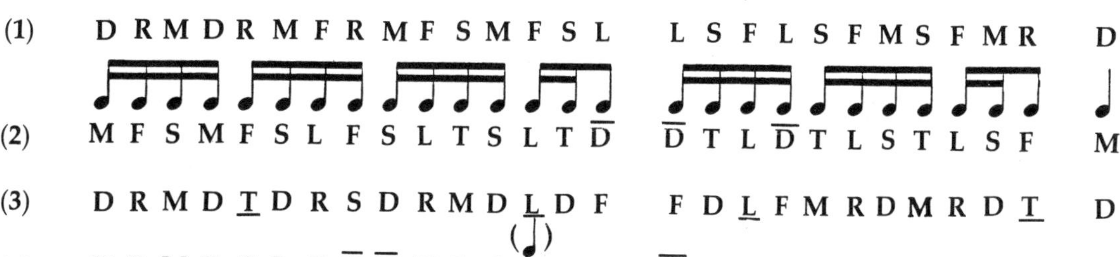

(2) M F S M F S L F S L T S L T $\overline{\text{D}}$ $\overline{\text{D}}$ T L $\overline{\text{D}}$ T L S T L S F   M

(3) D R M D $\underline{\text{T}}$ D R S D R M D $\underline{\text{L}}$ D F   F D $\underline{\text{L}}$ F M R D M R D $\underline{\text{T}}$ D

(♩)

(4) D R M F S L T $\overline{\text{D}}$ $\overline{\text{D}}$ T L S L $\overline{\text{D}}$ T L S F M R D R M R   D

Ex. 15

Two Sixteenths Followed by an Eighth

(1) D R M R M F M F S F   L S F S F M F M R D

(2) M F S F S L S L T L $\overline{\text{D}}$ T L T L S L S F M

(3) M R D F M R S F M L   F S L M F S R M F M

Ex. 16

Triplets

(1) D R M R M F M F S F   L S F S F M F M R D

(2) M F S F S L S L T L $\overline{\text{D}}$ T L T L S L S F M

Notated Chord Progressions

The harmonic patterns or *chord progressions* that you have sung in Exercises 1 through 16 are shown in notation in Exercises 17 through 35. Practice these using syllables or numbers and keeping a steady beat. Change parts as you have above. Read lines in unison as necessary.

Ex. 22

Ex. 23

S

A

T
(C)

B

i i i VI iv i v v i i

Ex. 24

S

A

T
(C)

B

i i i VI iv i V V i i

Ex. 25

S

A

T
(C)

B

i VI iv iv iv v v i

Ex. 26

S

A

T
(C)

B

i VI iv iv iv V V_7 i

SSA

Ex. 27 Ex. 28

Ex. 29

Ex. 30

Ex. 31

T B B

VOCABULARY

cadence	harmonic pattern	triad
chord	harmony	unison
chord progression	melody	

Overleaf ▶
South Houston High School Chamber Choir

PART 3

The Musical Literature

PART 3

The Musical Literature

The music on the following pages is your opportunity to explore the vast and exciting world of human musical sound. These pieces have been selected so that they represent all the major historical periods, many different styles, and a cross section of well-known and lesser-known composers.

Each piece of music has been selected because it expresses something about life. It communicates a feeling and a thought in an effective way. To understand what those feelings and thoughts are, it is necessary for you and other members of your choir to translate the musical symbols into sound. In the process of singing, you unlock the message of the music.

In this sense, then, the music on the following pages is like an adventure waiting to happen. You have before you a whole new musical world to explore and to investigate. Who knows what you will discover and what wonderful sounds you will learn to make?

The "literature" in this book is a collection of musical compositions for voices. It is organized in four sections according to the combination of voices required to perform it:

(1) **Rounds or Canons**. These eight pieces can be sung by any choir.

(2) **Music for Mixed Voices**. These songs have been arranged for male and female voices in two, three, or four parts.

(3) **Music for Treble Voices**. These works are scored for voices that sing in the range of the treble clef, whether female or unchanged male singers. The arrangements are in unison, two, and three parts.

(4) **Music for Boys' Voices**. These selections are arranged to be sung by changing or changed male voices.

Each piece is numbered so that you can find it easily. Within each of the four sections, the pieces are ordered alphabetically by title.

Your musical director will guide you through this grand tour. Enjoy!

Rounds or canons ("canon" means rule) are a special type of musical form in which the same exact melody is performed in strict imitation. By beginning the tune at different times, the parts overlap, and harmony results. Writing a round or canon is like solving a puzzle, because the melody must be created so that each of its sections will sound well together. That's no easy task, and if you don't believe it, try writing one!

1. Ah, Poor Bird

Old English Round

1 2 3 4
Ah, poor bird take your flight, Far a-bove the sor - rows of this sad night.

2. By the Rivers of Babylon

from *The Hallelujah*, 1854

(3 parts)

LOWELL MASON (1792-1872)

By the riv - ers of Ba - by - lon, There we sat down;

hanged our harps up - on the wil - lows in the midst there - of.

3. Canon

Thomas Ken

THOMAS TALLIS (c.1505-1585)

We wept, we wept, when we re - mem-bered Zi - on, We

All praise to Thee, my God, this night, For all the bless - ings
All praise to Thee, my God, this night, For
of the light; Keep me, oh keep me, King of Kings, be -
all the bless - ings of the light, Keep me, oh keep me,
neath Thine own Al - might - y wings.
King of Kings, be - neath Thine own Al - might - y wings.

Rounds

4. Ghost of Tom

Traditional Round

①
②
③
④
Have you seen the ghost of Tom? Long white bones with the
flesh all gone.
Oh,
Would - n't it be chil - ly with no skin on?

5. Hallelujah

①
②
Hal - le - lu - jah! Hal - le - lu - jah!
A - - - men, A - - - men.

6. Hey, Ho!

Old English

①
②
③
Hey ho! No - bod - y home. Meat nor drink nor mon - ey have I none,
Yet, I will be mer - ry. Hey ho! No - bod - y home.

7. Music Alone Shall Live

German Round

1
All things shall per - ish un - der the sky.

2
Mu - sic a - lone shall live, Mu - sic a - lone shall live,

3
Mu - sic a - lone shall live, nev - er to die.

8. Rise up, O Flame

MICHAEL PRAETORIUS (1571-1621)

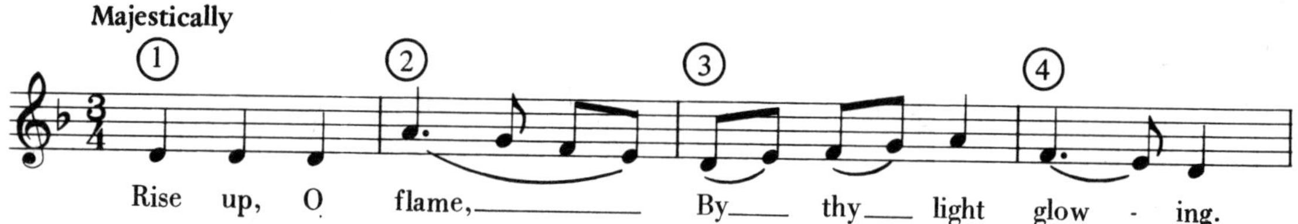
Majestically
1 2 3 4
Rise up, O flame, By thy light glow - ing.

Show to us beau - ty, vi - sion and joy.

9. Shalom, Chaverim

Israeli Round

1 2 3
Sha - lom, cha-ver-im! Sha - lom, cha-ver-im! Sha - lom, sha - lom. Le -

hit - ra - ot, le - hit - ra - ot, sha - lom, sha - lom.

Translation: Good-bye, friends, till we meet again.

10. America the Beautiful

for Mixed Voices, S.A.T.B., with Piano

Words by Katherine Bates

SAMUEL WARD
Arranged by Rob Landes

As one of the best loved patriotic songs, "America the Beautiful" is easier to sing than our national anthem, "The Star-Spangled Banner." For this reason some people have proposed that it should replace the present anthem. Arranger Rob Landes enhances this patriotic favorite with rich chords in the piano accompaniment.

7
am - ber waves of grain, For pur - ple moun - tain
am - ber waves of grain, For pur - ple moun - tain
am - ber waves of grain, For pur - ple moun - tain
am - ber waves of grain, For pur - ple moun - tain
mf
mp
10
cresc.
mf
maj - es - ties a - bove the fruit - ed plain. A -
cresc.
mf
maj - es - ties a - bove the fruit - ed plain. A -
cresc.
mf
maj - es - ties a - bove the fruit - ed plain. A -
cresc.
mf
maj - es - ties a - bove the fruit - ed plain. A -
cresc.
mf

13
mer - i - ca, A - mer - i - ca, God shed His grace on
mer - i - ca, A - mer - i - ca, God shed His grace on
mer - i - ca, A - mer - i - ca, God shed His grace on
mer - i - ca, A - mer - i - ca, God shed His grace on
16
thee, And crown thy good with broth - er-hood from
on thee, And crown thy good with broth - er-hood from
thee, And crown thy good with broth - er-hood from
on thee, And crown thy good with broth - er-hood from

19
f
sea to shin - ing sea.
f
sea to shin - ing sea.
f
sea to shin - ing sea.
f
sea to shin - ing sea.
f
22
mp
Oh, beau - ti - ful for
mp
Oh, beau - ti - ful for
dim.
mf
dim.
mp

25
mf
pil - grim feet, whose stern im - pas - sioned stress. A
mf
pil - grim feet, whose stern im - pas - sioned stress. A
mf
A
mf
28
thor - ough-fare for free - dom, beat a - cross the wil - der -
thor - ough-fare for free - dom, beat a - cross the wil - der -
thor - ough-fare for free - dom, beat
mp

31
mf
ness! A - mer - i - ca, A - mer - i - ca! God
mf
ness! A - mer - i - ca, A - mer - i - ca! God
mf
A - mer - i - ca, A - mer - i - ca! God
mf
A - mer - i - ca, A - mer - i - ca! God
mf
34
mend thine ev - 'ry flaw. Con - firm thy soul in
mend thine ev - 'ry, ev 'ry flaw. Con - firm thy soul in
mend thine ev - 'ry flaw. Con - firm thy soul in
mend thine ev - 'ry, ev - 'ry flaw. Con - firm thy soul in

37
self con-trol, Thy lib - er - ty in law!
self con-trol, Thy lib - er - ty in law!
self con-trol, Thy lib - er - ty in law!
self con-trol, Thy lib - er - ty in law!
40
rit.
Oh,
Oh,
Oh,
Oh,
rit.

43
a tempo
beau - ti - ful for pa - triot dream that sees be - yond the
a tempo
beau - ti - ful for pa - triot dream that sees be - yond the
a tempo
beau - ti - ful for pa - triot dream that sees be - yond the
a tempo
beau - ti - ful for pa - triot dream that sees be - yond the
a tempo
46
years, Thine al - a - bas - ter ci - ties gleam un -
years, Thine al - a - bas - ter ci - ties gleam un -
years, Thine al - a - bas - ter ci - ties gleam un -
years, Thine al - a - bas - ter ci - ties gleam un -

49
rit.
ff
a tempo
dimmed by hu - man tears! A - mer - i - ca, A -
rit.
a tempo
dimmed by hu - man tears! A - mer - i - ca, A -
rit.
a tempo
dimmed by hu - man tears! A - mer - i - ca, A -
rit.
a tempo
dimmed by hu - man tears! A - mer - i - ca, A -
rit.
ff
a tempo
52
mer - i - ca, God shed his grace on thee, And
mer - i - ca, God shed his grace on, on thee, And
mer - i - ca, God shed his grace on thee, And
mer - i - ca, God shed his grace on, on thee, And

55
crown thy good with broth - er-hood from sea to
crown thy good with broth - er-hood from sea to
crown thy good with broth - er-hood from sea to
crown thy good with broth - er-hood from sea to
58
shin - ing sea!
shin - ing sea!
shin - ing sea!
shin - ing sea!
no rit.
8va

11. Bright New Day

for Mixed Chorus, S.A.T.B., accompanied

Words and Music by ED ROBERTSON

This song in slow "pop" style conveys the message that hope comes with the dawn. The two verses are sung in unison, and the refrain is set in three parts with a short four-part ending. This gradual addition of voice parts is one way that composers have of adding variety to their songs.

M. M. ♩ = 72
Piano
mp
6
10
Unison mp
When the night is lone-ly, Dark-ness all a-round you,
When your dreams are shat-tered, And the world seems emp-ty,
14
When you feel for-sak-en, Long-ing for a home.
When you're feel-ing trou-bled, When you know de-spair.

18
When you start to tremble, Yearn-ing for the day-light,
When you are dis- cour-aged, Search-ing for an ans-wer,
22
When you start to wonder if day will ev - er come.
When you can't be certain if hope is an - y - where.
26
S.
A.
With the dawn comes the sun - light,
unis.
T.
B.
30
And the dark - ness fades a - way.

34
Lift your eyes in the still night,
38
And watch for a bright, new day!
div.
mp
mp
42
1.
2.
mp
rit.

12. Chorale

for Mixed Voices, S.A.T.B.

G.F. HANDEL (1685-1759)
Edited by John Rutter

George Frideric Handel (see page 347) was, with Bach, one of the two greatest composers of the first half of the eighteenth century. This chorale (the German name for a hymn) is part of Handel's *St. John Passion*, originally written to a German text by the poet Brockes.

A tempo giusto*
Soprano
Alto
Tenor
Bass
Keyboard

3
Lord, my spir - it longs to know thee;
Ach, wie hun - gert mein Ge - mü the,

*Literally 'at a just (i.e. correct or appropriate) speed'. 'Giusto' can also mean exact or accurate.

6
Friend of man, thy good-ness show me!
Men-schen freund, nach dei-ner Gü-te!
9
Ah! my hun-gry soul is yearn-ing,
Ach! wie pfleg' ich oft mit Thra-nen
12
Lord, for strength from thee re-turn-ing!
mich nach die-ser kost zu seh-nen!

15
Quench my thirst, and hear my cry - ing:
Ach, wie pfle - get mich su dür - sten
18
Of thy grace new life supply - ing,
nach dem Trank des Le - hens für - sten!
21
So, at last, my prayers re - quit - ed
wün - sche stets dass mein Ge - bei - ne

24
I may be with thee u - nit - ed.
sich durch Gott mit Gott ver - ei - ne.

27

13. Come Follow Me

S.A.T.B. with Piano and Optional Flute

Words by
Don Besig and Nancy Price (ASCAP)

Music by
DON BESIG (ASCAP)

This is a mellow song in a popular style. "Broken" chords called arpeggios are used in the piano part almost constantly throughout. The pleasant melody, flowing rhythm pattern, and familiar harmonies give a soothing effect that fits the text.

*Play cues in absence of flute.

(oo)
19
mf
High a-bove the trees I can
19
feel the gen - tle breeze; it's call - ing, "Come, fol - low

27
me."
In the morn-ing light I can
mp
Oo
27
watch the birds in flight;
they seem to say, "Fol - low
35
me."
All the world a - round me seems to
35

call my name; there is wonder in all I can
43
mf
see.
Ev-'ry-where I go there's a
mp
Oo
43
voice I think I know;
I hear it clear as can
I hear it clear as can

be:
"I'll be your guide, fol - low
55
me."
55

65
mf
I am all a - lone; you've been
65
mf
trav - 'ling on your own.
Why don't you

come, fol - low me?
73
We can make it through; there's so much that we can
73
do, if you will come, fol - low

81
me.
We will seek our
81
for - tunes, we will chase our dreams, and hold
fast to all we be - lieve!

89
Now we're on our way; don't look
89
back at yes - ter - day,
this is our
time to be free.
rit.
rit.
rit.

freely
ten.
99
stagger breathing
a tempo
Come, take my hand, fol - low me.
freely
ten.
a tempo
99
freely
ten.
a tempo
Oo
dim.
rit.
dim.
rit.
dim.
rit.

14. Come, Jesus, Holy Son of God

for Two-Part Mixed Voices, accompanied

G.F. HANDEL (1685-1759)
Arranged by Hal Hopson

Originally written by Handel for soprano and alto, this song is part of an oratorio, a sacred work of many sections for solo voices and chorus. The melodies of the two parts imitate and echo each other in continuous motion. Handel wrote many oratorios, the most famous being *Messiah* which contains the well-known "Hallelujah Chorus."

With a gentle flow
Accomp.
mf
A
SOPRANOS and ALTOS
mf
Come, Je - sus, Ho - ly Son of God, come.
TENORS and BASSES
mf
Come, Je - sus, Ho - ly Son of God,
Ho - ly Son of God, Thy truth un - seal. Thy love re -
Ho - ly Son of God, Thy truth un-seal. Thy love re - veal.

veal, truth un - seal,__ Thy love__ re - veal.
Thy truth un - seal,__ Thy love__ re - veal.
mf
B
mf
rit.
Lord, hear Thou in__ mer-cy our prayer to__Thee,
p
mf
rit.
a tempo
mf
Come, Je - sus, Ho - ly Son of God, come.
Come, Je - sus, Ho - ly Son of God,
a tempo

Ho - ly Son of God, Come in Thy might. Send forth Thy
Ho - ly Son of God, Come in Thy might. Send forth Thy light.
light, come in might, Come send forth Thy light.
Come_ in might, Come send forth Thy light.
Come, Je - sus,_ O
Lord, hear Thou_ in_ mer-cy, our prayer to_Thee.

mf
ho - ly Son of God. For Thee we long. Hear Thou our prayer.
For Thee we long. Hear Thou our
For Thee we long. O hear Thou our prayer. To Thee be glo - ry
prayer. O hear Thou our prayer. To Thee be glo - ry
now and ev - er - more.
mf
now and ev - er - more. Lord, hear Thou in mer - cy our prayer to Thee.
mf

D
mf
Come, Je - sus Ho - ly Son of God. To Thee be glo - -
To Thee be glo - -
- - - ry, To Thee be glo - ry ev - er -
più lento
- - - ry, To Thee be glo - ry ev - er -
più lento
Tempo I
more.
more.
Tempo I
f
rit.

15. Early One Morning

S.A.T.B., with Piano

English Folk Song

17th Century Tune
Arranged by Noble Cain

Noble Cain has made a dramatic arrangement of this fine old English folk song. The maiden in the song has obviously been left by an earlier love, so she begs her new love to be true. As the soprano line goes up the tenor or bass line goes down, and visa versa, building tension, then relaxing it. Dynamic contrasts add to the dramatic interest.

*May be sung S.A.A.B. by having low Altos sing Tenor

Oh, nev - er leave me, May thy love ne'er from me
oh, May thy love ne'er from me
oh, May thy love ne'er from me
oh, May thy love ne'er from me
espress.
piu p
go! So gay is the gar - land, and fresh are the ros - es I've
go! So gay is the gar - land, and fresh are the ros - es I've
go! So gay is the gar - land, and fresh are the ros - es I've
go! I've

mp
gath-ered from the gar - den to place on thy brow! Oh, don't de-
(pp)
gath-ered from the gar - den to place on thy brow! Oh,
(pp)
gath-ered from the gar - den to place on thy brow! Oh,
(pp)
gath-ered from the gar - den to place on thy brow! Oh,
cresc.
dim.
mp dolce
f
ceive me, Oh, nev - er leave me, May thy love ne'er
f
oh, May thy love ne'er
f
oh, May thy love ne'er
f
oh, May thy love ne'er
espress.
più p
f

from me go. Thus sang the pret - ty maid - en, her
from me go. Thus sang the pret - ty maid - en, her
from me go. Thus sang the pret - ty maid - en, her
from me go.
dim.
p
f
sor - rows re - call - ing, Thus sang the pret - ty maid - en in the
sor - rows re - call - ing, Thus sang the pret - ty maid - en in the
sor - rows re - call - ing, Thus sang the pret - ty maid - en in the
Thus sang the pret - ty maid - en in the
cresc.

f
p
val - ley be - low. Oh, don't de - ceive me, Oh, nev - er
val - ley be - low. Oh, don't de - ceive me, Oh, nev - er
val - ley be - low. Oh, don't de - ceive me, Oh, nev - er
val - ley be - low. Oh, don't de - ceive me Oh, nev - er
dim.
rit.
leave me, May thy love ne'er from me go.
leave me, May thy love ne'er from me go.
leave me, May thy love ne'er from me go.
leave me, May thy love ne'er from me go.
espress.
f cresc. poco a poco rit.

16. El Grillo

(The Cricket)
for Mixed Voices, S.S.A.B.

Edited and translated by
Gustav Reese

JOSQUIN DES PRES (c. 1440-1521)
Frottole libro tertio, 1505

Josquin was the most admired composer of his time. Along with important works for the church and royal courts, he wrote popular songs such as this. Josquin gave great care to expressing the meaning of the words in his music. It does not stretch the imagination to say that the cricket's singing is clearly heard in this song.

B
15
Dal - le be - ve gril - lo can - ta dal-le dal-le be-ve be-ve
From a pud - dle he is sing - ing; from a, from a, pud-dle, pud-dle
Dal - le be - ve gril - lo can - ta dal-le dal-le be-ve be-ve
From a pud-dle he is sing - ing; from a, from a, pud-dle, pud-dle
Dal - le be - ve gril - lo can - ta dal-le dal-le be-ve be-ve
From a pud-dle he is sing - ing; from a, from a, pud-dle, pud-dle
C
20
gril-lo gril-lo can-ta. El gril - - lo, el gril-lo è buon can - to - re.
he is, he is sing-ing. The crick - et sings while in the clo - ver sport - ing.
gril-lo gril-lo can - ta. El gril - - lo, el gril-lo è buon can - to - re.
he is, he is sing-ing. The crick - et sings while in the clo - ver sport - ing.
gril-lo gril-lo can - ta. El gril - - lo, el gril-lo è buon can - to - re.
he is, he is sing-ing. The crick - et sings while in the clo - ver sport - ing.

D
25
Ma non fa co - me gl'al-tri uc - cel - li, Co - me li han can - ta - to un
Van' de fat - to in al - tro lo - co, Sem - pre el gril - lo sta pur
He's un - like all of the oth - er chirp - ers: Birds fly off to a new lo -
Af - ter they have sung in one place brief - ly, But the crick - et stays at his
E
30
po - co, sal - do. Quan - do la mag - gior è'l cal - do Al -
ca - tion sta - tion. When the sum - mer heat's up - on us, He

35
hor can - ta sol per a - mo - - - - - - - re.
sings be - cause he is out a - court - - - - - - - ing.
hor can - ta sol per a - mo - - - - - - - re.
sings be - cause he is out a - court - - - - - - - ing.
hor can - ta sol per a - mo - - - - - - - re.
sings be - cause he is out a - court - - - - - - - ing.
F
40
El gril - - lo, el gril - lo è buon can - to - re Che
The crick - et sings while in the clo - ver sport - ing; He
El gril - - lo, el gril - lo è buon can - to - re Che
The crick - et sings while in the clo - ver sport - ing; He
El gril - - lo, el gril - lo è buon can - to - re Che
The crick - et sings while in the clo - ver sport - ing; He

45
tie - ne lon - go ver - - - - - - - - - so.
pipes a note and holds it.
G
50
Dal - le be - ve gril - lo can - ta dal-le dal-le be-ve be-ve
From a pud - dle he is sing-ing; from a, from a, pud-dle, pud-dle

H
55
gril-lo gril-lo can-ta. El gril - - lo, el gril-lo è buon can - to - re Che
he is, he is sing-ing. The crick - et sings while in the clo-ver sport - ing; He
gril-lo gril-lo can-ta. El gril - - lo, el gril-lo è buon can - to - re Che
he is, he is sing-ing. The crick - et sings while in the clo-ver sport - ing; He
gril-lo gril-lo can-ta. El gril - - lo, el gril-lo è buon can - to - re Che
he is, he is sing-ing. The crick - et sings while in the clo-ver sport - ing; He
60
tie - ne lon - go ver - - - - - - - - so.
pipes a note and holds it.
tie - ne lon - go ver - - - - - - - - so.
pipes a note and holds it.
tie - ne lon - go ver - - - - - - - - so.
pipes a note and holds it.

17. Je le vous dirai!

(I'll Say It Anyway!)

Chanson for Mixed Voices, S.A.T.B., a cappella

English Translation by C.C.H.

PIERRE CERTON (?-1572)

Edited by Charles C. Hirt

This popular French "chanson" (or song) about gossiping was first sung about 450 years ago. The first seven measures are like a refrain which is repeated twice. The verse-like section ("Il est un homme," etc) is also repeated. Composer Pierre Certon was a pupil of Josquin des Pres (see page 338).

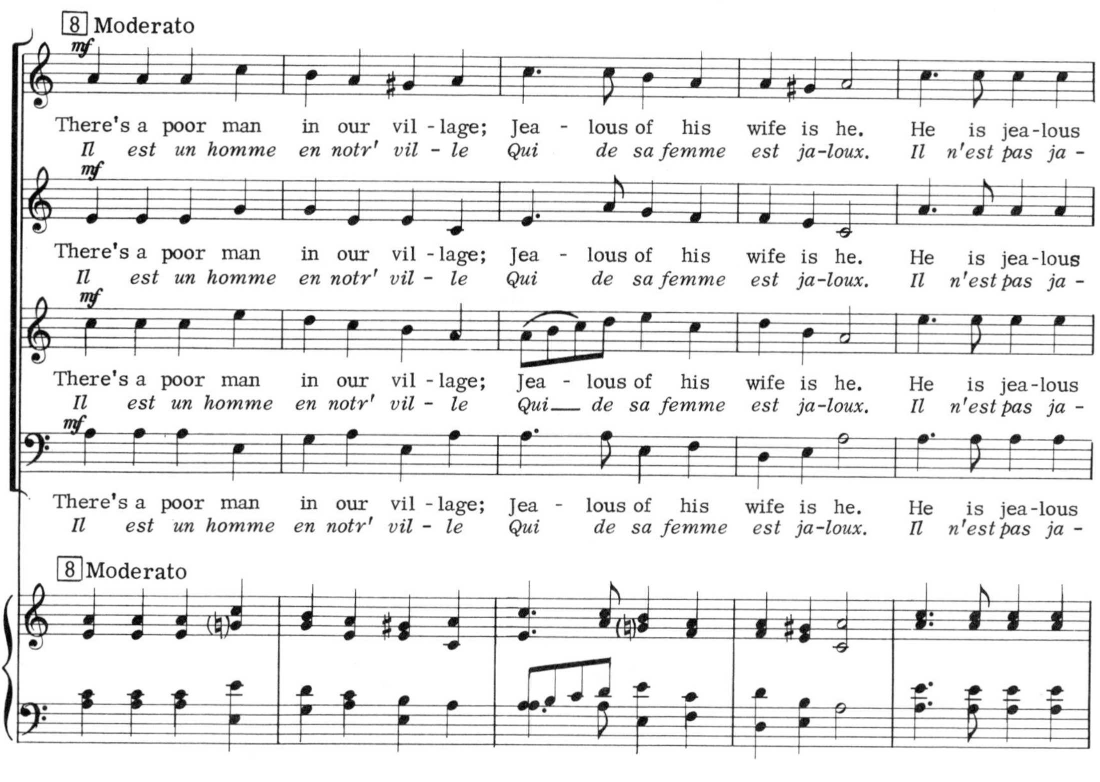
8 Moderato
mf
There's a poor man in our vil - lage; Jea - lous of his wife is he. He is jea-lous
Il est un homme en notr' vil - le Qui de sa femme est ja-loux. Il n'est pas ja -
mf
There's a poor man in our vil - lage; Jea - lous of his wife is he. He is jea-lous
Il est un homme en notr' vil - le Qui de sa femme est ja-loux. Il n'est pas ja -
mf
There's a poor man in our vil - lage; Jea - lous of his wife is he. He is jea-lous
Il est un homme en notr' vil - le Qui de sa femme est ja-loux. Il n'est pas ja -
mf
There's a poor man in our vil - lage; Jea - lous of his wife is he. He is jea-lous
Il est un homme en notr' vil - le Qui de sa femme est ja-loux. Il n'est pas ja -
8 Moderato

13
for good rea - son, For he is a sight to see! Heh, La, la, la, Do I
-loux sans cau - se, Mais il n'est pas beau du tout! et La, la, la, Je ne
for good rea - son, For he is a sight to see! Heh, La, la, la, Do I
-loux sans cau - se, Mais il n'est pas beau du tout! et La, la, la, Je ne
for good rea - son, For he is a sight to see! Heh, La, la, la,
-loux sans cau - se, Mais il n'est pas beau du tout! et La, la, la,
for good rea - son, For he is a sight to see! Heh, La, la, la,
-loux sans cau - se, Mais il n'est pas beau du tout! et La, la, la,
13

17 Tempo I
dare, don't I dare, Do I dare to say it? La, la, la,
l'o-, Je ne l'o-, Je ne l'o-se di - re, La, la, la,
dare, don't I dare, Do I dare to say it? La, la, la,
l'o-, Je ne l'o-, Je ne l'o-se di - re, La, la, la,
Do I dare, don't I dare, Do I dare to say it? La, la, la,
Je ne l'o-, Je ne l'o-, Je ne l'o-se di - re, La, la, la,
Do I dare, don't I dare, Do I dare to say it? La, la, la,
Je ne l'o-, Je ne l'o-, Je ne l'o-se di - re, La, la, la,
17 Tempo I
20
p
Tell me that I may, or La, la, la, I'll say it an - y - way!
Je le vous di - rai, et La, la, la, Je le vous di - rai!
p
Tell me that I may, or La, la, la, I'll say it an - y - way!
Je le vous di - rai, et La, la, la, Je le vous di - rai!
p
Tell me that I may, or La, la, la, I'll say it an - y - way!
Je le vous di - rai, et La, la, la, Je le vous di - rai!
p
Tell me that I may, or La, la, la, I'll say it an - y - way!
Je le vous di - rai, et La, la, la, Je le vous di - rai!
20

23 Moderato
mf
If to mar-ket she should ven-ture, He would al-ways go a-long, Nev-er from her
Il n'est pas ja-loux sans cau-se, Mais il n'est pas beau du tout. Il l'ap-prête et
If to mar-ket, she should ven-ture, He would al-ways go a-long, Nev-er from her
Il n'est pas ja-loux sans cau-se, Mais il n'est pas beau du tout. Il l'ap-prête et
23 Moderato
28
side to wan-der, Then he's sure she'll do no wrong! Heh, La, la, la, Do I
s'il la me-ne au mar-ché, s'en va à tout, et La, la, la, Je ne
side to wan-der, Then he's sure she'll do no wrong! Heh, La, la, la,
s'il la me-ne au mar-ché, s'en va à tout, et La, la, la,
28

32 Tempo I
dare, don't I dare, Do I dare to say it? La, la, la,
l'o-, Je ne l'o-, Je ne l'o - se di - re, La, la, la,
dare, don't I dare, Do I dare to say it? La, la, la,
l'o-, Je ne l'o-, Je ne l'o - se di - re, La, la, la,
Do I dare, don't I dare, Do I dare to say it? La, la, la,
Je ne l'o-, Je ne l'o-, Je ne l'o - se di - re, La, la, la,
Do I dare, don't I dare, Do I dare to say it? La, la, la,
Je ne l'o-, Je ne l'o-, Je ne l'o - se di - re, La, la, la,
32 Tempo I
35
poco rit. p
pp
Presto
Tell me that I may, or La, la, la, I'll say it an - y - way!
Je le vous di- rai, et La, la, la, Je le vous di- rai!
Tell me that I may, or La, la, la, I'll say it an - y - way!
Je le vous di - rai, et La, la, la, Je le vous di - rai!
Tell me that I may, or La, la, la, I'll say it an - y - way!
Je le vous di - rai, et La, la, la, Je le vous di - rai!
div.
Tell me that I may, or La, la, la, I'll say it an - y - way!
Je le vous di - rai, et La, la, la, Je le vous di - rai!
35
Presto
poco rit.

18. Jubilate, Jubilate

3-Part Mixed Voices, S.A.B., a cappella

Words by Samuel Longfellow (1819-1892)

Russian Air
Arranged by Joyce Eilers Bacak

This well-known Russian melody has English words by Samuel Longfellow. The texture is "homophonic" or hymn-like, with a melody that is harmonized. The even flowing rhythms and customary harmonies in this song contribute to the feeling of peace and calm which comes at sundown.

EASY CLASSICS SERIES
Conceived for the choir that needs to use compromise range for the male section, yet desires to use more classical masterworks for contest use or for worship.
This piece uses careful voice leading, limited ranges, and optimum use of dynamics, and retains the dignity without difficulty that is the essence of this masterwork.

Russian Air
Words by SAMUEL LONGFELLOW (1819-1892)
Arranged by JOYCE EILERS BACAK

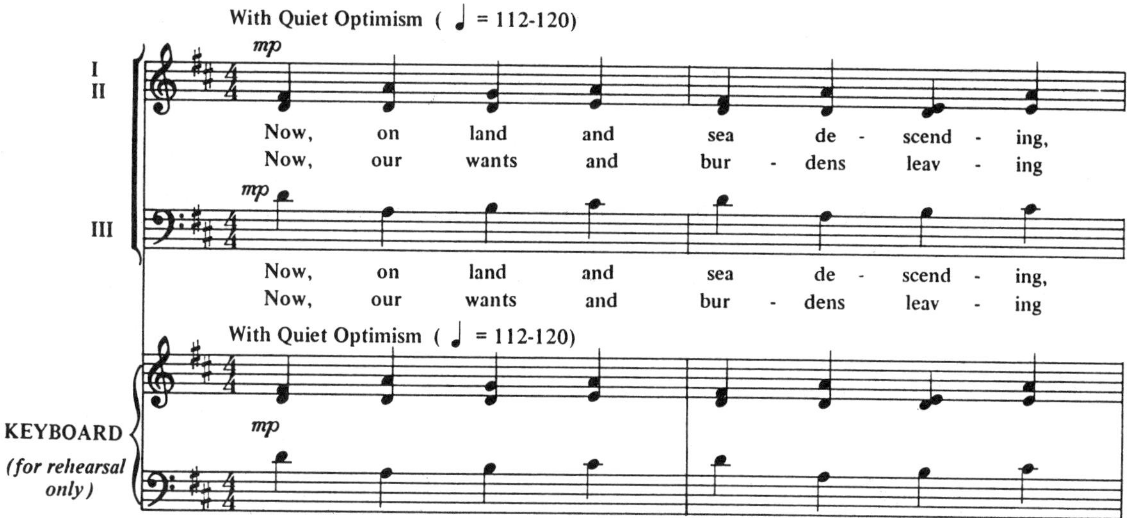

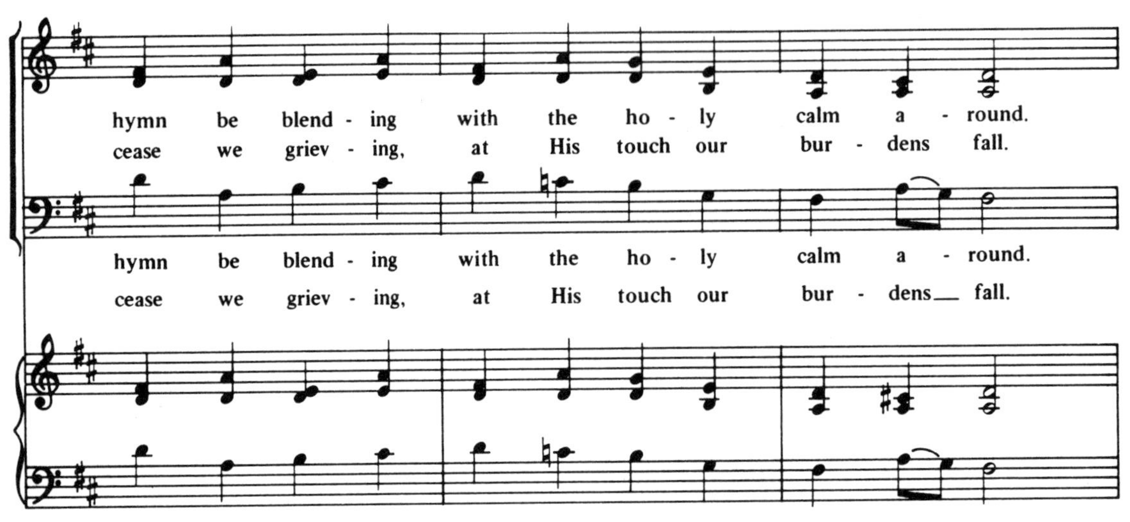
hymn be blend - ing with the ho - ly calm a - round.
cease we griev - ing, at His touch our bur - dens fall.
hymn be blend - ing with the ho - ly calm a - round.
cease we griev - ing, at His touch our bur - dens fall.

9
Joyful
mf
* Ju - bi - la - te! Ju - bi - la - te! Ju - bi - la - te!
mf
* Ju - bi - la - te! Ju - bi - la - te! Ju - bi - la - te!
9
mf

13
mp
A - men! Let our ves - per hymn be blend- ing
Cease we fear - ing, cease we griev - ing,
mp
A - men! Let our ves - per hymn be blend- ing
Cease we fear - ing, cease we griev - ing,
13
mp

* Pronounced "you - bih - lah - teh"

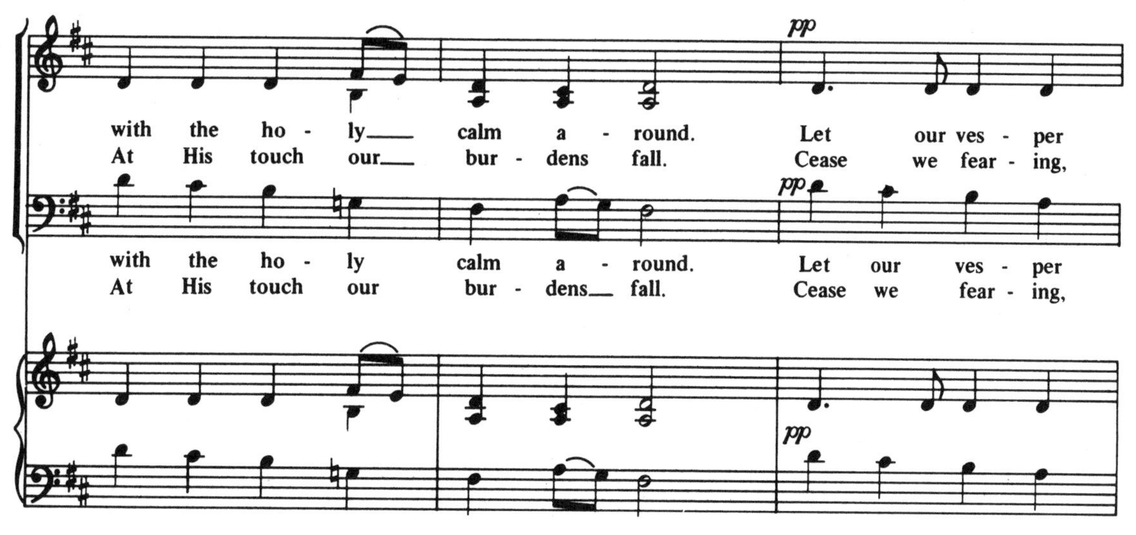
pp
with the ho - ly calm a - round. Let our ves - per
At His touch our bur - dens fall. Cease we fear - ing,
pp
with the ho - ly calm a - round. Let our ves - per
At His touch our bur - dens fall. Cease we fear - ing,
pp

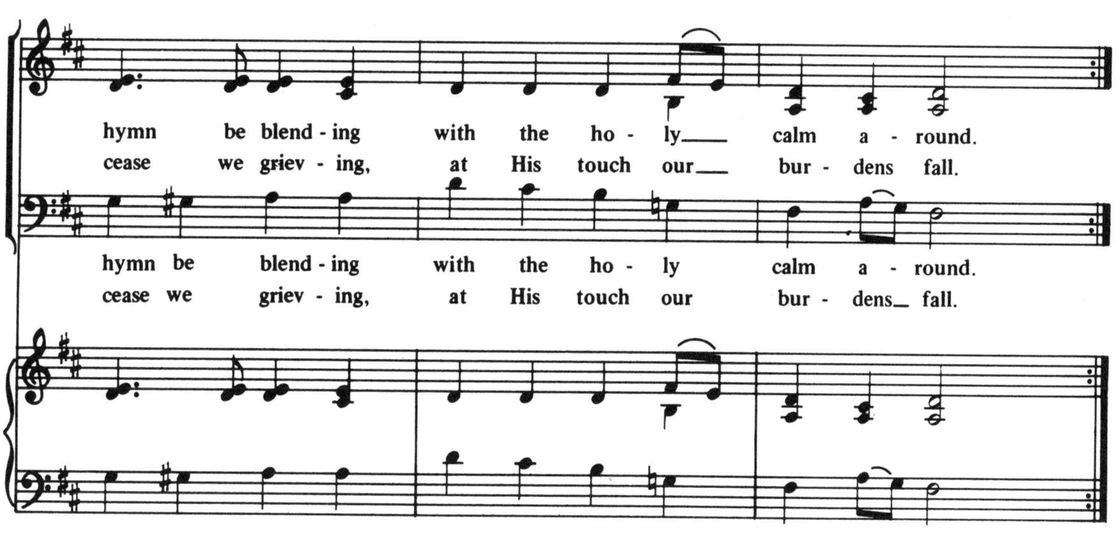
hymn be blend - ing with the ho - ly calm a - round.
cease we griev - ing, at His touch our bur - dens fall.
hymn be blend - ing with the ho - ly calm a - round.
cease we griev - ing, at His touch our bur - dens fall.

21
II
mp
As the dark - ness deep - ens o'er us, Lo! E - ter - nal stars a - rise.
21
mp

I
mp
Hope and faith and love rise glo - rious, shin - ing in the spir - it's skies.
mp
29
I & II
mf
Ju - bi - la - te! Ju - bi - la - te! Ju - bi - la - te!
mf
Ju - bi - la - te! Ju - bi - la - te! Ju - bi - la - te!
29
mf
33
A - men! Hope and faith and love rise glo - rious,
mp
A - men! Hope and faith and love rise glo - rious,
33
mp

pp
shin - ing in the spir - it's skies. Hope and faith and
pp
shin - ing in the spir - it's skies. Hope and faith and
pp

love rise glo - rious, shin - ing in the spir - it's skies.
love rise glo - rious, shin - ing in the spir - it's skies.

41
mp
Soon as dies the sun - set glo - ry, stars of heav'n shine
mp
Soon as dies the sun - set glo - ry, stars of heav'n shine
41
mp

mf
out a - bove. tell - ing still the an - cient sto - ry,
mf
out a - bove. tell - ing still the an - cient sto - ry,
mf

49
f
their Cre - a - tor's change - less love. Ju - bi - la - te!
f
their Cre - a - tor's change - less love. Ju - bi - la - te!
49
f

Ju - bi - la - te! Ju - bi - la - te! A - men!
Ju - bi - la - te! Ju - bi - la - te! A - men!

53
mf
Tell - ing still the an - cient sto - ry, their Cre - a - tor's
mf
Tell - ing still the an - cient sto - ry, their Cre - a - tor's
53
mf

pp
change- less love. Tell - ing still the an - cient sto - ry,
pp
change- less love. Tell - ing still the an - cient sto - ry,
pp

mp
their Cre - a - tor's change - less love. A - men.
mp
their Cre - a - tor's change - less love. A - men.
mp

19. The Messenger

from FOUR GERMAN FOLK SONGS
for Mixed Voices, S.A.T.B., with Piano

English Adaptation by R.R.

JOHANNES BRAHMS (1833-1897)
Edited by Ray Robinson

Johannes Brahms (see page 361) is one of a number of well-known composers who found great beauty in the folk music of his native land. The unfolding drama of this German folk song is highlighted by the increasing rhythmic motion Brahms creates from beginning to end, particularly in the piano part.

Allegretto
mf
p
Soprano
Alto
1. Es sass ein schnee-weiss Vö - ge - lein, Es sass ein
Up - on a small - tree sat a dove, there sat a
2. „Sag, willst du wohl mein Bo - te - sein?" „Sag, willst du
"Say, will you be my mes-sen- ger?" "To take a
Tenor
Bass
Allegretto
Keyboard
schnee-weiss Vö - ge - lein, auf ei - nem Dor - nen-bäu-me - lein, in der
snow - white lit - tle dove. Up - on a small tree in the Spring, when the
wohl mein Bo - te - sein?" „Ja - wohl, dein Bo - te will ich sein, in der
spe - cial word to her?" "Ah, yes your mes-sage I will bring, when the
dolce

Len-zes-zeit! auf ei-nem Dor-nen-bäu-me-lein, auf grün Heid!
rob-ins sing! Up-on a thorn tree in the Spring, rob-ins sing!
Len-zes-zeit! „Ja wohl, dein Bo-te will ich sein, auf grün Heid!“
rob-ins sing! "Ah, yes your mes-sage I will bring, in the Spring!"
1.
2.
3. Es nahm den Brief in sei-nen Mund, Es nahm den
She took the let-ter in her bill, the pre-cious
4. Zu Lieb-chens Tü-re hin es flog, Zu Lieb-chens
She flew to her with-out de-lay, flew off to

Brief in sei - nem Mund, flog fort, hin durch des Wal - des
mes - sage of good - will, A - way she flew through for - est
Tü - re hin es flog, „Schläfst, wachest du o - der bist du
her with - out de - lay; "Are you a - sleep or gone a -
Grund, in der Len - zes - zeit! flog fort, hin durch des Wal - des
green, when the rob - ins sing; a - way she flew through for - est
fort, in der Len - zes - zeit!" „Schläfst, wachst du o - der bist du
way, "when the rob - ins sing;" "Are you a - sleep or gone a -

Grund, auf grün Heid!
green, in the Spring.
fort,‹ auf grün Heid!
way," in the Spring.
5. „Ich schla - fe nicht, ich
"I do not sleep, I
6. „Bist du ge - traut seit
"If you were wed a
pp
wa - che nicht,“
do not watch,"
Jah - res Zeit,“
year a - go,"
„ich schla - fe nicht, ich
"I do not sleep, I
„Bist du ge - traut seit
"If you were wed a
wa - che nicht,“
do not watch,"
Jah - res Zeit,“
year a - go,"

„Ich bin ge - traut seit Jah - res Zeit," in der Len - zes - zeit!
"For I was wed a year a - go," when the rob - ins sang!
„Mich dünkt es ei - ne E - wig - keit," in der Len - zes - zeit!
"For me it seems e - ter - ni - ty," when the rob - ins sing!
p
„Ich bin ge - traut seit Jah - res Zeit," auf grün Heid!
"For I was wed a year a - go," in the Spring!
„Mich dünkt es ei - ne E - wig - keit," auf grün Heid!
"For me it seems e - ter - ni - ty," in the Spring!
p
pp

20. O Bella Fusa

(The Spinning Wheel)

for Mixed Voices, S.A.T.B., a cappella

English text by Don Hinshaw

ORLANDO DI LASSO (1532-1594)

Edited by Ray Robinson

A Netherlander by birth, Orlando di Lasso wrote part songs in German, French, and Italian. He was a truly international composer. In this Italian madrigal, the repetitious rhythms convey the endless turning of the wheel. For more information about di Lasso, see page 336.

10
p
O bel - la fu - sa, O bel - la fu - sa, O
Beau - ti - ful spin - dle, Beau - ti - ful spin - dle, How
O, O bel - la fu - sa, O bel - la fu - sa, O
O, O, beau - ti - ful spin - dle, beau - ti - ful, Beau -
O bel - la fu - sa, O bel - la fu - sa, O bel - la
Beau - ti - ful spin - dle, Beau - ti - ful spin - dle, Beau - ti - ful
O bel - la fu - sa, O bel - la fu - sa, O bel - la
Beau - ti - ful spin - dle, Beau - ti - ful spin - dle, Beau - ti - ful
15
f
bel - la fu - sa; chi ne vo-ac-ca - ta re? Noi le ven - di -
beau - ti - ful; What are you spin - ning to - day? If you will sell to
bel - la fu - sa; chi ne vo-ac-ca - ta re? Noi le ven - di -
ti - ful spin - dle; What are you spin - ning to - day? If you will sell
fu - sa; chi ne vo-ac-ca - ta re? Noi le ven - di -
spin - dle; Are you spin-ning to - day? If you will sell
fu - sa; chi ne vo-ac-ca - ta re? Noi le ven - di -
spin - dle; Are you spin-ning to - day? If you will sell

20
mo que - ste fu, que - ste fu, que - ste fu - s'in pro - va. Noi
us, we will buy, we will buy, we will buy it from you. If
mo que - ste fu, que - ste fu, que - ste fu - s'in pro - va. Noi
it, we will buy, we will buy, we will buy it from you. If
mo que - ste fu, que - ste fu, que - ste fu - s'in pro va. Noi
it, we will buy, we will buy, we will buy it from you. If
mo que - ste fu, que - ste fu, que - ste fu - s'in pro - va. Noi
it, we will buy, we will buy, we will buy it from you. If
25
le ven - di - mo que - ste fu, que - ste fu, que - ste fu - s'in pro -
you will sell to us, we will buy, we will buy, we will buy it from
le ven - di - mo que - ste fu, que - ste fu, que - ste fu - s'in pro -
you will sell it, we will buy, we will buy, we will buy it from
le ven - di - mo que - ste fu, que - ste fu, que - ste fu - s'in pro -
you will sell it, we will buy, we will buy, we will buy it from
le ven - di - mo que - ste fu, que - ste fu, que - ste fu - s'in pro -
you will sell it, we will buy, we will buy, we will buy it from

30
p cresc.
mp
va. Son fu, son fu, son fu, son fu - sa no - va, Son fu, son
you. The spin-ning wheel, the spin-ning wheel is spin - ning. The spin - ning
va. Son fu, son fu, son fu, son fu - sa no - va, Son fu, son
you. The spin-ning wheel, the spin-ning wheel is spin - ning. The spin - ning
va. Son fu, son fu, son fu, son fu - sa no - va, Son fu, son
you. The spin-ning wheel, the spin-ning wheel is spin - ning. The spin - ning
va. Son fu, son fu, son fu, son fu - sa no - va, Son fu, son
you. The spin-ning wheel, the spin-ning wheel is spin - ning. The spin - ning
35
mf
p
fu, son fu, son fu - sa no va! Voi le pro - va - re. Ve - ni tel - l'a pi -
wheel, the spin-ning wheel is spin - ning, The wheel is spin - ning. The wheel is spin - ning,
fu, son fu, son fu - sa no va! Voi le pro - va - re. Ve - ni tel - l'a pi -
wheel, the spin-ning wheel is spin - ning, The wheel is spin - ning. The wheel is spin - ning,
fu, son fu, son fu - sa no va! Voi le pro - va - re. Ve - ni tel - l'a pi -
wheel, the spin-ning wheel is spin - ning, The wheel is spin - ning. The wheel is spin - ning,
fu, son fu, son fu - sa no va! Voi le pro - va - re. Ve - ni tel - l'a pi -
wheel, the spin-ning wheel is spin - ning, The wheel is spin - ning. The wheel is spin - ning,

40
f
glia - re! Ve - ni tel - l'a pi - glia - re! Le dam in pro - va. Voi le pro - va - re, Ve -
spin-ning, the wheel is spin-ning, spin-ning, is spin - ning, it spins. The wheel is spin - ning, The
glia - re! Ve - ni tel - l'a pi - glia - re! Le dam in pro - va. Voi le pro - va - re, Ve -
spin-ning, the wheel is spin-ning, spin-ning, is spin - ning, spin - ning. The wheel is spin - ning, The
45
rit.
ni tel - l'a pi - glia - re, ve - ni tel - l'a pi - glia - re; le dam in pro - va.
spin-ning wheel is spin - ning, the spin-ning wheel is spin - ning, the wheel spins and spins.
spin-ning wheel is spin - ning, the spin-ning wheel is spin - ning, the wheel is spin - ning.

21.

O Lord Our God

S.A.T.B., a cappella

Text adapted from Scripture by K.K.D.

WILLIAM BYRD (1543-1623)
Arranged by Katherine K. Davis

Music from the Renaissance period is sung by many school choirs because of its beauty and the fact that it is so singable. Good musicians enjoy performing this music because each voice part is independent and takes its turn being prominent and important.

earth, of all the earth and
of all the earth, of all the earth and
Thou King of all the
earth, of earth and
1.
2.
f
heav'n.
f
heav'n.
f
heav'n.
f p
heav'n. Thy word is
f
heav'n.
f
heav'n.
p
Thy word is
f
heav'n.
f p
heav'n. Thy word is ho - ly, is
1.
2.
f
f p

mf
f
Thy word is ho - ly. We
ho - ly. Thy word is ho - ly. We
ho - ly. Lord, Thy word is ho - ly. We
ho - ly. Thy word is ho - ly. We
lift up our hearts to bless Thy
lift up our hearts to bless Thy
lift up our hearts to bless Thy
lift up our hearts to bless Thy

mf
name ev - er - more.
mf p
name ev - er - more. Thy word is
mf p
name ev - er - more. Thy word is
mf p
name ev - er - more. Thy word is ho - ly, is
mf p
mf
Thy word is ho - ly. We
mf f
ho - ly. Thy word is ho - ly. We
mf f
ho - ly. Lord, Thy word is ho - ly. We
mf f
ho - ly. Thy word is ho - ly. We
mf f

lift up our hearts to bless Thy
lift up our hearts to bless Thy
lift up our hearts to bless Thy
lift up our hearts to bless Thy
rall. f mf
name ev - er - more. A - men.
name ev - er - more. A - men.
name ev - er - more. A - men.
name ev - er - more. A - men, A - men.

22. O Music, Thou Most Lovely Art

(O Musik dein ganz lieblich Kunst)

for Mixed Voices, S.A.T.B., a cappella

JOHANN JEEP (1581-1644)

Edited by Ray Robinson

Many songs in praise of music have been written throughout the centuries. This short German "lied" (or song) receives many performances each year by school choirs. The imitative entrances and the measures of triple meter near the end give particular interest.

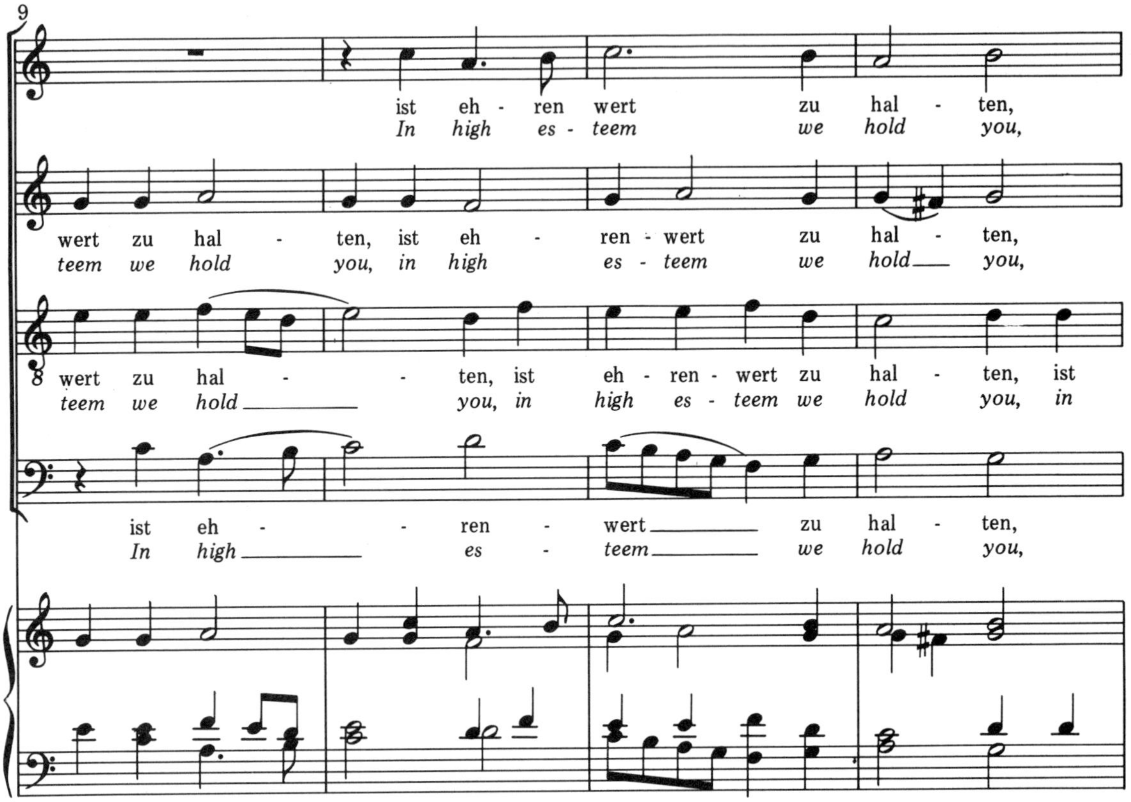

9
ist eh - ren wert zu hal - ten,
In high es - teem we hold you,
wert zu hal - ten, ist eh - ren - wert zu hal - ten,
teem we hold you, in high es - teem we hold you,
wert zu hal - ten, ist eh - ren - wert zu hal - ten, ist
teem we hold you, in high es - teem we hold you, in
ist eh - ren - wert zu hal - ten,
In high es - teem we hold you,

13
p
ist eh - ren-wert zu hal - ten, hat bil - lig
in high es-teem we hold you, we play that
ist eh - ren - wert zu hal - ten,
in high es - teem we hold you,
eh - ren - wert zu hal - ten,
high es - teem we hold you,
ist eh - ren - wert zu hal - ten,
in high es - teem we hold you,
p

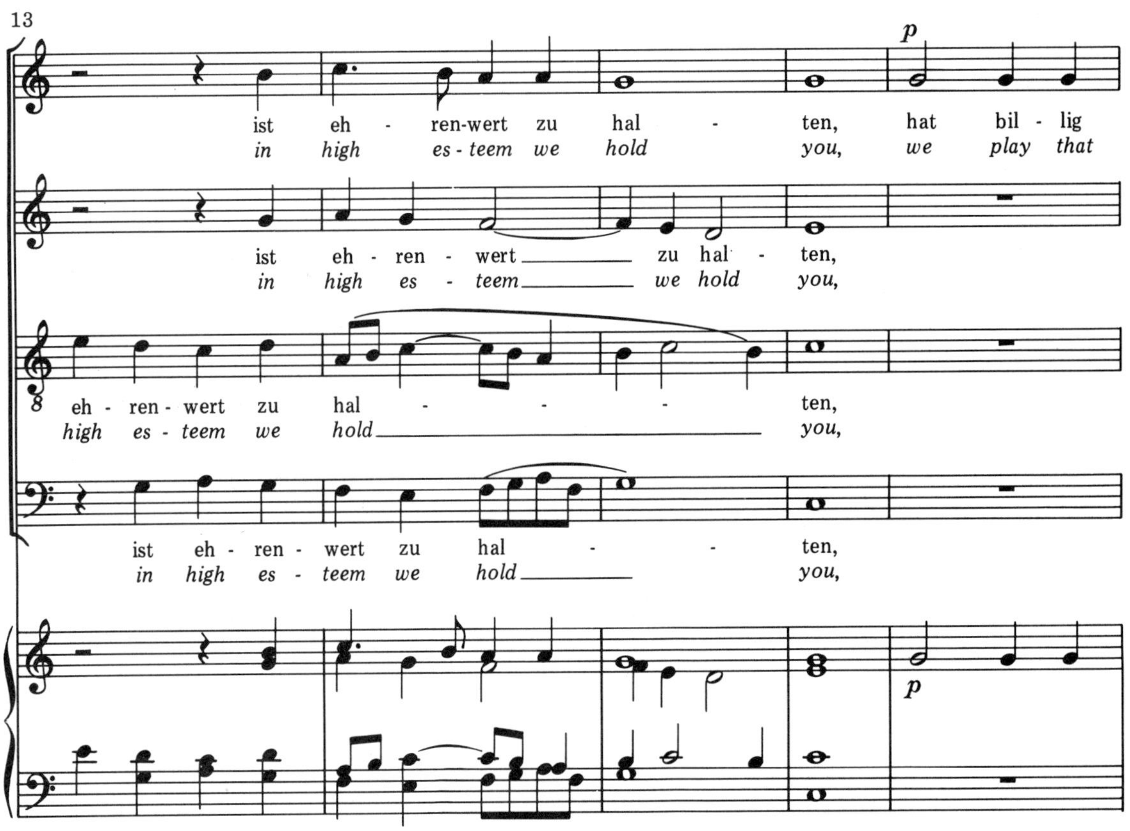

18
all - ent - hal - - - - ben Gunst, hat bil - lig
you will not de - part, we pray that
hat bil - lig all - ent - hal - ben Gunst, hat bil - lig
We pray that you will not de - part, we pray that
hat bil - lig all - ent -
We pray that you will
hat bil - lig
We pray that

22
all - ent - hal - ben Gunst,
you will not de - part,
all - ren - hal - - ben Gunst, bei Jun - gen und bei Al -
you will not de - part, with young and old we praise
hal - - - ben Gunst, bei Jun - gen und bei Al -
not de - part, with young and old we praise
all - ent - hal - ben Gunst, bei Jun -
you will not de - part, with young

26
bei Jun - gen und bei Al - ten, bei
with young and old we praise you, with
ten, bei Jun - gen und bei Al - ten, bei
you, with young and old we praise you, with
- ten, bei Jun - gen und bei Al - ten, bei Jun - gen und bei
- you, with young and old we praise you, with young and old we
- gen und bei Al - ten, bei Jun - gen
- and old we praise you, with young and

30
Jun - gen und bei Al - ten. Sie frischt das Herz, welchs
young and old we praise you, Lift - ing the hearts when
Jun - gen und bei Al - ten. Sie frischt das Herz welchs
young and old we praise you. Lift - ing the hearts when
Al - - - ten. Sie frischt das Herz welchs
praise you. Lift - ing the hearts when
und bei Al - - ten. Sie frischt das Herz welchs
old we praise you. Lift - ing the hearts when

35
lei - det Schmerz, tut all uns Mut ver - trei - -
pain and tears have filled our lives with sad - -
lei - det Schmerz, tut all uns Mut ver - trei - ben,
pain and tears have filled our lives with sad - ness,
lei - det Schmerz, tut all uns Mut ver - trei - -
pain and tears have filled our lives with sad - -
lei - bet Schmerz, tut all uns Mut - - ver - trei -
pain and tears have filled our lives with sad

39
ben, lasst trau - rig nie - mand blei - ben.
ness, you bring us joy and glad - ness.
lasst trau - rig nie - mand blei - ben.
you bring us joy and glad - ness.
ben, lasst trau - rig nie - mand blei - ben.
ness, you bring us joy and glad - ness.
ben, lasst trau - rig nie - mand blei - ben.
ness, you bring us joy and glad - ness.

23. Ride the Chariot

for Mixed Voices, S.A.T.B., Conga Drum (optional)

Spiritual
Arranged by Andre Thomas

The arranger has taken this simple spiritual and dressed it up for a concert presentation. Insistent syncopated rhythm patterns move the song forward. Audiences respond well to spirituals, particularly if they are sung with the same honest religious fervor which they express.

*Conga Drum: Lower pitch - Stems down.
Higher pitch - Stems up.

8
morn - ing,
Ride the cha-riot in the morn-ing Lord,
morn - ing,
Ride the cha-riot in the morn-ing Lord,
Oh, ride,
Oh, ride,
11
ride the cha-riot in the morn - ing. I nev - er shall for -
ride the cha-riot in the morn - ing. Oo,
ride the cha-riot in the morn - ing. Oo,
ride the cha-riot in the morn - ing. Oo,

14
get that day,
Ride the cha-riot in the morn - ing,
Ride the cha-riot in the morn - ing,
Ride the cha-riot in the morn - ing,
Ride the cha-riot in the morn - ing, When
17
Oo,
Ride the cha-riot in the
Oo,
Ride the cha-riot in the
Oo,
Ride the cha-riot in the
all my sins were ta-ken a - way,
Ride the cha-riot in the

20
morn - ing,
Ride the cha-riot in the morn-ing, Lord,
morn - ing,
Ride the cha-riot in the morn-ing, Lord,
morn - ing,
Ride the cha-riot in the morn-ing, Lord,
morn - ing, I'm gon-na
Ride the cha-riot in the morn-ing, Lord, I'm gon-na
23
Ride the cha-riot in the morn-ing, Lord,
Get rea-dy for that
Ride the cha-riot in the morn-ing, Lord,
Get rea-dy for that
Ride the cha-riot in the morn-ing, Lord,
Get rea-dy for that
ride, ride the cha-riot in the morn-ing, Lord, I'm get-tin' rea - dy for that

Judgement Day.
Ride on,
ride on. My
Judge-ment Day.
Ride on,
Ride on.
Judge-ment Day.
Ride on, you bet-ter ride, ride on.
Judge-ment Day.
Ride on,
ride on.
29
feet were snatched from the mi - ry clay,
Ride the cha-riot in the
Oo,
Ride the cha-riot in the
Oo,
Ride the cha-riot in the
Oo,
Ride the cha-riot in the

32
morn - ing,
Oo,
morn - ing,
Oo,
morn - ing,
Oo,
morn - ing, I'll serve my Lord till Judge-ment Day,
35
Ride the cha-riot in the morn - ing, Lord.
Ride the cha-riot in the
Ride the cha-riot in the morn - ing, Lord.
Ride the cha-riot in the
Ride the cha-riot in the morn - ing, Lord.
Ride the cha-riot in the
Ride the cha-riot in the morn - ing, I'm gon-na ride the cha-riot in the

38
morn-ing, Lord,— Ride the cha-riot in the morn-ing, Lord.—
morn-ing, Lord,— Ride the cha-riot in the morn-ing, Lord.—
morn-ing, Lord,— Ride the cha-riot in the morn-ing, Lord.—
morn-ing, Lord,— I'm gon-na ride, the cha-riot in the morn-ing, Lord.— I'm get - tin
41
Get rea - dy for that Judge-ment Day.— Ride— on,—
Get rea - dy for that Judge-ment Day.— Ride— on,—
Get rea - dy for that Judge-ment Day.— Ride on,— you bet-ter
rea - dy for that Judge-ment Day.— Ride on,—

44
ride on. Are you rea-dy my bro - ther? Ride, ride in the
ride on. Oh, my bro - ther? Ride, ride in the
ride,ride on. Oh, my bro - ther? Ride, ride in the
ride on. Oh, my bro - ther? Ride, ride in the
48
morn - ing.
morn - ing.
morn - ing. Are you rea-dy my sis - ter?
morn - ing. Are you rea-dy my sis - ter?

51
Yes, I'm rea - dy for the Judge-ment day.
Yes, I'm rea - dy for the Judge-ment day.
Are you rea - dy for that
Yes, for the Judge-ment day?
54
I'm rea - dy for that jour - ney, Oh, ride, on,
I'm rea - dy for that jour - ney, Oh, ride, on,
jour - - ney? Oh, ride, on,
I'm rea - dy for that jour - ney, Oh, ride, on,

57
ride on, ride on, my Lord, Oh,
ride on, ride on, my Lord, Oh,
ride on, ride on, my Lord, Oh,
ride on, ride on, my Lord, Oh,
60
ride on, ride on, ride on,
ride on, ride on, ride on,
ride on, ride on, ride on,
ride on, ride on, ride on,

63
my Lord. Ride the cha-riot in the morn-ing. Lord,
my Lord. Ride the cha-riot in the morn-ing. Lord,
my Lord. Ride the cha-riot in the morn-ing. Lord,
my Lord. Ride the cha-riot in the morn-ing. Lord,
66
Ride the cha-riot in the morn - ing. Ride!
Ride the cha-riot in the morn - ing. I'm get - tin' rea-dy,
Ride the cha-riot in the morn - ing. I'm get - tin' rea-dy
Ride the cha-riot in the morn - ing. I'm gon-na ride,

69
Ride!
Ride on the judge-ment day!
I'm get-tin' rea-dy for that, get - tin' rea-dy for that judge-ment day!
I'm get-tin' rea-dy for that, get - tin' rea-dy for that judge-ment day!
Ride!
Ride on the judge-ment day!

24. Ring the Bells

for Three-part Mixed Choir, S.A.B., with Piano, Claves and Orchestral Chimes (handbells) optional

Words by Jane Foster Knox

Music by MARK WILSON

The Caribbean flavor of this Christmas song comes from the syncopation in the principal melody and the use of claves, a popular Latin-American percussion instrument. The song has one melody and two countermelodies. Can you identify them?

* Cue notes may be played by either orchestral chimes or handbells.

C
Ring the bells so mer - ri - ly;
Let their mus-ic re-
Al - le - lu -
mf
lay.
Peace and joy to all the earth
ia!
Al - le -
On this Christ-mas Day.
lu - ia!
mf
Claves tacet to E

D
unis. mp
In the cold De - cem - ber,
Swing - ing to and
mp
8va
fro,
Bells in hap - py cho - rus
to div.
loco
S. A. unis.
will set our spir-its a - glow!
E
mf
Oh, Ring the bells so
T. B. unis.
will set our spir-its a - glow!
Oh, Al -
mf
Claves

mer - ri - ly; Sound a car-ol to say,
le - lu - ia!
simile to end
"Peace and joy to all the earth on this Christ - mas
Al - le - lu -
F f
Soprano
Day!" Al - le - lu - ia,
Alto
Day!" Oh, Ring the bells so mer - ri - ly;
T. B.
ia! Oh, Al - le -

Al - le - lu - ia! Al - le -
Let their mus-ic re - lay. Peace and joy to
lu - ia! Al -
lu - ia, Al - le - lu - ia!
all the earth On this Christ-mas Day!
le - lu - ia!

G
mp
Al - le - lu - ia! Al - le -
Ring the bells so mer - ri - ly! Sound a car-ol to
Al - le - lu -

lu - ia! Al - le - lu - ia!
say, "Peace and joy to all the earth
ia! Al - le -

p
Al - le - lu - ia!
On this Christ-mas
p
On this Christ-mas Day!"
On this Christ-mas
lu - ia!
p

Day!
On this Christ - mas Day!
Day!
On this Christ - mas Day!
Chime
rit.

25. Sanctus

for Mixed Voices, S.A.T.B., a cappella

GIOVANNI DA PALESTRINA (c. 1525-1594)
Edited by John Rutter

This work is a movement from one of Palestrina's masses, called the *Missa: Ave Regina Caelorum (Mass: Hail Queen of Heaven)* because it is based on an old Gregorian chant having that text. Much of the choral music of Palestrina's time (see page 338) was written in polyphonic ("many-voiced") style, meaning that all the parts or melodies are equally important.

Source: *Missarum Liber Nonus* (1599). Original pitch a whole step higher.

5
mp smoothly
San - - - - - - - ctus, San -
Ho - - - - - - - ly, Ho -
mp smoothly
San - - - - - - - -
Ho - - - - - - - -
- - - - - ctus, San - -
- - - - - ly, Ho - -
- - ctus,
- - ly,
10
- - - ctus,
- - - ly.
- - ctus, San - - ctus,
- - ly, Ho - - ly,
- - - ctus, San - - -
- - - ly, Ho - - -
San - - - - - - -
Ho - - - - - - -

14
mf
San
Ho
San
Ho
ctus
ly
ctus
ly
mf
Do - mi -
Lord of
mf
mf
18
ctus
ly
mf
Do -
Lord
ctus
ly
mf
Do - mi - nus De - us Sa - ba -
Lord of hosts, Lord of hosts, of
mf
Do - mi - nus De - us Sa - ba -
Lord of hosts, Lord of hosts, of
nus De - us Sa - ba - oth, Sa - ba -
hosts, Lord of hosts, Lord God of hosts, Lord

22
- mi - nus De - us Sa - ba - - - - - -
of hosts, Lord God, Lord of hosts, Lord of
- oth, Do - mi - nus De - us Sa - ba - oth,
hosts, Lord of hosts, Lord of hosts, of hosts,
- oth, Sa - - ba - oth, Do - mi - nus De - us Sa - ba - oth,
God, Lord of hosts, Lord God of hosts, Lord God of hosts,
- - oth, Do - mi -
of hosts, Lord of
26
- oth, Do - mi - nus De - us Sa - ba - - -
hosts, Lord of hosts, Lord of hosts, Lord God of
Sa - ba - oth, Do - mi - nus De - us Sa - ba - oth.
Lord God of hosts, Lord of hosts, Lord God of hosts.
Do - mi - nus De - us Sa - - - ba - oth, Sa - ba - -
Lord of hosts, Lord of hosts, of hosts, Lord God of
- nus De - us Sa - - - - ba - oth, Sa - ba -
hosts, Lord of hosts, Lord God of

31
f
- oth. Ple - ni sunt cae - li
hosts. Heav - en and earth, heav -
Ple - ni sunt cae - li et ter - - ra glo - ri -
Heav - en and earth are filled with your glo - -
- oth. Ple - ni sunt
hosts. Heav - en and
- oth. Ple - ni sunt cae - li et ter -
hosts. Heav - en and earth are filled with
35
et ter - ra glo - ri - a
- en and earth are filled with your
- a tu - a, glo - - ri - a tu -
- ry, your glo - ry, glo - - ry, filled with your glo - ry, with
cae - li et ter - - - - ra glo - ri -
earth are filled with your glo - ry, with your
- - - ra glo - ri - a tu - a, glo -
your glo - ry, with your glo - ry, filled

39
(f) more marked
tu - a. Ho - san - na in ex - cel - sis, ho -
glo - ry. Ho - san - na in the high - est, ho -
(f) more marked
tu - a. Ho - san - na in ex - cel - sis, ho -
your glo - ry. Ho - san - na in the high - est, ho -
(f) more marked
a tu - a. Ho - san - na in ex - cel - sis, ho -
glo - ry. Ho - san - na in the high -
f more marked
ri - a tu - a. Ho -
with your glo - ry. Ho -
43
- san - na in ex - cel - sis.
- san - na in the high - est, in the high - est.
- san - na in ex - cel - sis.
- san - na in the high - est.
- san - na in ex - cel - sis.
- est, ho - san - na in the high - est.
- san - na ho - san - na in ex - cel - sis.
- san - na ho - san - na in the high - est.

26.

Your Voices Tune

for Mixed Voices, S.A.T.B., with Keyboard

G.F. HANDEL (1685-1759)
Edited by John Rutter

This brief chorus can be a rousing curtain-raiser for a choral concert. It comes from Handel's *Alexander's Feast* (1736), an extended ode in honor of St. Cecilia, the patron saint of music. For a short biography of Handel, see page 347.

*'at a lively walking pace'

5
till they ech - o from the vault - ed
7
sky the blest Ce - ce - lia's name:
9
mu - sic to heav'n and her we owe, the

11
great - est bless - ing that's be - low; sound

13
loud - ly then her fame.

27.

All Things Bright and Beautiful

for Two-Part Choir, with Keyboard

Words by Mrs. C.F. Alexander (1823-1895) JOHN RUTTER (1945-)

John Rutter's music is sung by choral singers on both sides of the Atlantic. He is one of the most prominent English composers writing at present. The text of this anthem is used in several church hymnals. The piano part is the "glue" that keeps the syncopated rhythm flowing and helps the singers change from one key to another.

15
A
cresc.
Each lit-tle flow'r that o - pens,
Each lit-tle bird that sings,
cresc.
18
mf
He made their glow - ing co - lors, He
mf
21
(mf)
made their ti - ny wings.
All things bright and
(mf)
24
beau-ti-ful, All crea - tures great and small,

*The lower voice here and elsewhere is optional.

39
mp
bright - ens up the sky; The cold wind in the
mp
42
win - ter, The plea - sant sum - mer sun, The
sim.
45 cresc.
mf
poco rit.
ripe fruits in the gar - den, He made them ev - 'ry one;
poco rit.
cresc.
mf
49 C a tempo
mf
All things bright and beau-ti - ful, All crea - tures great and
a tempo
mf

52
small,
All things wise and wonder-ful,
The Lord God made them all.
56
cresc.
He gave us eyes to see them, And
cresc.
59
div.
f
lips that we might tell
How great is God Al-
f
62
unis.
-might-y, Who has made all things well.

65
D
(f)
All things bright and beau-ti-ful, All crea - tures great and
(f)
sim.
68
div.
small, All things wise and won - der - ful,
71
rall.
mp
dim.
The Lord God made them
mf dim.
l.h.
mp
dim.
a tempo
75
p
rall.
all.
p
pp

28. The Arrow and the Song

for Treble Voices, Three-Part

Henry Wadsworth Longfellow

DEDE DUSON

The text of this song is by one of America's finest poets — Henry Wadsworth Longfellow (1807-1882). Notice how the sound and the meaning of the words guide this composer in her choice of pitches and rhythms—particularly on words like "air" and "flight." Also notice the use of a triplet on the word "afterward."

With thoughtful fantasy (♩ = c.52)
Treble 1
Treble 2
Treble 3
(rehearsal only)
mp
I shot an ar-row in-to the air, it fell to earth, I
5
know not where; for so swift-ly it flew the sight could not fol-low in its
8
flight, I shot an ar-row in-to the

11
air.
I breathed a song in-to the
pp
15
air,
it fell to earth I knew not where; for
p
18
who has sight so keen and strong that it can fol-low the flight of
cresc.
poco
a
poco
who has sight so keen and strong that it can fel-low the flight of
who has sight so keen and strong that it can fol-low the flight of

21
mf
mp
song? Long af-ter-ward in an oak,
mf
dim.
mp
song, of song? Long, long, long af-ter-ward in an oak,
mf
dim.
pp
song, of song? Long, long, long
mf
dim.
mp
pp
25
pp
p
the ar-row, un-broke; and the
mp
p
I found the ar-row still un - broke; and the
mp
p
af-ter-ward in an oak, I found the ar-row still un - broke; and the
pp
mp
p
29
Slower
mp
mf
song, and the song, from be-gin-ning to end, I found a - gain in the
mp
mf
song, and the song, from be-gin-ning to end, I found a - gain in the
mp
mf
song, and the song, from be-gin-ning to end, I found a - gain in the
Slower
mp
mf

33
Still slower
heart of a friend, the
heart of a friend, in the heart of a
heart of a friend, in the heart of a
Still slower
37
a tempo
heart of a friend. I shot an ar-row in-to the air;
friend. I
friend. I
a tempo
42
div.
a song!
breathed a song in-to the air, a song!
breathed a song in-to the air, a song!

29. Butterfly Roses

for Treble Voices, S.S.A., with Piano and Optional Guitar

Words and Music by RON MYERS

Arranged by Larry Norred

This is a love song in triple meter. Many composers have combined waltz rhythm with love poems. What is unusual is the minor key. To give variety in the three verses, the arranger uses unison, then two-part harmony, and then the melody with a counter-melody above.

13
SI
SII
A
When pres - ence my heart gai - ly sings, of
In your_ pres - ence my heart gai - ly sings, of
In your_ pres - ence my heart gai - ly sings, of
Dm
Eb
ros - es with but - ter - fly wings.
ros - es with but - ter - fly wings.
ros - es with but - ter - fly wings.
Dm
A7
Dm
21
mf
Do you see on - ly what oth - ers can see? Are
Do you see on - ly what oth - ers can see? Are
Do you see on - ly what oth - ers can see? Are
Bb
C7
F

flow - ers just flowers? A tree just a tree?
flow - ers just flowers? A tree just a tree?
flow - ers just flowers? A tree just a tree?
C7
Dm
29
When we're to - geth - er do things change their form?
When we're to - geth - er do things change their form?
When we're to - geth - er do things change their form?
B♭
C7
F
To Coda
Hint - ing of life in a time not yet born!
Hint - ing of life in a time not yet born!
Hint - ing of life in a time not yet born!
G7
C
Dm7
E♭o
C7
C+7

37
SI
SII
A
mp
God shows lov - ers,
mf
But - ter - fly Ros - es with pet - als like wings,
Dm
Eb
Myst - er - ies hid - den from oth - ers,
Rare is the feel - ing your gen - tle kiss brings,
Dm
A7
45
Has He shown you,
When in your pres - ence my heart gai - ly sings, of
Dm
Eb

D.S. al Coda
SI
ros - es with but - ter - fly wings.
SII
A
ros - es with but - ter - fly wings.
Dm
A7
Dm

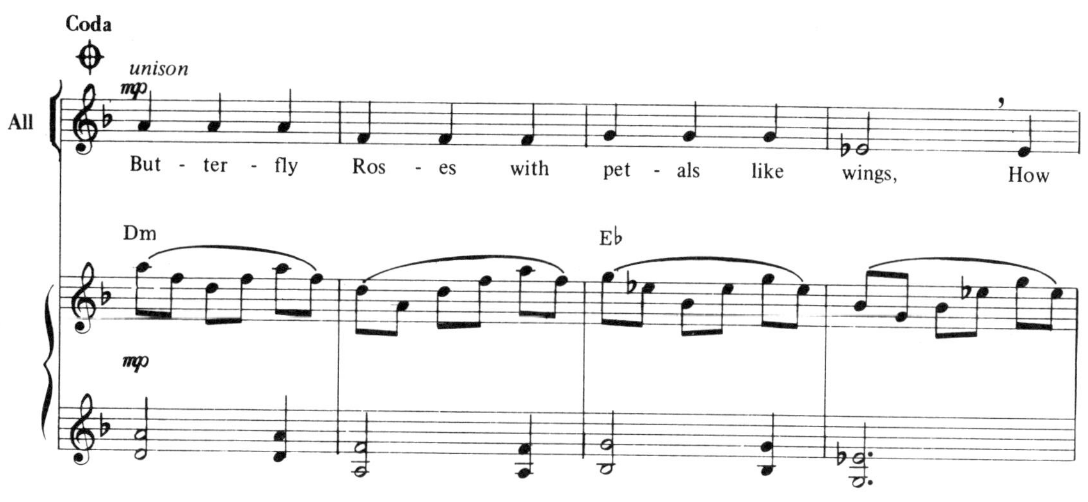
Coda
unison
mp
All
But - ter - fly Ros - es with pet - als like wings, How
Dm
Eb
mp

frag - ile the frag - rance that some - how still clings, De -
Dm
A7

61
SI
SII
A
stroy not with rough - ness the vis - ion love brings, of
stroy not with_ rough - ness the vis - ion love brings, of
stroy not with_ rough - ness the vis - ion love brings, of
Dm
E♭
rit.
a tempo
But - ter - fly Ros - es with pet - als like wings.
But - ter - fly Ros - es with pet - als like wings.
But - ter - fly Ros - es with pet - als like wings.
Dm
A7
Dm
rit.
a tempo
A7
rit.
R.H.
L.H.
L.H.

30.

Christmas Is a Feeling

for Unison or Two-Part Chorus, accompanied

N.S.

NATALIE SLEETH

The message of Christmas continues to attract the attention of composers, poets, and artists of all kinds. Composer Natalie Sleeth has skillfully combined the basic melody that is sung by Part I throughout the song with counter-melodies. Listen and you will hear three traditional carols floating above this tune.

16
cheer, it reach - es out to touch you as the hol - i - day draws near.
brings good cheer, it reach-es out as the hol - i - day draws near.
21
Obbligato
mf
It's mis - tle-toe and fall -ing snow and
It's
26
can - dles burn - ing bright; It's a feel - ing that we're hap - py on a
mis - tle - toe and can - dle - light, feel - ing hap - py a - gain on a

30
cold win - ter night; It's glad no - els and chim-ing bells and
cold win - ter night; It's car - ing and shar - ing and
34
pres - ents by the tree; It's the spi - rit of giv - ing in
pres - ents by the tree; It's the spi - rit of giv - ing in
38
poco rall.
a tempo
you and in me, For Christ - mas is a feel - ing
you and in me, For Christ - mas, Christ - mas,

42
fill - ing the air, it's love and joy and laugh - ter of
Christ - mas fills the air, it's love and joy of
46
peo-ple ev - 'ry where; But if Christ - mas is a feel - ing
peo-ple ev - 'ry where; But it Christ - mas is a feel - ing
50
bring-ing such good cheer, Then why, O why don't you and I
bring-ing such good cheer, Then why, O why don't you and I

54
try to make it last all year?
try to make it last all year?
59
rall.
Why can't it last all year?
Why can't it last all year?
rall.
ped.

31. Der Gang Zum Liebchen

(The Way to My Beloved)
Treble Voices, Unison

Translation by Anne Grossman

JOHANNES BRAHMS (1833-1897)

Like other Romantic composers, Johannes Brahms (see page 361) often chose love poems to set to music. The poem's anxious mood is conveyed by the wide intervals, the minor key, and the "animato" marking, as well as the rhythm changes in the piano part as it shifts between a feeling of three and then two.

Con grazia (With grace)
1. Es glänzt der Mond nie - der, ich soll - te doch wie - der zu mei - nem
2. Es ging der Mond un - ter, ich eil - te doch mun - ter, und eil - te, dass
1. The moon-beams were shin - ing, my spir - it was pin - ing To see my be -
2. The moon has re - ced - ed, I has-tened, I speed - ed, I hur - ried that
p
Lieb - chen, wie mag es ihr gehn?
kei - ner mein Lieb - chen ent führt.
lov - ed, the one I a - dore.
no one would steal her a - way.
animato
Ach weh, sie ver -
Ihr Täub - chen, o
She's moan - ing and
So rob - ins, keep
animato
p

za - get und kla - get, und kla - get, dass sie mich nim - mer im
gir - ret, ihr Lüft - chen, o schwir-ret, dass kei - ner mein Lieb - chen, mein
cry - ing, she's weep - ing and sigh - ing; She feared I was gone and she'd
sing - ing, and breez - es, keep wing - ing so no one will steal my be -

Le - ben wird sehn!
Lieb - chen ent führt!
see me no more.
lov - ed a - way.

32. Die Schwalben

(The Swallows)

Treble Voices, Two-Part

ROBERT SCHUMANN (1810-1856)

Translation by Anne Grossman

In this Romantic part song, Robert Schumann (see page 359) captures the feeling of swallows in flight—climbing, diving, and darting—by tone painting. On the word "high" (*hoch*), the pitch goes up. On "diving" (*nieder*), the pitches move down. The restless darting is expressed by the fast tempo and the changing rhythms and keys.

cresc.
kom-men sie, da kom - men sie wie-der und su - chen, und su - chen ihr
year is gone a - gain they'll be ar - riv - ing, And seek - ing and seek - ing their
cresc.
cresc.

1., 2.
3.
vo - ri-ges Haus.
own___ lit-tle house.
sf
f

2. Sie gehen jetzt fort in's neue Land,
Und ziehen jetzt eilig hinüber;
Doch kommen sie wieder, sie wieder herüber,
Das ist einem Jeden, Jeden bekannt.

3. Und kommen sie wieder zu uns zurück,
Der Bauer geht ihnen entgegen,
Sie bringen ihm vielmal, ihm vielmal den Segen,
Sie bringen ihm Wohlstand, ihm Wohlstand und Glück!

2. They're now going forth to untried lands,
For half the year sojourning.
But they'll be returning, but they'll be returning,
As certainly everyone understands.

3. And in the springtime when they come back,
The peasant's delight is unceasing.
The swallow's returning will bring him a blessing.
They bring him good fortune, good fortune and luck.

33. Die Zufriedenheit

(Happiness)

Treble Voices, Unison

WOLFGANG AMADEUS MOZART (1756-1791)

Translated by Anne Grossman

Since the film *Amadeus*, Mozart has become even more highly regarded by the American public. This small song illustrates a characteristic of music of the Classical period—the practice of decorating melodies with ornaments. These ornaments in both the vocal and piano parts add a flourish of notes that quickly turn about each other. For more about Mozart, see page 349.

fp
f
p
1. Wie sanft, wie ru - hig fühl' ich hier des Le - bens Freu - den
1. My life is hap - py when I'm here; my lit - tle world is
oh - ne Sor - gen, und son - der Ah - nung
free from sor - row; all pain and an - guish

leuch - tet mir will - kom - men je - der Mor - gen. 2. Mein
dis - ap - pear, I wel - come each to - mor - row. 2. My
fro - hes, mein zu - fried' - nes Herz tanzt nach der Me - lo -
heart when in this par - a - dise, re - sponds to na - ture's
die der Hai - ne, und an - ge - nehm ist
tune - ful meas - ure. The tears that cloud my
selbst mein Schmerz, wenn ich vor Lie - be wei - ne.
brim - ming eyes are on - ly tears of pleas - ure.
f
p

3. *Wie sehr lach' ich die Grossen aus,*
Die Blutvergiesser, Helden, Prinzen!
Denn mich beglückt ein kleines Haus,
Sie nicht einmal Provinzen.

4. *Wie wüten sie nicht wider sich,*
Die göttergleichen Herr'n der Erden:
Doch brauchen sie mehr Raum als ich,
Wenn sie begraben werden?

3. I laugh at all that princely band,
those greedy lords of highest station;
I'm happy with my bit of land —
they're not content with nations.

4. They fight for land, they do or die,
those angry lords, so hot and harried.
But will they need more than than I
when they are dead and buried?

34. Flying Free

for Treble Voices, S.S.A. with piano and flute*

Words and Music by DON BESIG (ASCAP)

The text of this piece discloses the poet/composer's philosophy, namely, that although he might wish for a carefree life (flying free, like a bird), he knows that life will hold pain as well as happiness.

Performance time: approx. 4:00

* Dotted slur means no breath.

C
SOPRANO
f
Like the bird a - bove the trees
ALTO
f
mf
dim.
glid - ing gen - tly on the breeze,
(opt. div.)
dim.
dim.
D
(a few voices)
mp
Oo
mf
S. & A. UNISON
I wish that all my life I'd be with - out a
mp

F .4 6
E
(div.)
care, and fly - ing free!
(Flute)
mf
(mp)
F
SOPRANO
mp
But life is not a dis - tant sky
ALTO
mp
mp

with-out a cloud,
with-out rain,
(opt. div.)
G
mp
And I can nev-er hope that I
mp
cresc.
can trav-el on
with-out pain.
cresc.
cresc.

H
mf
Time goes swift - ly on its way.
mf
mf
mf
dim.
All too soon we've lost to - day.
dim.
dim.
I
mp
I can - not wait for skies of blue
mp
mp
mp

J
— or dream so long that life is through.
(opt. div.)
mf
K
mf
So life's a song, a gift of
mf
So life's a song that I must sing, — a gift of
mf

love I must share.
mf
L
And when I see, my spir - its
And when I see the joy it brings, my spir - its
cresc.
soar through the air.
cresc.
mf
mf
cresc.

M
f
Like that bird up in the sky,
f
life has taught me how to fly.
N
For now I know what I can be and now my
mp

O
dim.
heart is fly - ing free!
Oo
(opt. div.) dim.
mf
dim.
rit. e dim.
p
dim.
p
rit. e dim.
p

35.

Frühlingslied

(Spring Song)

Treble Voices, Unison

Translation by Anne Grossman

FELIX MENDELSSOHN (1809-1847)

> This is a typical Romantic art song. Romantic composers like Mendelssohn (see page 359) often chose poetry that speaks of nature and love. The song has three verses and a refrain. The verse starts low. As the notes climb higher, a feeling of excitement is created. The refrain starts high, then descends, creating a feeling of relaxation.

Allegro vivace
1. Es
2. Die
1. The
2. The
dim.
bre - chen im schal - len - den Rei - gen die Früh - lings stim - men
Knos - pen schwel - len und glü - hen und drän - gen sich an das
voi - ces of spring - time are peal - ing, Their joy can no long - er
blos - soms are swell - ing and burst - ing To grace our bloom - ing

los, sie kön - nen's nicht län - ger ver-schwei - gen, die
Licht und war - ten in seh - nen dem Blü - hen, dass
wait; No long - er their pro - mise con - ceal - ing, Their
land. The buds of the pe - tals are thirst - ing For
cresc.
sf
Won - ne ist gar zu gross, die Won - ne, die
lie - ben - de Hand sie bricht, dass lie - ben - de,
rap - ture is far to great, Their rap - ture, their
touch of a loved one's hand, For touch, for
p
p
Won - ne ist gar zu gross!
lie - ben - de Hand sie bricht.
rap - ture is far too great.
touch of a loved one's hand.
f
f
(1., 2.) Wo -
(1., 2.) And
sf
sf

3. *Und Frühlingsgeister, sie steigen*
hinab in der Menschen Brust
Und regen da drinnen den Reigen
der ew'gen Jugendlust,
der ew'gen, ew'gen Jugendlust.

Wohin, wir ahnen es selber kaum,
Es rührt uns ein alter, ein süsser Traum,
Ein alter, ein süsser Traum!

3. The spirit of springtime is waking
within every human breast;
And mankind, its sorrows forsaking,
with infinite youth is blest,
with infinite, infinite youth is blest.

And what is bidding our spirits rise?
The dream, half-forgotten, of springs gone by;
Forgotten, of springs gone by.

36. Glück, Glück Zum Neuen Jahr

(Good Luck, a Happy New Year)

Three-Part Canon

Translation by Anne Grossman

LUDWIG VAN BEETHOVEN (1770-1827)

While he composed mainly for instruments, Ludwig van Beethoven, favorite composer of Charlie Brown's friend Schroeder, did write a few fine pieces for voices. In this lighthearted three-part canon, he uses one simple melody to create harmonies as the voices overlap. For more about Beethoven, see page 352.

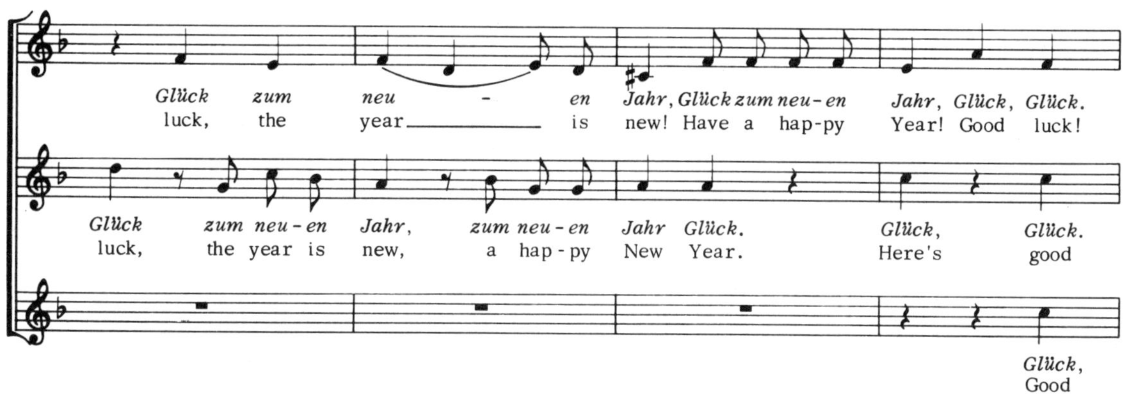

Glück zum neu-en Jahr, zum neu-en Jahr Glück. Glück, Glück,
luck, the year is new, a hap-py New Year. Here's good
Glück, Glück zum neu-en Jahr, Glück, Glück zum neu-en Jahr, Glück,
Good luck, the year is new, Good luck, the year is new, Good
Glück zum neu - en Jahr, Glück zum neu - en Jahr, Glück, Glück.
luck, the year is new! Have a hap-py year! Good luck!
Glück zum neu - en Jahr, Glück zum neu-en Jahr, Glück, Glück.
luck, the year is new! Have a hap-py year! Good luck!
Glück zum neu-en Jahr, zum neu-en Jahr Glück. Glück, Glück.
luck, the year is new, a hap-py New Year. Good luck!
Glück, Glück zum neu-en Jahr, Glück, Glück zum neu-en Jahr Glück.
Good luck, the year is new, Good luck, a hap-py New Year!

37. Hasten Shepherds On

(Vamos Pastorcillos)
Treble Voices, Two-Part

Arranged by Juan Pablo

Whether sung in English or Spanish, *Vamos Pastorcillos* "sounds" Hispanic. Why? Because it contains some of the musical characteristics of that culture: the use of syncopation, an emphasis of the interval of a third in the harmony, the constant repetition of certain tonal patterns, and an accompaniment of claves, maracas, and guitar.

* Maracas - alternating

Lul - la - bies to sing, He wno lies be - fore you Is Heav-'n's gra-cious
pron-tos a mar - char pres-tos y con brí - os el pa - so a - lar-
F♯m A7 F♯m A7 F♯m
King. Shep-herds, leave the moun - tain, Has-ten to the stall Where
gar. Va - mos, pas - tor - ci - llos, va - mos a Be - lén, que el
A7 D
lies the Ho - ly Child Who is born to save us all. Where lies the Ho - ly
Ni - ño ha na - ci - do pa - ra nues - tro bien, que el Ni - ño ha na -
A7 F♯m D
Child Who is born to save us all.
ci - do pa - ra nues - tro bien.
A7 D+6 G+6 D+6 Em
* Maracas
tr

mf
S.
Shep - herds, leave the moun - tain, Has - ten to the
Va - mos, pas - tor - ci - llos, va - mos a Be -
p
A.
La, la, la, la, la, la, la, la, la, la, la, la,
D
simile
stall Where lies the Ho - ly Child Who is
lén, que el Ni - no ha na - ci - do
la, la, la, la, la, la, la, la, la, la, la, la,
born to save us all, Where lies the Ho - ly
pa - ra nues - tro bien, que el Ni - ño ha na -
la, la, la, la, la, la, la, la, la, la, la, la,
A7
D

Child Who is born to save us all.
ci - do para nues - tro bien.
la, la, la, la, la, la, la, la, la, la, la, la.
A7
D
Hear the choir-ing voic - es An - gels from on
Con ce - les - tes voc - es he oí - do en - to -
tr
A7
D
tr
high, "Glo - ria in ex - cel - sis"
nar: Glo - ria en las al - tu - ras
A7
D
tr
A7

D
A7
Ech-oes from the sky. La, la, la, la, la, la,
ya los hom-bres paz.
la, la, la, la, la.
diminuendo
pp
diminuendo
tr
Tutti
Shep-herds, leave the moun-tain, Has-ten to the stall Where
Va-mos, pas-tor-ci-llos, va-mos a Be-lén, que el
D
G
D
8va
f staccato

Translation by Miriam L. Transue

38. In dulci jubilo

Treble Voices, Two-Part

Edited by Noah Greenberg
Translated by Hubert Creekmore

MICHAEL PRAETORIUS (1571-1621)
Musae Sionae IX (1611)

This Christmas song is nearly 400 years old, but the origin of the melody is even older. Originally a chant, it was first changed into a hymn or chorale. Then Praetorius made it into a two-part "polyphonic" work in which the two melodies interweave and imitate each other—but not exactly. Works in two languages were not uncommon at that time.

25
ne, un - sers Her - zens Won - -
one, our heart's joy, our dear
Won - ne, un - sers Her - zens Won -
dear one, our heart's joy, our dear
30
- - - - ne leit in prae - se - pi -
one, Safe in the man - ger
- - ne leit in prae - se - pi - o,
one, Safe in the man - ger lies
35
o, und leuch-tet als die Son - ne, und
lies And shines out like the clear sun, and
und leuch-tet als die Son - ne, und leuch-tet als die Son - ne,
And shines out like the clear sun, and shines out like the clear sun,
40
leuch-tet als die Son - ne ma - tris in gre - mi - o.
shines out like the clear sun In Ma - ry's lap a - sleep.
und leuch-tet als die Son - ne ma - tris in gre - mi -
and shines out like the clear sun In Ma - ry's lap a -
45
Al - pha es et O,
Al - pha es et O,
o. Al - pha es et
sleep. Al - pha es et

Al - pha es, Al - pha es et O, ___ Al - pha
Al - pha es, Al - pha es et O, ___ Al - pha

O, ___ Al - pha es et O, Al - pha es et O, ___
O, ___ Al - pha es et O, Al - pha es et O, ___

es et O, ___ Al - pha es et O,
es et O, ___ Al - pha es et O,

___ Al - pha es et O, Al - pha es et
___ Al - pha es et O, Al - pha es et

Al - pha es et O, ___ Al - pha es et O, ___
Al - pha es et O, ___ Al - pha es et O, ___

O, ___ Al - pha es et O, ___ Al - pha
O, ___ Al - pha es et O, ___ Al - pha

Al - pha es, Al - pha es et O, Al - pha es ___ et O.
Al - pha es, Al - pha es et O, Al - pha es ___ et O.

es et O, Al - pha es, Al - pha es et O.
es et O, Al - pha es, Al - pha es et O.

Note: "*Alpha es et O(mega)*," an abbreviated usage which means, "In God is the beginning and the end."

Original Chorale
In dul - ci ju - bi - lo, ___ nun sin - get und seid froh, ___ un - sers
Her - zens Won - ne leit in præ - se - pi - o ___ und leuch - tet als die Son - ne
ma - tris in gre - mi - o. ___ Al - pha es et O, ___ Al - pha es et O.

39. Linden Lea

for Treble Voices, S.S.A., with Piano

W. Barnes

RALPH VAUGHAN WILLIAMS (1872-1958)
Arranged by Douglas E. Wagner

This piece was originally a solo song. It has been arranged here for treble voices in three parts. There is a distinctly English "feel" to this song: the poem is filled with references to the countryside and to nature; the music bristles with rich, but at the same time folk-like, harmonies. To read about this composer, see page 367.

HMC-944

8
moot, the shin - ing grass blades, tim - ber shad - ed, now do
copse, and paint - ed birds do hush their sing - ing, up up -
moot, the shin - ing grass blades, tim - ber shad - ed, now do
copse, and paint - ed birds do hush their sing - ing, up up -
11
qui - ver un - der foot; And birds do whis - tle o - ver -
on the tim - ber tops; And brown leaved fruit's a - turn - ing
qui - ver un - der foot; And birds do whis - tle o - ver -
on the tim - ber tops; And brown leaved fruit's a - turn - ing
f
mf
14
head, and wa - ter's bub - bling in its bed; And there for
red, in cloud-less sun - shine o - ver head, with fruit for
head, and wa - ter's bub - bling in its bed; And there for
red, in cloud-less sun - shine o - ver head, with fruit for
mf
mp

17
me, the ap-ple tree do lean down low in Lin - den Lea.
me, the ap-ple tree do lean down low in Lin - den Lea.
me, the ap-ple tree do lean down low in Lin - den Lea.
me, the ap-ple tree do lean down low in Lin - den Lea.
21
Animato
Let oth-er folk make mon-ey
Let oth-er folk make mon-ey
rit.
a tempo
25
fast - er, in the air of dark-roomed towns; I don't dread a pee-vish
fast - er, in the air of dark - roomed towns; I don't dread a pee-vish

29
mf
risoluto
mas - ter, though no man may heed my frowns. I be free to go a -
mf
mas - ter, though no man may heed my frowns. I be free to go a -
mp
33
poco rall.
p
broad, or take a - gain my home-ward road, to where, for me, the ap - ple
p poco rall.
mf
broad, or take a - gain my home-ward road, to where, for me, the ap - ple
p poco rall.
mp
37
rall.
Lea.
mp
tree do lean down low in Lin - den Lea, Lin - den Lea.
rall.
mp
tree do lean down low in Lin - den Lea, Lin - den Lea.
rall.
p

40. Little by Little

for Two-Part Choir, accompanied

N.S. NATALIE SLEETH

Unlike most composers, Natalie Sleeth usually writes her own poetry. Here the poet/composer advises singers and listeners to be the best they can be, little by little. The music is delivered in "patter" (um-pah) style. Two melodies are presented individually, then combined.

18
got the will, and lit-tle by lit - tle you're there! If you can't swim an o -cean, then
22
ford a stream! Just "re-mod-el" your bas-ic scheme; Don't give up 'till you
26
reach your dream, and lit - tle by lit - tle you're there! Good things that are
30
here to stay don't get done in just one day. Once you start you're

34
on your way, so keep on go - ing. If you can't make a mil-lion, don't draw a blank!
39
Just keep fill - ing your pig - gy bank! You'll have on - ly your - self to thank, when
43
lit - tle by lit - tle you're there! Ev' - ry rose was once a bud,
47
One small rain - drop starts a flood, A - corns plant-ed in the mud will

51
grow, you know! If you can't walk a mile — take one long stride, —
55
move a - long with a sense of pride, — step by step 'till you're sat - is - fied, and
59
lit - tle by lit - tle you're there!
63

68
Part I
mf
If you can't climb a moun - tain, then climb a hill! That's much bet-ter than
Part II
mf
Climb a hill if you will, pick a bright
72
stand - ing still, There's a way if you've got the will, and
daf - fo - dil! To the top, nev - er stop, and
75
lit - tle by lit - tle you're there! If you can't swim an o - cean, then
lit - tle by lit - tle you're there! Ford a stream,

78
ford a stream, Just "re-mod-el" your ba-sic scheme, Don't give up 'till you
keep your dream, pro-gress brings self es-teem, move a - long,
82
reach your dream, and lit-tle by lit - tle you're there! Good things that are
sing a song, and lit-tle by lit - tle you're there! Don't
86
here to stay don't get done in just one day. Once you start you're
de-lay, but start to-day, once you're

90
on your way, so keep on go - ing. If you can't make a mil - lion don't
on your way, just keep on go - ing. Cent by cent,
94
draw a blank,— Just keep fill - ing your pig - gy - bank!— You'll have on - ly your -
saved, not spent, one day soon pays the rent. Rev - e - nue
98
self to thank, when lit - tle by lit - tle you're there! Ev' - ry rose was
will ac - crue, and lit - tle by lit - tle you're there! Ros -
legato

102
once a bud, One small rain-drop starts a flood, A - corns plant-ed
- es grow, and rain - drops flow, A - corns
106
in the mud will grow, you know! If you can't walk a mile, take
turn one day to oaks, you know! So, take a stride,
110
one long stride, move a - long with a sense of pride,
walk with pride, set your course, you de - cide!

113
mp cresc.
step by step 'till you're sat - is - fied, and lit - tle by lit - tle by lit -
mp cresc.
Don't re - treat, move your feet, and lit - tle by lit - tle by lit -
mp cresc.
116
- tle by lit - tle by lit - tle by lit - tle, you'll be
- tle by lit - tle by lit - tle by lit - tle, you'll be,
119
there, lit - tle by lit - tle you're there!
ff
Inch by inch, day by day, lit - tle by lit - tle you're there!
ff
ff
8va

41. Old Joe Clark

Treble Voices, Three-Part

American Folk Song
Arranged by Mary Goetze

Originally, "Old Joe Clark" was a fiddle tune played at dances by American pioneers. As sometimes happens with good dance tunes, someone put words to it so that people would have the pleasure of singing it. In this arrangement, the melody is passed quickly from voice to voice.

Chorus
18
mf
Old Joe Clark, I say now
f
mf
Round and round Old Joe Clark, Round and round.
mf
f
Round and round it's round and round I say.

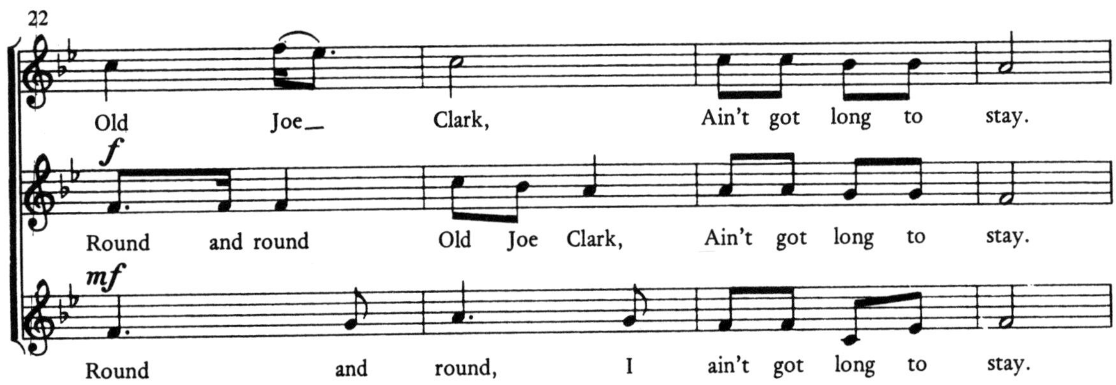
22
Old Joe Clark, Ain't got long to stay.
f
Round and round Old Joe Clark, Ain't got long to stay.
mf
Round and round, I ain't got long to stay.

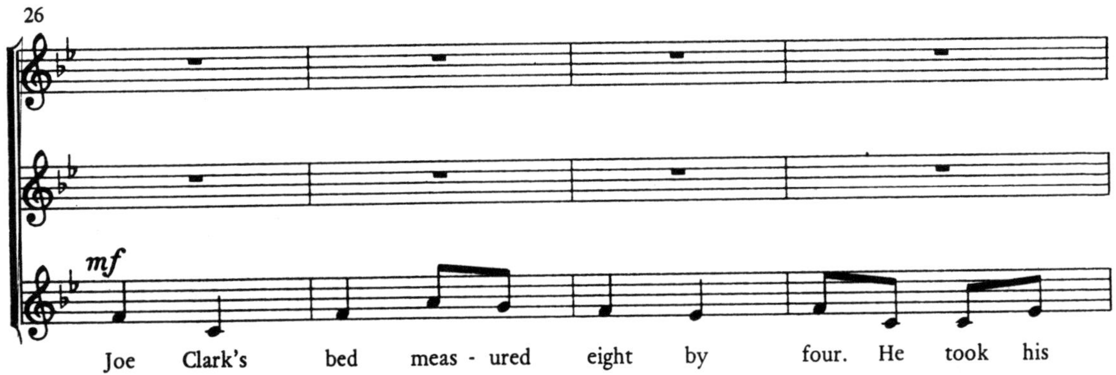
26
mf
Joe Clark's bed meas - ured eight by four. He took his

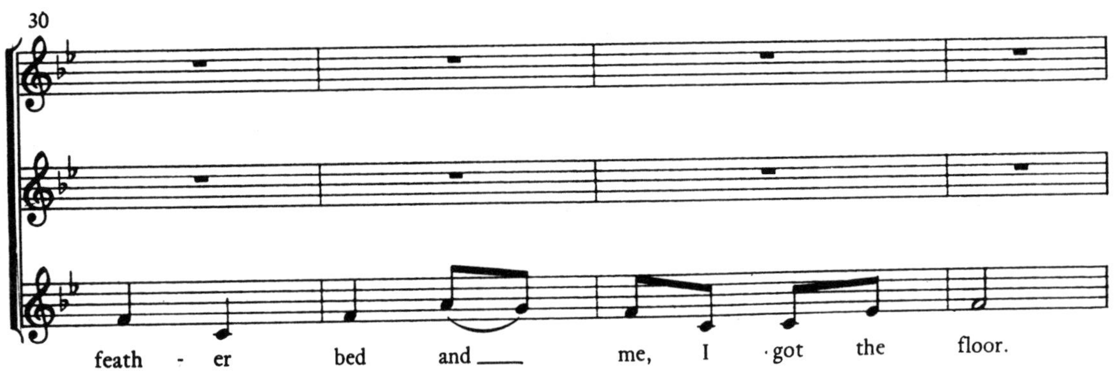
30
feath - er bed and me, I got the floor.

34
mf
Old Joe Clark had a feath - er bed.
p
Joe Clark's bed meas - ured eight by four. He got the
38
He got the bed and I got the floor.
feath - er bed and me, I got the floor.
Verse 2
42
mf
I went down to Joe Clark's house, Nev - er been be - fore.
p
Old Joe Clark had a feath - er bed.
p
Joe Clark's bed meas - ured eight by four. He got the
46
He slept on the feath - er bed and I slept on the floor.
He got the bed and I got the floor.
feath - er bed and me, I got the floor.

Chorus
50
Old Joe Clark, I say now
Round and round Old Joe Clark, Round and round.
Round and round it's round and round I say.
54
Old Joe Clark, Ain't got long to stay.
Round and round Old Joe Clark, Ain't got long to stay.
Round and round I ain't got long to stay.
58
Pling pling - a pling pling - a pling pling - a pling pling (etc.)
61

65
f
Pom pom pom pom pom pom (etc.)
69
74
Verse 3
f
Joe Clark had a vi - o - lin, he fid - dled all the day.
mf
mf
78
An - y - bod - y start to dance and Joe would start to play.

Chorus
82
mf
Old Joe_ Clark, I say now
f
Round and round Old Joe Clark, Round and round.
mf
Round and round it's round and round I say.
86
Old Joe_ Clark, Ain't got long to stay.
Round and round Old Joe Clark, Ain't got long to stay.
Round and round I ain't got long to stay.
90
pp
Old Joe_ Clark, I say now
mp
Round and round Old Joe Clark, Round and round.
Round and round it's round and round I say.
94
Slowly
Old Joe_ Clark, Ain't got long to stay.
Round and round Old Joe Clark, Ain't got long to stay.
Round and round, Ain't got long to stay.

42. Personet Hodie

(On This Day, People Sing)

for Treble Voices, S.A., with Keyboard, (Flute, Percussion, Optional)

Words and melody from *Piae Cantiones*, 1582

English Text, D.H.

**Arranged by Don Hinshaw*

The 400-year-old text of this work tells of the celebration of the birth of Jesus in a way that brings to mind the determined and hopeful journey of the Wise Men or a stately Christmas festival in a large cathedral. The strong duple meter invites us to join the procession.

Introduction**
Allegro (𝅗𝅥 = 92)
2 Flutes or Recorders
a 2
Finger Cymbals
simile
p
Hand Drum
p
8
Fl. 1
mf
Fl. 2
mf
mf
16
23
Soprano (a cappella)
mp
1. Per - so - net ho - di - e Vo - ces pu - e - ru - lae, Lau - dan - tes ju - cun - de
On this day peo - ple sing, sing - ing praise to the King, Joy - ful - ly now we sing
29
S.
A.
Qui no - bis est na - tus, Sum - mo De - o da - tus, Et de vir, vir, vir,
to the King of Glo - ry, To the King of Glo - ry. He is born, born, born,
35
Et de vir, vir, vir, Et de vir - gi - ne - o ven - tre pro - cre - a - tus.
He is born, born, born, He is born on this day, Glo - ria in ex - cel - sis.

*Based on an arrangement by K. Lee Scott (CHRIST IS NOW ARISEN, HMC-830)

**This arrangement may be used as a processional. Flutes and drums should be in the procession. If instruments are not available, choir begins with stanza 1.

42 S.
mf
A.
2. In mun - do na - sci - tur, Pan - nis in - vol - vi - tur,
All on earth now re - joice, To the King lift your voice,
mp
46
Prae - se - pi po - ni - tur Sta - bu - lo bru - to - rum, Rec - tor su - per -
He is born on this day in a sta - ble low - ly, Glo - ria in ex -
51
mf
no - rum, Per - di - dit - dit, - dit, Per - di - dit, - dit, - dit,
cel - sis, He is born, born, born, He is born, born, born,
mf
56
Per - di - dit spo - li - a prin - ceps in - fer - no - rum.
He is born on this day, Glo - ria in ex - cel - sis.

60
Flutes a 2
S.
mf
A.
3. Ma - gi tres ve - ne - runt,
From the East wise-men came,
p
66
Par - vu-lum in - qui-runt, Beth - le-hem ad - e - unt, Stel - lu - lam se - quen - do,
"Where is he who is born, born to-day, born to-day in a low-ly man - ger?
72
f
Ip - sum a - do - ran - do, Au - rum, thus, thus, thus, Au - rum, thus, thus, thus,
We have come to wor-ship. We bring gifts, gifts, gifts, We bring gifts, gifts, gifts,

78
Au-rum, thus,
er myrr-ham
e - i
of - fe - ren - do.
Frank-in-cense,
myrr and gold
we will of - fer to him."

83
f
f
4. Om-nes cle -
All the peo -
f
Finger Cymbals
f
Hand Drum
f

87
simile
ri - cu - li, Pa - ri - ter pu - e - ri, Can - tent ut
ple that dwell on the earth now re - joice, Join the an -
91
an - ge - li: Ad - ve - ni - sti mun - do, Lau - des ti - bi fun - do.
gel's re - frain: "Glo - ria in ex - cel - sis, Glo - ria in ex - cel - sis!"

96
ff
ff
I - de - o, - o, - o, I - de - o, - o, - o,
He is born, born, born, He is born, born, born,
ff
100
(opt. div.)
I - de - o, glo - ri - a in ex - cel - sis De - o.
He is born, glo - ri - a in ex - cel - sis De - o.

43.

Prepare Thyself Zion

for Two-Part Choir, accompanied

J.S. BACH (1685-1750)
Edited and arranged by Lucy Hirt

Johann Sebastian Bach, one of the great master composers of the Baroque period (see page 345), originally wrote this piece for alto solo as part of his *Christmas Oratorio*. Bach conveys the feeling of haste with eighth and sixteenth notes that are always in motion. This is a "Da capo" or A-B-A form in which the first part is repeated.

20
fec - tion the pur - est, the fair - est this day to re - ceive, the
fec - tion the pur - est, the fair - est this day to re - ceive,
25
pur - est,
the fair - est, Pre - pare thy-self,
30
with ten - der af - fec - tion,
Zi - on,
tr
f
p
f

35
Pre - pare Thy-self, Zi - on, with ten - der_ af -
Pre - pare Thy-self, Zi - on, with ten - der_ af -
tr
p
40
fec - tion, the pur - est,_the_ fair - est this day to_ re - ceive, Pre -
fec - tion, the pur - est,_the_ fair -est this day to_ re - ceive, Pre -
45
pare thy-self, Zi - on,_with ten -der af - fec- tion,_the pur- est, the
pare, O Zi - on, with great af - fec - tion, the pur - est, the

50
fair - est, this day to — re - ceive. the pur - est,
fair - est, this day to re - ceive, the
p
55
Pre - pare thy-self, Zi - on,
fair - est, Pre - pare thy - self, Zi - on,
f
60
with ten - der af - fec - tion, Pre -
with ten - der af - fec - tion,
tr
p
f
p

65
pare thy - self, Zi - on, — with ten - der af - fec - tion, — the
the
69
pur - est, the fair /- est, this day to — re - ceive.
pur - est, the fair - est, this day — to re - ceive.
73
tr
tr
77

81
Fine
89
Thou must meet Him with a heart — with love — o'er - flow - ing,
95
With a heart — with love — o'er - flow - ing, Haste then with

100
ar - dour the Bride-groom to wel -come. Haste, then, haste
Haste, then
105
then with ar - dour the Bride - groom, Haste to
haste with ar - dour the Bride-groom to wel - come, to
110
D.C. al fine
wel -come. Haste, then, O haste, the Bride-groom to wel -come.
D.C. al fine
wel -come. O haste then, O haste, then the Bride-groom to wel- come.
D.C. al fine

44. Sing a Song

for Two-part Choir, with Piano, Bells, Triangle, Tub Drum, or Bongo Drum

Words and Music by ED ROBERTSON

This work is full of interesting musical ideas—the continual change of meters in the principal melody which creates an off-balance rhythmic effect that is appealing; the use of various instruments to add to the rhythmic interest; and the addition of new melodies to be sung and/or played at the same time.

♩= 76 (♪♪=♪ throughout)
Piano
5
Unison
Sing a song, sing a song as you go a-long your way.
7
Sing a song, sing a song, you'll feel bet-ter all the day. Sing a song, oth-ers
10
soon will sing a-long. Sing a song, sing a song.

13
Beat a drum, beat a drum, you can real-ly feel the beat.
Tub-drum
16
Beat a drum, beat a drum, makes you want to tap your feet. Beat a drum, lis-ten.
19
to the rum-pa-dum. Beat a drum, beat a drum.
Drum
22
Let's make mu - sic!
Triangle
Drum

25
Live - ly mu - sic! Come a - long!
29
Bells*
Here we go! Ring a bell, ring a bell, you can
33
make a hap-py sound. Ring a bell, ring a bell, and you'll spread some cheer a-round.

*Glockenspiel, handbells, etc.

36
Ring a bell, Let the mu-sic cast a spell. Ring a bell, ring a bell.
41
Part I.
I like mu - sic! Live - ly
Part II.
Tra-la-la, tra - la-la, tra-la, La-la-la-la-la, Tra-la-la, Tra-la - la, tra-la,
Drum
Clap

44
mu - sic! Come a - long! Sing a song, sing
la-la-la-la-la, Tra-la-la, la-la, Tra-la-la-la-la, Sing a song, sing
48
shouted
a song! Tra - la!
shouted
a song! Tra - la!

45. Tanzen Und Springen

(Dancing and Springing)

for Treble Voices, Three-Part, S.S.A.T.B., or Unison

Edited by Noah Greenberg
Translated by Charles Canfield Brown

HANS LEO HASSLER (1564-1612)
Lustgarten, 1601

Usually dance music is written for instruments, but the gagliarda—an Italian 16th-century dance—is written for voices. It is very doubtful that singers could sing and dance this work at the same time, because the music moves very quickly, and the dance requires athletic leaps that would leave a singer breathless.

*The top voice may be omitted when it is sung in unison by all voices.

5
fa - la - la - la, fa - la - la - la, fa - la - la. Lau - ten und
Fa - la - la - la, Fa - la - la - la, Fa - la - la. Strum - ming and
fa - la - la - la, fa - la - la, fa - la - la. Lau - ten und
Fa - la - la - la, Fa - la - la, Fa - la - la. Strum - ming and
fa - la - la - la, fa - la - la, fa - la - la. Lau - ten und
Fa - la - la - la, Fa - la - la, Fa - la - la. Strum - ming and
10
15
Gei - gen solln auch nicht schwei - gen; zu mu - si - zie - ren und ju - bi -
bow - ing With none fore - go - ing; Such mu - sic mak - ing And cel - e -
Gei - gen solln auch nicht schwei - gen; zu mu - si - zie - ren und ju - bi -
bow - ing With none fore - go - ing; Such mu - sic mak - ing And cel - e -
Gei - gen solln auch nicht schwei - gen; zu mu - si - zie - ren und ju - bi -
bow - ing With none fore - go - ing; Such mu - sic mak - ing And cel - e -

20
lie - ren steht mir all mein Sinn. Fa - la - la - la, fa - la -
brat - ing Will ev - er suit me. Fa - la - la - la, Fa - la -
lie - ren steht mir all mein Sinn. Fa - la - la - la, fa - la -
brat - ing Will ev - er suit me. Fa - la - la - la, Fa - la -
lie - ren steht mir all mein Sinn. Fa - la - la - la, fa - la -
brat - ing Will ev - er suit me. Fa - la - la - la, Fa - la -
25
la, fa - la - la, fa - la - la - la, fa - la - la fa - la - la
la, fa - la - la, Fa - la - la - la, Fa - la - la, fa - la - la.
la, fa la la, fa - la - la - la, fa - la - la, fa - la - la.
la, fa - la - la, Fa - la - la - la, Fa - la - la, fa - la - la.
la, fa - la - la, fa - la - la - la, fa - la - la, fa - la - la.
la, fa - la - la, Fa - la - la - la, Fa - la - la, fa - la - la.

46. The Trout

(Die Forelle)

for Treble Voices, Two-Part

FRANZ SCHUBERT (1797-1828)

Arranged by Ray Robinson

Franz Schubert (see page 358) is known as a great "melodist," a composer who had a great gift for writing beautiful melodies. Schubert liked this "Trout" melody so much that he also used it as a main theme in a string quintet of the same name.

NMC-941

20
Ba - de im kla - ren Bäch-lein zu, des mun - tern Fisch - leins
shad - y, the trout so quick and wise, The wa - ters cool and
rel - le mit sei - ner An - gel nicht, so fängt er die Fo -
held it, the trout is safe and sure. So pleased as I be -
Ba - de im kla - ren Bäch - lein zu, des mun - tern Fisch - leins
shad - y, the trout so quick and wise, The wa - ters cool and
rel - le mit sei - ner An - gel nicht, so fängt er die Fo -
held it, the trout is safe and sure. So pleased as I be -
24
Ba - de im kla - ren Bäch - lein zu.
shad - y, the trout so quick and wise.
rel - le mit sei - ner An - gel nicht.
held it, the trout is safe and sure.
Ba - de im kla - ren Bäch - lein zu.
shad - y, the trout so quick and wise.
rel - le mit sei - ner An - gel nicht.
held it, the trout is safe and sure.
28
1. D.S. 2.
Ein Doch
With But
1. D.S. 2.
Ein Doch
With But
1. D.S. 2.

32
end - lich ward dem Die - be die Zeit zu lang.
then the cru - el fish - er stepped off the bank.
end - lich ward dem Die - be die Zeit zu lang.
then the cru - el fish - er stepped off the bank.
simile
36
Er macht das Bach - lein tü - ckisch trü - be, und eh ich es ge -
He stirred and dimmed the pure clear wa - ter, And quick - er than a
Er macht das Bäch - lein tü - ckisch trü - be, und eh ich es ge -
He stirred and dimmed the pure clear wa - ter, And quick - er than a
p
40
dacht, so zuck - te sei - ne Ru - te, das Fisch - lein, das
wink the fish - ing rod was bend - ing, the young trout, the
dacht, so zuck - te sei - ne Ru - te, das Fisch - lein, das
wink, the fish - ing rod was bend - ing, the young trout, the

44
Fisch - lein zap - pelt dran, und ich mit re - gem Blu - te sah
trout had seized the bait. And I with sad re - flec - tion had
Fisch - lein zap - pelt dran, und ich mit re - gem Blu - te sah
trout had seized the bait. And I with sad re - flec - tion had
simile
48
die Be-trog - ne an, und ich mit re - gem Blu - te sah die Be-trog - ne
viewed the cru - el fate, And I with sad re - flec - tion had viewed the cru - el
die Be - trog - ne an, und ich mit re - gem Blu - te sah die Be - trog - ne
viewed the cru - el fate, And I with sad re - flec - tion had viewed the cru - el
an.
fate.
an.
fate.

47. Village Festival

(Mura Matsuri)
for Two-Part Choir, with Piano

Japanese Folk Song

Arranged by Grayston Ives

Many cultures celebrate the harvest. Japanese villagers celebrate a bountiful harvest at the village shrine with song, dance, and instruments. In the United States, we call our celebration Thanksgiving.

*Here, imitate instrument noises. Similarly in vv. 2 and 3.

*Imitate instrument noises, as before.

45
All voices, *unison*
f
Come, join the
f
50
fes - ti - val and light your lan - terns bright; Crowds gath - er round and sing 'til
55
day turns in - to night.
60
Sing, dance and play to - geth - er on this hap - py day!
ff

48. Jesu, Joy of Man's Desiring

CBB with Optional Handbells

J.S. BACH (1685-1750)
Arranged by Bobby L. Siltman
Piano Score by John Campbell

This is a very well known religious piece composed by the renowned composer J.S. Bach more than 200 years ago. The triple figure in the accompaniment gives a flow that contrasts with the hymn-like passages for the singers. The accompaniment can be played on a piano or organ and is especially effective when played by handbells.

joy of man's de - sir - ing,
Thee, our soul's as - pir - ing,
joy of man's de - sir - ing,
Thee, our soul's as - pir - ing,
joy of man's de - sir - ing,
Thee, our soul's as - pir - ing,

15
Ho - ly wis - dom,
Soar to un - cre -
Ho - ly wis - dom,
Soar to un - cre -
Ho - ly wis - dom,
Soar to un - cre -

love most bright.
a - ted light.
love most bright.
a - ted light.
love most bright.
a - ted light.
20
20

25
mf
Word of God, our flesh that
Word of God, our flesh that
Word of God, our flesh that

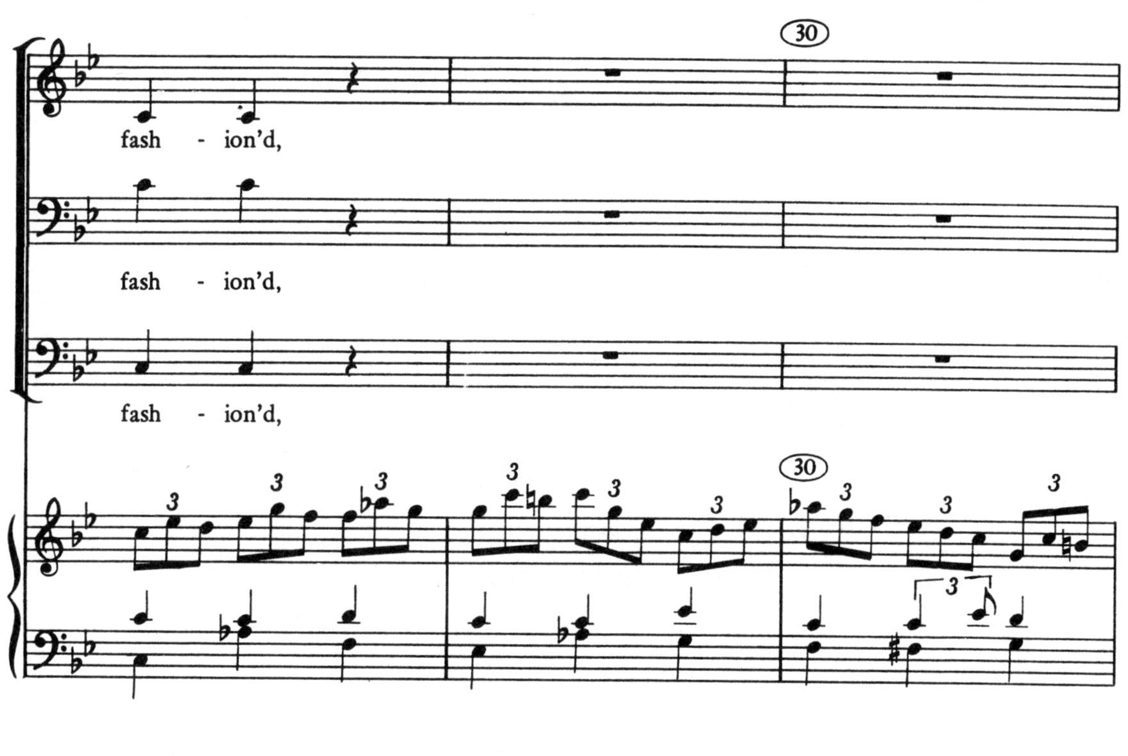
30
fash - ion'd,
fash - ion'd,
fash - ion'd,
30

mf
With the glow of faith im -
With the glow of faith im -
With the glow of faith im -

35
pas - sion'd.
pas - sion'd.
pas - sion'd.
35

mp
40
Striv - ing still to truth un - known,
mp
Striv - ing still to truth un - known.
mp
Striv - ing still to truth un - known.
40

mp
Life at - tain - ing
mp
Life at - tain - ing
mp
Life at - tain - ing

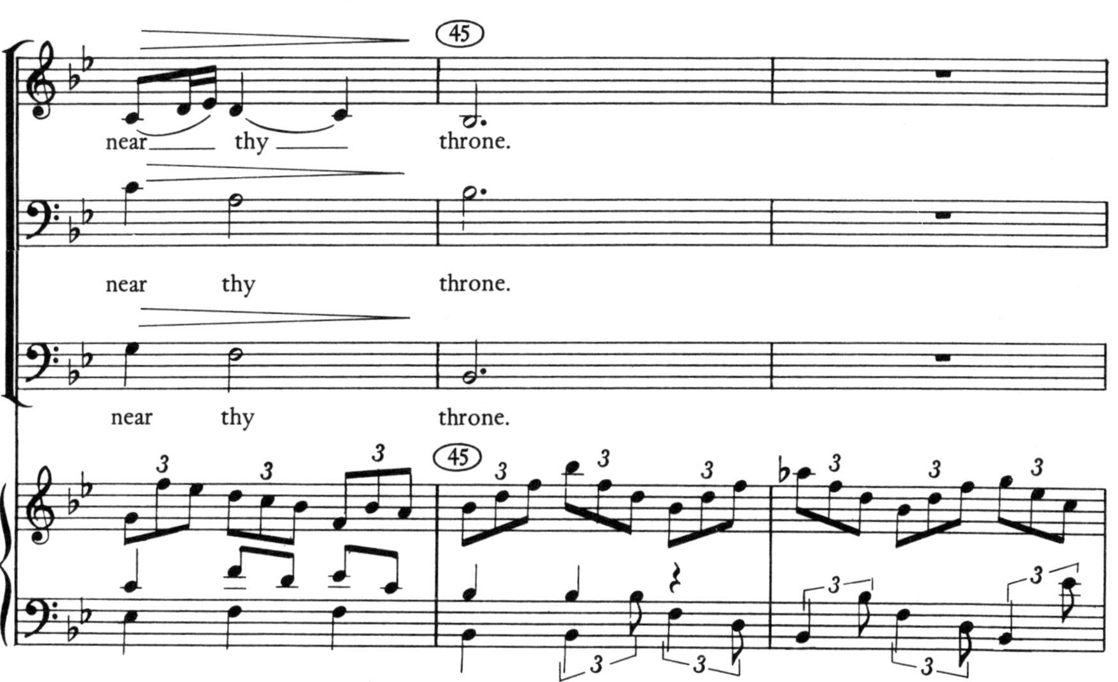
45
near thy throne.
near thy throne.
near thy throne.
45

50

55
rit.

49. My Lord, What a Morning

TB with Optional Accompaniment

Arranged by Lois Land

Spirituals, like jazz, are an original American musical expression. They originated in the South during the 19th century as a religious expression of Negro slaves. Many of these spirituals, like this one, cry out for a better life after death.

15
na - tions un - der - ground,
look - ing to God's right hand when the
look to God's right hand when the
(After Verse 1, D.S.)
(After Verse 3, go to last Refrain)
mf
20
stars be-gin to fall.
(2) hear the sin - ners mourn to wake the
mf
You'll hear the sin - ners
(After Verse 1, D.S.)
(After Verse 3, go to last Refrain)
mp
na - tions un - der - ground,
look - ing to God's right hand, when the
mourn,
mourn,
look to God's hand,

25
D.S. Refrain (after Verse 3)
stars be-gin to fall.
p
My Lord, what a morn-ing,
D.S.
mp
30
My Lord, what a morn-ing,
Slower
mp
when the
mf
My Lord, what a morn-ing,
Slower
ten. ten.
35
stars be-gin to fall when the stars be-gin to fall.
ten. ten.
The stars be-gin to fall.
ten.
ten.
pp
ten. ten.

*Opt.

50. This Train

(CBB)

American Folk Song

Arranged by Bobby L. Siltman
Piano Score by Tom Stoker

An old American folk/gospel song in a new version with catchy, syncopated rhythms. Bobby L. Siltman, music supervisor and choral director in Abilene, Texas is successful in composing and arranging music for boys' choirs because of his long experience in working with such choirs.

20
This train don't car-ry no gam - blers, This Train.
mf
This train done car-ried my moth-er, well, This Train.
mf
25
mf Baritone I
This train done car-ried my moth-er, well, This Train.
mf
Cambiata
mf
30
mp
This train done car-ried my moth - er, well my moth-er, my fa-ther, my
mp
This train done car-ried my moth - er, well my moth-er, my fa-ther, my
mp
mp

sis-ter and my brother-er, This train done car-ried my moth - er, well,
sis-ter and my brother-er, This train done car-ried my moth - er, well,
35
mp
Slowly
This Train.
This train, she's
mp
This Train.
This train, she's
mp
Slowly
mp
poco accel.
40
mf
bound for glo - ry, well, This Train.
This train she's
mf
bound for glo - ry, well, This Train.
This train she's
mf
poco accel.
mf

poco accel.
45
f
bound for glo - ry, well, This Train.
This train, she's
f
bound for glo - ry, well, This Train.
This train, she's
f
poco accel.
f
bound for glo - ry, well, This Train.
This train, she's
bound for glo - ry, well, This Train.
This train, she's
50
rit.
bound for glo - ry, if you want to get to heav-en, well you've got to be ho - ly.
bound for glo - ry, if you want to get to heav-en, well you've got to be ho - ly.
rit.

mp a tempo
55
mf
This train, she's bound for glo - ry, well, This train, she's
mp
mf
This train, she's bound for glo - ry, well, This train, she's
mp
mf
a tempo
mp
mf
f
rit.
bound for glo - ry, well, This Train, she's bound for glo - ry, Well,
f
bound for glo - ry, well, This Train, she's bound for glo - ry, Well,
f
rit.
f
ff a tempo
This Train.
ff
This Train.
ff
a tempo
ff

51. We Sail the Ocean Blue

for Three-Part Male Choir, T.B.B., with Piano

From "H.M.S. Pinafore"
GILBERT and SULLIVAN
Adapted and arranged by Ruth Artman

This is a "medley" of two famous sailor songs—"We Sail the Ocean Blue" (from England) and "Anchors Aweigh" (from the United States). The first is from an operetta by Gilbert and Sullivan (see page 360). In the days of sailing vessels, songs like these served to raise the spirits of the men and to help them perform their tasks.

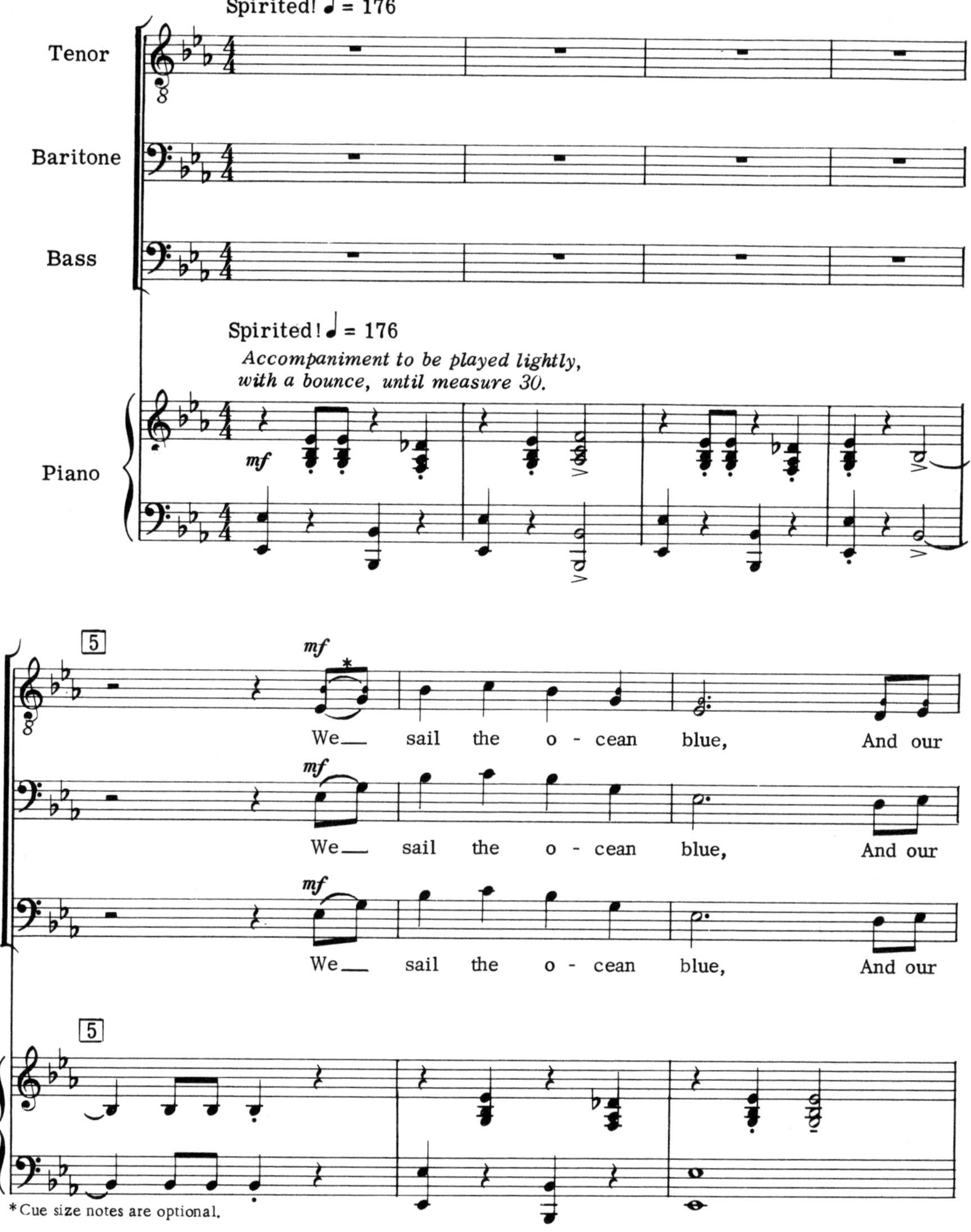
Spirited! ♩ = 176
Tenor
Baritone
Bass
Spirited! ♩ = 176
Accompaniment to be played lightly, with a bounce, until measure 30.
Piano
mf
5
mf
We__ sail the o - cean blue, And our
mf
We__ sail the o - cean blue, And our
mf
We__ sail the o - cean blue, And our
5

*Cue size notes are optional.

8
sau - cy ship's a beau - ty! We're sturd - y men and
melody
sau - cy ship's a beau - ty! We're sturd - y men and
melody
sau - cy ship's a beau - ty! We're sturd - y men and
8

11
true, And at - ten - tive to our du - ty! When the
melody
true, And at - ten - tive to our du - ty! When the
melody
true, And at - ten - tive to our du - ty!
11

14
Opt.
balls whis-tle free o'er the bright blue sea, We stand by our guns all the
balls whis-tle free o'er the bright blue sea, We stand by our guns all the
We stand by our guns all the
14

17
day. When at an - chor we ride on the eve - ning tide, We've
day. When at an - chor we ride on the eve - ning tide, We've
day. When at an - chor we ride on the eve- ning tide, We've
17

20
plen-ty of time for play. A-hoy! A - hoy! The balls_whis-tle
plen-ty of time for play. A-hoy! A - hoy! The balls whis-tle
plen-ty of time for play. A - hoy! A -
20

23
free! A-hoy! A - hoy! O'er the bright_ blue_ sea! We
free! A-hoy! A - hoy! O'er the bright blue sea!
hoy! A - hoy! A - hoy! Ship a-hoy!
23

26
stand by our guns, by our guns all day, by our guns all day!
We stand by our guns all day, by our guns all day!
We stand by our guns all day!
26
30 Marcato (♩ = 138)
(Shout and point)
ff
SHIP!
With vigor!
An - chors a -
(Shout and point)
ff
SHIP A - HOY!
An - chors a -
(Shout and point)
ff
SHIP A - HOY!
An - chors a -
30 Marcato (♩ = 138)
With vigor!
ff

33
weigh, my boys; An - chors a - weigh! We're a
weigh, my boys; An - chors a - weigh! We're a
weigh, my boys; An - chors a - weigh! We're a
33
36
salt - y crew through and through, and we sail at the break of
salt - y crew through and through, and we sail at the break of
salt - y crew through and through, and we sail at the break of
36

39
day. Sail - ing, sail - ing,
melody
day. An - chors a - weigh, my boys;
melody
day. An - chors a - weigh, my boys;
39
42
o - ver the bound - ing main! We're a salt - y crew
An - chors a - weigh! We're a salt - y crew
An - chors a - weigh! We're a salt - y crew
42

45
melody
through and through; It's an - chors a - weigh, a - weigh!
through and through; It's an - chors a - weigh, a - weigh!
through and through; It's an - chors a - weigh, a - weigh!
45
48 Spirited, a tempo (♩ = 176)
48 Spirited, a tempo (♩ = 176)
(Accompaniment light, bouncy, as initially)
f

52
f
We sail the o - cean blue, And our
f
We sail the o - cean blue, And our
f
We sail the o - cean blue, And our
52

55
sau - cy ship's a beau - ty! We're sturd - y men and
melody
sau - cy ship's a beau - ty! We're sturd - y men and
melody
sau - cy ship's a beau - ty! We're sturd - y men and
55

58
true, And at - ten - tive to our du - ty! Our
melody
Opt.
true, And at - ten - tive to our du - ty! Our
melody
true, And at - ten - tive to our du ty!
58

61
sau-cy lit-tle ship's a beau - ty!
sau-cy lit-tle ship's a beau - ty! We're at - ten - tive to our
We're at - ten - tive to our
61

*NOTE: One voice may hold the word "true" on and on, until, in exasperation, another singer may punch him to make him stop!

Overleaf ▶
"Singing Gallery," upper panel, relief sculpture by Italian sculptor Luca della Robbia (c.1400–1482), Cathedral, Florence, Italy.

PART 4

Singing through the Ages

PART 4

Singing through the Ages

Just as various species of birds sing their own particular song, different human cultures have produced their own particular kind of music. While it is true that all people sing, it is also true that they do not all sing exactly the same way. The character of a society and of a country is expressed in the way the people dress, eat, work—and sing. The music of Africans, of Hispanics, of Europeans, of Arabians, of Indians, and of Chinese is vastly different. So, too, is the music of various historical periods. As times change, so, too, do musical tastes.

Music is one way that we give identity to ourselves and to our times. It is an expression of our character—our style. Just as you can tell the year and the make of an automobile by observing its appearance, you can identify the historical origins of a piece of music by its characteristics. As we live, so do we sing—or so it seems.

The world of vocal music contains many forms and styles—from ancient chants to operatic arias, from old folk tunes to today's "pop" songs. All this music can be ours to understand and to enjoy. It is part of our heritage—one of the riches we inherit because we are alive right now. Each age has its own personality, and that's part of the fun of it. That personality comes through the music. It is as if a bit of history comes alive again, when we sing the music of these other ages. The chapters that follow will help you to understand these different times and peoples and the type of music they produced. And remember, all these types of vocal music use the same basic materials—melody, rhythm, and words performed on the musical instrument we all possess, our voice.

Chapter 8

Our Singing Heritage

No one knows exactly when or how the first music was made. But we have indications in painted pictures on the walls of caves some 30,000 years ago that people made music long before any kind of writing was invented. Music appears to be part of the human mind, just as it is innate to birds, whales, and certain insects. Early humans may have invented song by imitating the sounds of nature. They evidently found that song could soothe them, could lighten work, and could help them to celebrate.

Early cave drawings that date back to the Stone Age some 60,000 years ago depict hunting scenes and other aspects of human life. Unfortunately, there is no record of the music of these peoples. At that time and for many thousands of years after, there was no way to preserve sounds or to write them down. Our human ability to record and to replay sound is barely more than 100 years old, and systems for writing music down are a little more than 2,000 years old. What we know of music among these early peoples is limited to what they showed us in their paintings and what remains of their musical instruments.

North African cave painting showing music-making in this early civilization

Early Civilizations

If we travel today to the modern country of Iraq, we will be in an area of the world that was called Mesopotamia in ancient days. Some of our earliest musical instruments that date back to the time of the Sumerians in 3,000 B.C. have been found in this area, the cradle of civilization.

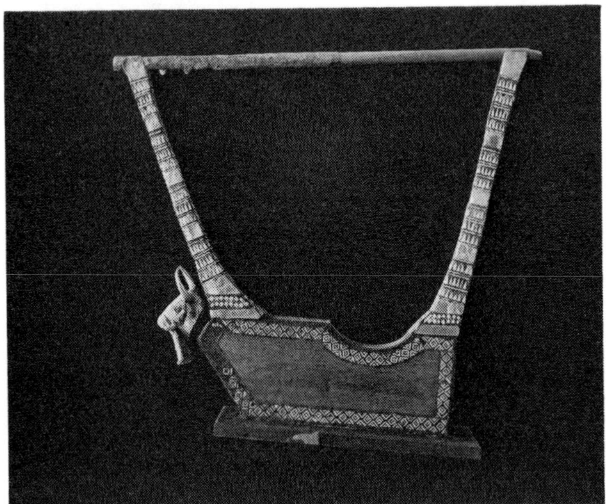

The Golden Harp from Ur, which dates back to about 3,000 B.C.

We know of the importance of music to the Pharaohs in Egypt. Musicians are pictured in royal tombs. Among the most famous of Egyptian singers was Amon who, in 1,000 B.C., accompanied himself on a ten-string harp.

Besides singing for entertainment or when chanting their poetry, the people of these early civilizations believed music had magical powers. They used it in their temples or in warlike ceremonies. They even thought they could influence nature with music. There is a Chinese legend that tells of a musician who played the "scale" of winter on a hot summer day. Immediately, an icy wind blew and lakes froze!

VOCABULARY

antiphonal	monophonic	scale
modes	responsorial	

Another type of ancient music dates back to the songs and psalms of the Hebrews. King David, who lived a thousand years before Jesus, was a composer and performer. His songs and harp playing are mentioned in the Old Testament. The Hebrews used professionally trained musicians—soloists and choirs—for performances in their temple services. In responsorial music, the soloist was answered by the choir. In antiphonal music, the choir was divided into two groups that sang alternately back and forth.

Ancient Greek Pottery, dating from around 500 B.C., showing figures dancing.

Music was highly important in ancient Greece. Greek pottery, carvings, and writings provide proof of the prevalence of music in this society. Drawings on pottery often show people playing musical instruments. The Greeks believed that good music helped to build character, and they therefore required all young people to study it. The Greeks invented musical "scales" or "modes," and they named the pitches of the scale by the first seven letters of the alphabet—A, B, C, D, E, F, and G. Only fragments of their songs remain, but they indicated that these were simple, one-voiced (monophonic) melodies. Much of our present musical system can be traced directly back to the ancient Greeks.

The Middle Ages

Music during the Middle Ages was closely associated with monasteries and churches. When the Christian Church was becoming established, the members always sang religious songs in their services. The texts of these songs were taken mostly from the Book of Psalms in the Old Testament and were chanted (almost recited) in Latin and were sung in unison without instruments. The chants were sung to smooth flowing melodies that centered on a few tones and followed the rhythm of the text. The melodies of these chants probably came originally from Hebrew and Greek music. Later, these melodies sometimes became melismatic—quite elaborate with many notes sung to one syllable of text.

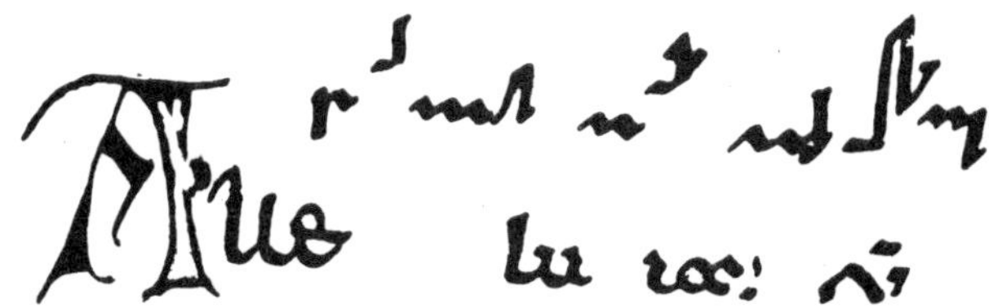

Alleluia, Plate VI, Monte Cassino, 11th Century

By the 6th Century, so many chants had been invented for the church services that attempts were made by several popes to collect these melodies. The organization of these chants was finally completed during the reign of Pope Gregory the Great (540-604) and was given his name. Gregorian chant, also called "plainsong," is still a form of music used in some church services.

In the early days, chants had to be learned by memory (rote) because they were not written down. This took a long time. It also became increasingly difficult as the numbers of chants increased, and it was hard to remember all of them. Because of this, the church musicians sought a way to write the chants down. Between the sixth and eighth centuries, a method of notation was invented that placed marks called "neumes" over the words to show the direction of the melodic line. "Neume" means "sign" in Greek. These signs were hooks and wiggles that were placed above the syllables of a text to remind singers of the direction of the melody in chants they already knew. These marks weren't definite enough for singers to use to learn to sing a new chant.

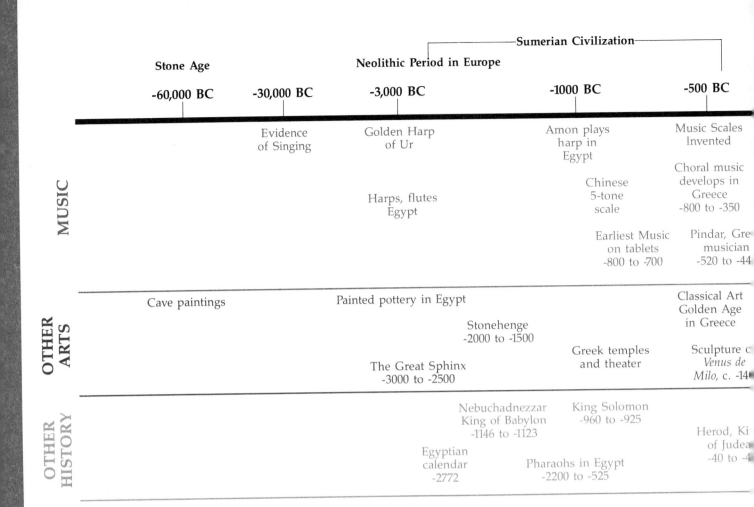

	Stone Age		Neolithic Period in Europe / Sumerian Civilization		
	-60,000 BC	-30,000 BC	-3,000 BC	-1000 BC	-500 BC
MUSIC		Evidence of Singing	Golden Harp of Ur Harps, flutes Egypt	Amon plays harp in Egypt Chinese 5-tone scale Earliest Music on tablets -800 to -700	Music Scales Invented Choral music develops in Greece -800 to -350 Pindar, Gre musician -520 to -44
OTHER ARTS	Cave paintings		Painted pottery in Egypt Stonehenge -2000 to -1500 The Great Sphinx -3000 to -2500	Greek temples and theater	Classical Art Golden Age in Greece Sculpture c *Venus de Milo*, c. -14
OTHER HISTORY			Nebuchadnezzar King of Babylon -1146 to -1123 Egyptian calendar -2772	King Solomon -960 to -925 Pharaohs in Egypt -2200 to -525	Herod, Ki of Judea -40 to -4

Alleluia from the *Liber Usualis*

A horizontal line was then added to give a reference point for the moving melodies. By the end of the 12th Century, three more lines had been added. Sometimes these were in different colors. For example, F was red, and middle C was yellow. Square notes were substituted for neumes, and clefs were written on any line. The reason the notes were square was that the quill pens used for hand writing had square tips. These made either square shapes or straight lines. Eventually, musicians settled on the five lines that we have on our staff today.

Easter Alleluia chant in modern notation

GUIDO D'AREZZO

Once music was written down, people had to learn how to read it. The first system designed for this purpose was invented by Guido d'Arezzo (c.995-1050) or Guido of Arezzo, a town in Italy. Guido was a Benedictine monk and choirmaster who was a music theorist. His contributions were many, but he is remembered today primarily for the system he invented for sight singing. His idea was to give names to the different pitches of the scale. He took his syllable names from an eighth-century hymn to St. John. In this hymn the beginning notes of each phrase move up the first six notes of the C-major scale. The Latin syllable that was sung with the note became the name of that note. This is how Guido invented what is now called "solmization" or "solfeggio," the do, re, mi's that we know today. SI (later TI) was added a century later to complete the scale. By using his system, Guido claimed that a singer could learn in five months what had taken ten years before! For this reason, he can truly be called the "Father of Music Theory."

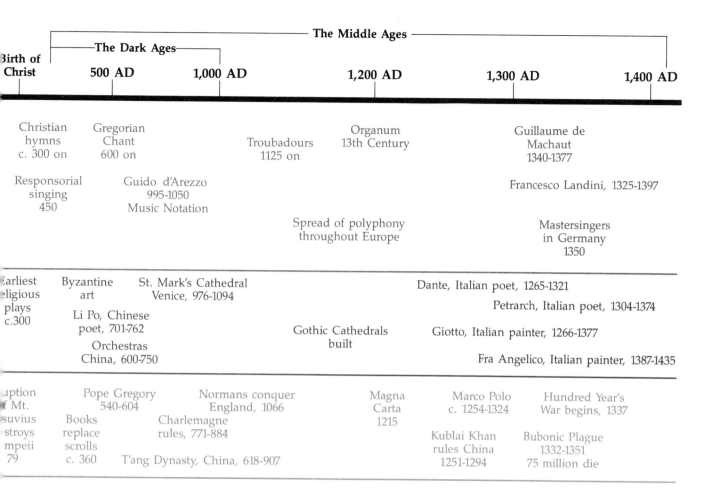

The Middle Ages

The Dark Ages

Birth of Christ — 500 AD — 1,000 AD — 1,200 AD — 1,300 AD — 1,400 AD

Christian hymns c. 300 on

Gregorian Chant 600 on

Troubadours 1125 on

Organum 13th Century

Guillaume de Machaut 1340-1377

Responsorial singing 450

Guido d'Arezzo 995-1050 Music Notation

Francesco Landini, 1325-1397

Spread of polyphony throughout Europe

Mastersingers in Germany 1350

Earliest religious plays c.300

Byzantine art

St. Mark's Cathedral Venice, 976-1094

Dante, Italian poet, 1265-1321

Petrarch, Italian poet, 1304-1374

Li Po, Chinese poet, 701-762

Gothic Cathedrals built

Giotto, Italian painter, 1266-1377

Orchestras China, 600-750

Fra Angelico, Italian painter, 1387-1435

Eruption of Mt. Vesuvius destroys Pompeii 79

Pope Gregory 540-604

Normans conquer England, 1066

Magna Carta 1215

Marco Polo c. 1254-1324

Hundred Year's War begins, 1337

Books replace scrolls c. 360

Charlemagne rules, 771-884

Kublai Khan rules China 1251-1294

Bubonic Plague 1332-1351 75 million die

T'ang Dynasty, China, 618-907

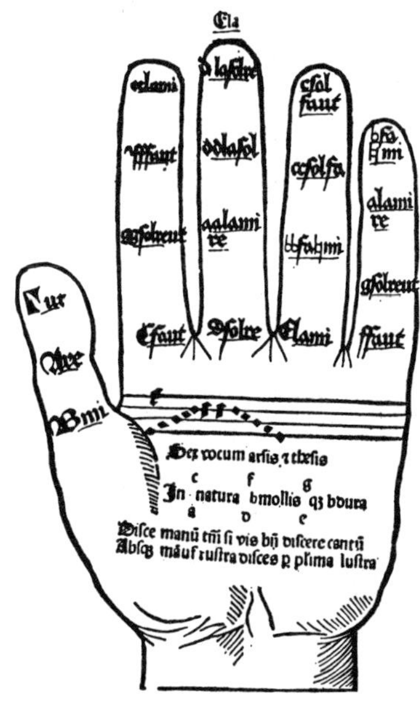

In the eleventh century, Guido invented this hand to help his pupils remember the syllables and how they could be shifted from one key to another.

Important political figures then, as now, could have great influence on musical developments if they showed an interest in them. One such leader in the early history of music was Charlemagne who was the Emperor of what was called the Holy Roman Empire. Beginning with his reign in 800, many singers were trained and music schools were established.

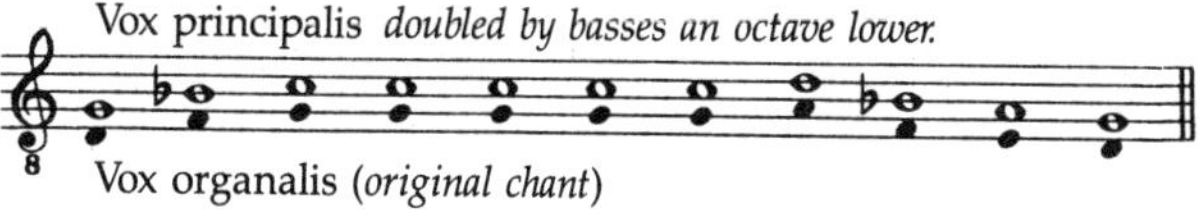

An example of parallel organum

Throughout these early years, singing was all done in unison (monophonic). Then, in the 9th Century, singers started to sing parts of the chants in parallel parts spaced a fourth or fifth apart. This "organum" was the first attempt at singing in harmony. Later, the voices began to move more freely, first using fourths, fifths, and octaves, then with one part singing a melismatic or highly florid melody against a second part singing the slow moving chant. By the 13th Century, musicians discovered that voices could imitate each other, and rounds came into being. There were many rules to be followed as harmony and counterpoint (the combination of two of more

America as it would sound in parallel organum

A
294

independently moving melodies) developed, but such beginnings as these prepared the way for our choral singing today.

Another development during the Middle Ages was the use of instruments with voices. In churches, the organ was used. Outside, string and wind instruments were used with voices in processions and ceremonies. At first these instruments played only the melodies that the voices were singing. They did not play independent parts.

In addition to singing Latin sacred music, people sang secular (non-religious) music in their own (vernacular) language. Some performers of these songs were known as minstrels and troubadours. They traveled to towns and castles entertaining people with their songs and dances. They sang about beauty and love and historical events. They also told folk stories and conveyed the local news in song in much the same way as some of our popular touring singers do now. But instead of today's guitar, they accompanied themselves on the lute.

Toward the end of the Middle Ages, a new way of life was developing known as the feudal society. Much time was spent by lords of large tracts of land in defending their property and the vassals and serfs who worked the land. Heroic knights on horseback fought in wars and in competitions. The troubadours wrote many songs about life during these colorful and distressing times, and they gave special honor to the women of the society. Music was a counterpart to life in all its aspects much as it is today.

FRANCESCO LANDINI

The most famous musician of the late Middle Ages was Francesco Landini (1325-1397) of Italy whose father was a painter. Landini was blinded as a young child, but he overcame this handicap to become a greatly admired composer and organist. He turned early to music, taking lessons on lute, guitar, flute, and organ and becoming expert at playing all of them. He wrote poems and set them to music in the form of madrigals and other nonsacred songs. He also wrote church music and for many years served as organist at the Church of Lorenzo in Florence. Some 150 of his works still exist, and they amount to more than one-third of the existing Italian music of the 14th century.

VOCABULARY

clef	monophonic	secular
counterpoint	neumes	solfeggio
Gregorian chant	organum	solmization
harmony	plainsong	staff
interval	round	unison
	sacred	

◀ Egyptian Music Making

Chapter 9

The Age of the Renaissance c. 1400-1600

During the Renaissance in Europe, Columbus landed his ships in the New World.

When Christopher Columbus reached the shores of America in 1492 and Vasco Da Gamma completed his voyage to India in 1497, the Renaissance in Europe was well underway. This was a time when many artists, inventors, and composers came forth with a fresh, new creative spirit. Because of this, the Age of the Renaissance became a time of renewal and human achievement.

Arts and Invention

Michelangelo was an outstanding painter, sculptor, and architect of the period. If you go to Italy today, you will see many statues and paintings created by this genius. Among his works that people most want to see are the statue of David in Florence and the ceiling of the Sistine Chapel in Rome. He created the dome of St. Peter's church by imbedding chains in the mortar—the first reinforced concrete.

During the Renaissance, architects designed spacious public buildings and churches that glittered with golden mosaics. Composers began to write vocal music to fill these vast spaces. In the great Cathedral of St. Mark's in Venice, Giovanni Gabrieli divided his singers and placed choirs in opposite locations so that they could sing back and forth in alternation or imitation (antiphonal). The music he composed was polychoral. It required two or more choirs performing together. In addition, each of the choirs might be accompanied by an organ and other instruments, making a highly dramatic effect. This music might be thought of as the beginning of "stereo" sound. Gabrieli's music is still a favorite with modern choirs and, when it is performed today, the musicians try to imitate the way it must have echoed in the Renaissance by separating the different choirs and instrumentalists.

Italian painter Raphael (1483-1520) depicts the "Marriage ▶ of the Virgin," using the rules of perspective and symmetrical balance. The rejected suitor symbolically breaks the staff at lower right.

·RAPHAEL·VRBINAS·
M DIIII

	1400	1450	1500
MUSIC	Guillaume Dufay, Dutch composer, 1400-1478	Josquin des Prez, Dutch composer, 1450-1521	
		Johannes Okegham, Dutch composer, 1430-1494	
		The Netherlands becomes center of music	
		Dufay develops tonic-dominant cadence which will affect harmony for hundreds of years	Ottavio de Petrucci of Venice prints first music with moveable type 1500
OTHER ARTS		Botticelli paints *Birth of Venus* 1480	Raphael paint *Marriage of the Virgin* 1504
		Raphael, Italian painter, 1483-1520	
	Leonardo da Vinci, 1452-1519		Everyman Morality Play c. 150(
	Luca della Robbia, Italian sculptor, 1399-1482		DaVinci paints *Mona Lisa*, 1503
OTHER HISTORY	Joan of Arc burned at stake 1431	Florence Italy under rule of Medici becomes center of Renaissance, 1450	Columbus lands in New World 1492
			Balboa discovers Pacific Ocean 1500
		Guttenberg invented moveable type c. 1450	
		End of Hundred Years War, 1453	Vasco da Gamma completes voyage to India, 1497

Another great visual artist of the period was Leonardo da Vinci. His paintings of the *Last Supper* and *Mona Lisa* stand out in the history of art as masterworks. Leonardo was also a scientist who is best known for his studies in human anatomy (parts of the body). As a physicist, his experiments with what he called his "flying machine" are amazing when compared to the development of twentieth-century aviation. Michelangelo and Da Vinci were truly "renaissance" men; their interests and their greatness were in several fields, not just one.

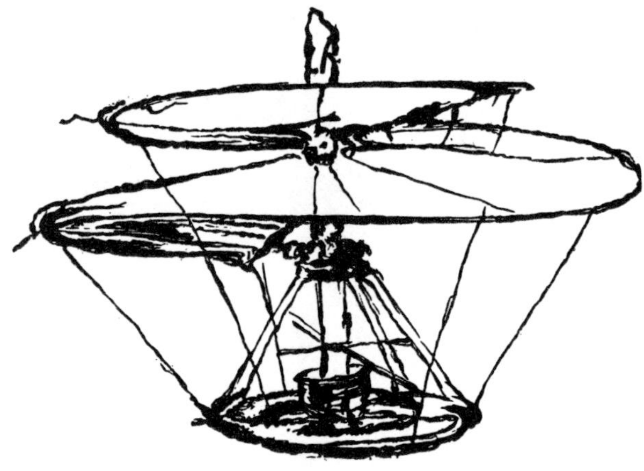

Leonardo's "flying machine"

In literature, the many plays of William Shakespeare (1564-1616)—*Hamlet*, *Romeo and Juliet*, *Macbeth*, and *A Midsummer Night's Dream*, to name a few—comprise the greatest collection of master works in the history of dramatic theater. Now, almost 400 years after they were written, Shakespeare's plays are still performed and enjoyed throughout the world. In fact, his plays, many of which contain references to music, continue to be a source of inspiration for artists today. (The Broadway musical *West Side Story* tells the story of *Romeo and Juliet* in today's terms.)

The Renaissance was a period of abundant creativity and invention. More music was being written and increasing numbers of people were becoming involved in performance. Still, each piece or part of music had to be copied by hand. What was needed was a quicker way to reproduce words and music. The method to reproduce words was invented by Johann Gutenberg in Germany in 1454. This was the printing press. The method to reproduce music followed. Ottaviano Petrucci, an Italian, printed the first collection of music in 1501. Printing provided a faster and cheaper way to make copies, permitting more and more people to enjoy singing in their churches and homes.

1550 | 1600

Giovanni da Palestrina, Italian composer, 1526-1594

Michael Praetorius, German composer, 1571-1621

William Byrd, English composer, 1543-1623

Orlando di Lasso, Dutch composer, 1532-1594

Hans Leo Hassler, German composer, 1564-1612

Orlando Gibbons, English composer, 1583-1625

Madrigals begin to be written in Italy c. 1533

Giovanni Gabrieli, Italian composer, c. 1554-1612
Polychoral Music

William Shakespeare, 1564-1616

Michelangelo Buonarotti, Italian painter, sculptor, 1475-1564

Martin Luther, 1483-1546

Michelangelo sculpts *Pieta*, 1555

Kabuki Theatre begins in Japan 1586

Tintoretto, Italian painter, 1518-1594

Shakespeare's *Romeo and Juliet* 1594

Magellan sails around world 1519-1522

Spain at peak of power c. 1550-1600

Elizabeth I reigned in England, 1558-1603

Galileo, inventor of telescope, 1564-1642

Protestant Reformation begins, 1517

First Christmas tree 1539

Sir Frances Drake voyage around the world, 1577

Sir Walter Raleigh discovers Virginia 1584

The Gutenberg press, about 1454

The interior of St. Mark's Cathedral in Venice. From these balconies, the music of composer Giovanni Gabrieli rang from multiple choirs, echoing in the huge space.

ORLANDO di LASSO

For more than a hundred years, composers from the Netherlands dominated musical Europe. Orlando di Lasso (1532-1594) was the last of these great composers. Born in what is now Belgium, di Lasso, or "Lassus," as he is sometimes called, began to sing in church choirs when he was very young. At the age of twelve, he went to Italy where he sang in and directed choirs for more than ten years. In 1555, he moved to Antwerp where his first collections of madrigals were published. The next year, he became composer to King Albert V of Bavaria. He then moved to Munich where he lived for the rest of his life.

Di Lasso wrote masses, sacred motets, and hundreds of shorter sacred works for voices. He also wrote many non-sacred works—French chansons, Italian madrigals, and German part songs that are lighthearted. In all, he composed more than 2,000 works, and he was highly regarded in his day.

Music in Daily Life

During the Renaissance, music was woven into the daily lives of the people—at weddings, funerals, festivals, and celebrations. Trumpeters welcomed important visitors and accompanied processions and hunting expeditions. Even the kings and queens became good singers and instrumentalists. Ordinary people began singing in their homes for entertainment in the way we watch television or listen to our stereos. Paintings from those times reveal how widespread the practice of music must have been.

Often a family or group of friends would gather around a table after dinner and sing. Many of the songs these people enjoyed were called madrigals. These were usually non-religious (secular) songs for a small number of singers. Until printed books became more available, they used one large book. One part was printed on each of four sides so that the singers could sit facing their side of the page.

The rhythms of some madrigals were based on the lively dance tunes of the time. The voice parts came together on refrains using syllables such as "fa la la" at the end of each verse. Prior to this time, music had been thought of as primarily horizontal; that is, as a melodic line or lines. Now the sounding together of these horizontal lines of independent melodies (polyphonic music) began to create an interest

During this period, people began to get together in small groups at home to sing madrigals. This painting by Italian painter Lorenzo Costa (c. 1459-1535) depicts "A Concert." Look for it in the National Gallery in London.

in the combined or vertical sounds that resulted. This new musical delight paved the way for the development of chordal harmony, the combining of vertical sounds to support one melody (homophonic music).

Music in England

Many of the most popular madrigals are associated with the country of England. Queen Elizabeth I was especially interested in music. She performed and danced and offered encouragement to composers. In fact, Queen Elizabeth I was such a vibrant leader in both cultural matters and politics that her reign during the second half of the 16th century has been given her name—the "Elizabethan Age."

Queen Elizabeth had her own Royal Chapel with professional musicians. One organist and composer there was Thomas Tallis. He wrote many church motets which are vocal settings of religious texts without accompaniment. Motets could be written for many voice parts and more than one choir. Tallis wrote a motet for eight choirs that has a total of 40 voice parts!

Two other leading English composers were church organists in the large cathedrals in London. Thomas Morley (1557-1602) and Orlando Gibbons (1583-1625) composed much church music as well as many madrigals.

WILLIAM BYRD

In 1588, William Byrd (1543 - 1623) published his book of *Psalms, Sonnets, and Songs of Sadness and Pietie*. In a foreword to the last of these, he says "Since singing is so good a thing, I wish all men would learne to sing." Byrd, who lived at the same time as the poet and dramatist William Shakespeare, was the greatest English composer of the Elizabethan period. He excelled at composing church music: masses, motets, anthems, and other sacred works. He was also a masterful composer of madrigals, solo song, chamber music, and music for keyboard instruments—the organ and the virginal, the latter a forerunner of the piano.

Byrd may have acquired his great skill as an organist and composer by studying with Thomas Tallis, another great composer of the period. He was appointed organist of London's Lincoln Cathedral in 1563, and in 1572 he assumed the post of organist of the Chapel Royal, a position he shared with Tallis. In 1575, Queen Elizabeth granted Byrd and Tallis a patent for the exclusive right to print music and sell music paper for 21 years. The business failed, but the two continued to be favored by the Queen.

Byrd led a very colorful life. He was often involved in disputes and lawsuits. He dared to be a devout Catholic at a time when Catholics were being seized and jailed. Only the high respect he commanded as a composer prevented him from being persecuted. Byrd wove vocal lines with great skill, and his religious music still conveys his strong spiritual belief.

The Reformation

The Protestant Reformation which was begun in Germany by Martin Luther in 1517 was one of the most significant events of the Renaissance. It brought important developments in religion and politics, and, at the same time, changed the course of music. Because of it, vocal music was expanded and altered for all time.

Luther loved music and believed it was a "Gift from God." He also believed that the Latin language should no longer be the only language used for worship as it had been since the Middle Ages. Luther translated the Bible into German so that the people could read it for themselves. He composed hymns in the German (vernacular) language so that the congregation could sing these as an important part of religious services and ceremonies. One of his best known hymns is "Ein feste Burg"—"A Mighty Fortress." The four-part harmonic settings of these hymns are called "chorales," a form that many later composers used. Chorales are sung today in the churches of many denominations and are included in concert programs of choral groups.

Other Leading Composers

One of the greatest composers of the Renaissance was Josquin des Pres. Like many other composers of this period and later times, he began his musical training as a church choirboy. During his long life Josquin composed many vocal works. He promoted the use of imitation, a type of repetition in which a musical motive or phrase introduced in one part is repeated in another part exactly or with some alteration. Through his effective use of this device, imitation became a basic technique in composing music, and composers who came after Josquin continued its use.

JOSQUIN DES PRES

Josquin des Pres (born about 1440, died 1521) was the greatest master of the contrapuntal style of writing that flourished in the Netherlands during the fifteenth and sixteenth centuries. He was a master at weaving together two or more melodies to create expressive and beautiful vocal music. The voices often imitate each other, the same melody being sung by various voices in turn, often overlapping. This kind of writing required great technical ingenuity. Josquin's music was sung everywhere at that time, and he was widely admired.

Josquin wrote 30 masses and many shorter religious works. He also wrote hundreds of chansons—delightful songs with simple melodies and suggestions of dance rhythms. Sometimes these move along in chords, more like music of a later time. Because of these chordal sections, Josquin is sometimes called the "father of modern harmony."

Born in the province of Hainault, in what is now Belgium, he was a boy chorister in the Collegiate Church at St. Quentin. He later became choirmaster there. In his twenties, he studied music in Italy. For eight years (1486-1494), he sang in the Papal choir in Rome. (During this same period, Columbus landed in America.) Later, he returned to Burgundy where he was considered the greatest composer of his time. His good friend and musician, Martin Luther, who led the Protestant Reformation in Germany, said of him: "Josquin is the master of the notes; others are mastered by the notes."

GIOVANNI DA PALESTRINA

Palestrina is the name of a small town near Rome where Giovanni Pierluigi (born 1525, died in 1594) was born. This great composer of Roman Catholic church music has become known by the name of his home town. His musical training began at the age of seven when he became a choirboy in the local cathedral. When the bishop of Palestrina was made archbishop of the church of Saint Maria Maggiore in Rome, he took Palestrina with him and entered him in the choir school there. In 1539, at the age of about 14, his voice changed, and he returned home, But he was soon back in Rome studying music, and in 1544 was appointed to his first position as organist and choirmaster at the cathedral in Palestrina.

When the bishop of the cathedral became pope, he brought Palestrina to Rome as choirmaster of the Cappella Giulia in the Vatican. Palestrina held this honored post for the rest of his life.

Among his 619 vocal-works, Palestrina composed 93 masses, appoximately 200 motets, and more than 100 hymns and offertories. His complete works fill 34 volumes. He mastered the art of composing "a cappella" music—works for unaccompanied voices. His music is calm and peaceful. He wrote long and flowing melodies that gently rise and fall. He was a master of polyphony, combining two or more melodies, often with the voice imitating each other. For contrast, he sometimes interrupted the flow with chantlike blocks of chords. But mainly, his music is deeply religious which may explain why his works have continued to be sung for 400 years. When Palestrina died in 1594, it is said that all of Rome must have mourned for him since so many people attended his funeral.

During the Renaissance, composers made special efforts to bring out the meaning of the words. For example, the word "death" might have a downward melody, or "rise up" might have an upward motion. This is called "tone painting." A composer who often used this technique was Orlando Lassus (1532-1594). He was so highly regarded that many musicians of his day referred to him as the "Prince of Music."

Another of the great composers of the Renaissance, and one of the greatest choral composers of all time, was Giovanni Palestrina (c. 1525-1594). Palestrina spent most of his career in Rome as the major composer of St. Peter's Catholic Basilica in the Vatican where the pope lives. He was a master of polyphony—the art of combining two or more melodies and interweaving the various voice parts using imitation.

By the end of the Renaissance, the sounds and textures of choral music had become richer and more interesting than ever before. As civilization became more complex, so did music. The range and depth of musical expression had been greatly extended. More people could participate in singing because there were now music books in print. Composers created new types of songs using new combinations of melodies and rhythms. Harmony became more varied and choral pieces contained several voice parts. Congregations sang hymns and chorales in church during the worship services, and people sang secular songs at home.

The Renaissance years should be remembered as a time of the flowering of vocal music. Composers discovered the expressive possibilities of the human voice. This was a period when singing spread among the people, and composers of that time have left us with a glorious heritage of choral works and other art that we can continue to enjoy.

Block print depicting musicians of the Renaissance.

MICHAEL PRAETORIUS

Michael Praetorius (1571–1621) was a great German musician, composer, and music theorist. He studied organ in Frankfurt. When he was in his early thirties, he went into the service of the Duke of Braunschweig. In 1612, at the age of 41, he became organist and choirmaster in Wolfenbuttel where he remained until his death.

His vocal music is scored from one to 21 voice parts. The music is generally contrapuntal although the voices do not exactly echo each other. During the years 1605 through 1610, Praetorius compiled a collection of 1,244 vocal numbers in 9 parts. Many other works followed. He composed motets, psalms, hymns, madrigals, church songs, and songs of peace and rejoicing.

His writings about music are as important as his music. In 1618, he completed the second book in a three-volume series that describes in detail the musical instruments of this period. The organ was given extensive treatment, and many woodcuts picturing all the instruments were included. Today this remains the most important source of information about the instruments of that day.

VOCABULARY

a cappella	homophonic	motet
anthem	hymn	polychoral
antiphonal	imitation	polyphonic
chorale	madrigal	tone painting

Chapter 10

The Baroque Period c. 1600-1750

During the years when our own country was being founded, music in Europe continued to grow and to change. There, the vocal forms became more elaborate and expressive. Here, singing was simpler, but it was an important part of church services and, upon occasion, of home entertainment.

The American Colonies

Beginning in 1619, small groups of people made the arduous voyage across the Atlantic Ocean to settle in the new found land. These early colonists brought their music with them—hymns for their church services and songs and dances for entertainment. The first colonists to reach Massachusetts were Puritans from England. Religious music was so important to them that they printed their own hymn book in 1640, only ten years after they arrived. This *Bay Psalm Book*, as it was called, was the first book of any kind to be printed in the American colonies.

Because the melodies of the Puritan hymns were very familiar, only the words were contained in the earliest editions of the *Bay Psalm Book*. Later on, printed melodies were included that used four syllables for sight reading—fa, sol, la, and mi. The note for each of these syllables was given a different shape:

FA SOL LA MI

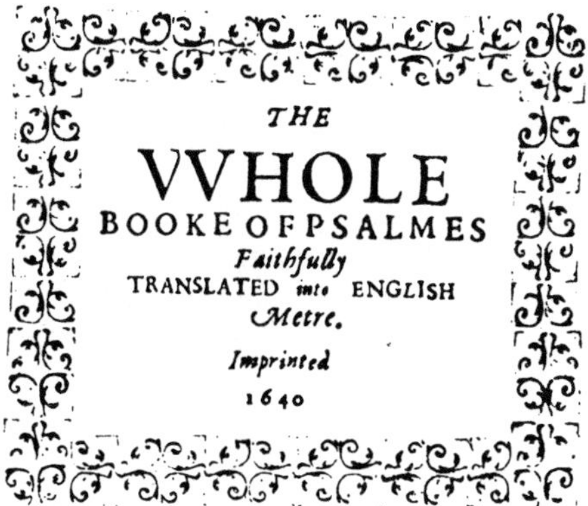

THE
VVHOLE
BOOKE OF PSALMES
Faithfully
TRANSLATED into ENGLISH
Metre.
Imprinted
1640

The Massachusetts *Bay Psalm Book*

◄The Italian sculptor Bernini (1598-1680) depicts the "Ecstasy of Saint Theresa" with exaggerated emotion. The figure emotes as if acting on a stage, and the elaborate, flowing robes look as if the body is in motion.

This "shape note" system helped people to read new hymns. Although the system is not in common use today, it is still used by some congregations in the rural south.

Europe

While the American colonies were being settled, the Baroque period in Europe was a time of expanding horizons. Great minds searched for new knowledge about all aspects of life. There were discoveries in science, the arts, and other fields.

In astronomy, Galileo Galilei (1564-1642) perfected the telescope and used it to prove that the earth revolves around the sun and is not the center of the universe as had been believed. Another interesting fact about Galileo is that his father was a well-known musician.

HANS LEO HASSLER

Like many other composers of the period, Hans Leo Hassler (1564-1612) received his early musical training as an organist and showed remarkable ability at a young age. He was among the first German composers to study in Italy. At the age of 20, he went to Venice to study with Andrea Gabrieli, the great composer of antiphonal music—music that echoed from two or more choirs. During his year in Venice, he became friendly with Giovanni Gabrieli, the composer's nephew, who also composed choral music in the Italian style. Hassler was greatly influenced by their music.

He returned to Germany, serving in a variety of musical posts as a chamber musician, as leader of a town band, and as an organist. At the same time, he engaged in the business of manufacturing and installing musical clocks. He is remembered today for applying his knowledge of Italian musical techniques to create German songs and other music with a strong national feeling.

	1600		1650	
MUSIC	Claudio Monteverdi, Italian composer, c. 1567-1643 Heinrich Schutz, German composer, 1585-1672	*Bay Psalm Book* First book published in the New World 1640	Anton Stradivarius, stringed instrument maker, 1644-1737	Alessandro Scarlatti Italian composer 1659-1725 Henry Purcell, English composer, 1659-1695
OTHER ARTS	Rembrandt van Rijn, Dutch painter, 1606-1669 Anthony Van Dyck, Dutch painter, 1599-1641 Peter Paul Rubens, Dutch painter, 1599-1645	King James version of The *Bible*	Bernini sculpts *Ecstasy of St. Teresa* 1644	The young King Louis XIV of France appears in a court ballet, 1651
OTHER HISTORY	Jamestown, Va. founded, 1607 Pilgrims land at Plymouth Rock, 1620	Peter Minuit buys Manhattan Island from Indians, 1626	Harvard College founded, 1636	Louis XIV marries Maria Teresa, 1660

A Baroque church organ

Later in the period, Isaac Newton (1642-1727) studied the motion of objects and formulated the "law of gravity." The success of these and other scientists influenced musicians to apply scientific methods to music. As a result, "theoretical treatises" explained how music is constructed and how to build instruments so pitches would be more in tune.

In the visual arts, painters produced large-scale works that expressed intense feelings. The Spanish painter El Greco used dramatic color and lighting, and the Dutch painter Rembrandt used dark hues in his portraits to probe the personality of his subjects. In architecture, massive buildings of an irregular plan with curved surfaces and richly decorated columns took the place of the balanced plan and straight lines of buildings in the Renaissance.

Much of the style of life during this period was set by the royalty. They controlled law and authority—and the arts. The center for much of the cultural life in Europe from 1643 to 1715 was the Palace at Versailles, near Paris, the home of Louis XIV, the "Sun King," who ruled France during those years. The French language became the one that diplomats and other political leaders used in their communications, and French composers developed a nationalistic spirit that gave their music a clear distinction.

1700

1750

First performance
Handel's *Messiah*
1741

Johann Sebastian Bach, German composer, 1685-1750

George Frideric Handel, German composer, 1685-1759

Domenico Scarlatti, Italian composer and harpsichordist, 1685-1767

Christofori invents piano
1709

Milton Writes
Paradise Lost,
1667

Christopher Wren
begins rebuilding
St. Paul's Cathedral
London, 1675

John Bunyan writes
Pilgrim's Progress, 1678

Development of
Kabuki Theatre
in Japan, 1700

Work begins
on Buckingham
Palace
1703

Daniel Defoe writes
Robinson Caruso
1719

Jonathan Swift writes
Gulliver's Travels
1726

Louis XIV reigns King of France, 1643-1715

Isaac Newton's Theory of Gravity, 1687

Salem witchcraft trials, 1692

Philadelphia founded by William Penn, 1682

New Amsterdam becomes New York, 1664

One of the elaborate court entertainments of Louis XIV, King of France. Here he is pictured in the center, back to us, viewing a ballet accompanied by orchestra.

The Opera

Another very important center for the development of Baroque music was Northern Italy, especially the art-loving city of Florence. Here, there were poets, composers, and musical performers who formed a group called the "Camerata." These men shared ideas about musical composition, drama, and literature. They decided to place more emphasis on the words and the dramatic ideas behind the music than had been done in the Renaissance. This led to the creation of dramatic musical plays with soloists, chorus, and orchestra—the beginning of opera.

In these early operas, singers used their voices in two ways to get the story over to the audience. In the first, called "recitative," they recited words that told the action of the story on a few pitches using very simple accompaniment. In the second, called "aria," they sang a song of flowing melody and moving rhythms to convey the emotion of the story's events. As opera grew, a new style of singing also developed, called "bel canto" meaning "beautiful song." In this style, the sound of the voice itself and the singer's vocal technique became more important than the story or the dramatic meaning of the music. Because of such vocal skill, opera singers were the "box office" stars of their day.

The first great opera composer was the Italian, Claudio Monteverdi (1567-1643), now called the "Father of Opera." His first opera was *Orfeo*, the Greek story of Orpheus, a musician who went down to the underworld to bring his wife back from the dead. The vocal writing portrays joy, grief, terror, and triumph, according to the story. When *Orfeo* was first performed in 1607, the people loved it so much that they rose to their feet and cheered.

Monteverdi's operas were performed in Venice which was the first city to open a public opera house. The year was 1634. So many people attended these operas that 16 new theaters were opened by the end of the century, and more than 350 different operas

The Italian painter Pannini depicts an opera being performed in one of the new opera houses in Rome.

were produced. This tells us how much the people of Venice, a city of only 150,000 people, enjoyed the opera.

At the age of 14, a young composer named Jean Baptiste Lully (1632-1687) left Florence, Italy and went to France. Fortunately he became a friend of the 15-year-old "Sun King." Eventually he started composing operas for the court of Louis XIV, creating a new form of French opera. Lully was a fine violinist, dancer, and actor. Because of his many talents, he included ballet dancing and many dramatic effects in his operas. The King's favorite dance was the minuet, and Lully composed many of them for his operas. Lully is an example of a person who was born as a humble miller's son but rose to be a brilliant musician and composer. He was also a real-estate dealer!

The opera that began in Italy continued to spread and to flourish throughout Europe. It is one of the most important vocal developments of the Baroque period. Opera brings singing, instrumental music, dancing, and drama together to heighten the emotion of story-telling. Today, it remains a powerful form of musical expression in which singers display their vocal artistry and their dramatic skill.

Other Musical Developments

Two other vocal forms were invented during the Baroque period, and each one is associated with a master composer. In England, George Frideric Handel (1685-1759) invented the oratorio as a substitute for opera. Handel, who was born in Germany but became an English citizen, wrote more than 40 operas of the Italian style, but the form fell out of favor with audiences. The stories were based on old legends, had very little action, and were difficult to sing and to stage. In one opera, for example, Handel called for statues to rise out of a trap door surrounded by fire while cupids fly about in mid-air. Perhaps now, with the electronic advances of television and lasers, Handel's operas will be revived!

Handel took to writing oratorios which can be thought of as religious operas without any acting. They tell Biblical stories and can be performed in churches or concert halls. His best known oratorio is the *Messiah* which contains the famous *Hallelujah Chorus*. When this chorus is sung, the audience always stands up. This is a tradition that began when King George II first heard the work. He liked it so much that he stood up, and when the king stands, so does everyone else.

Handel traveled widely, but despite these journeys, he never met the other great composer of religious music, Johann Sebastian Bach (1685-1750), who hardly traveled at all. Bach was a master of counterpoint, but now he gave as much attention to the harmony (vertical) as to imitation and the combination of melodies (horizontal). He composed choral music of many types, organ and harpsichord pieces, orchestral works, and pieces for solo instruments.

Like other composers of this time, Bach was a performing musician, in this case, a virtuoso organist. As director of music for St. Thomas' Lutheran Church in Leipzig, Germany, he wrote over 300 cantatas for church services. The cantata is a vocal

JOHANN SEBASTIAN BACH

The greatest composer of the late Baroque period was Johann Sebastian Bach (1685-1750). He was born in Eisenach in the small state of Thuringia which is now part of the Republic of East Germany. In his early years, Bach studied stringed instruments with his father, a violinist. But before he was ten, both his parents died, and he was cared for by his eldest brother, Johann Christoph, an organist, with whom he studied keyboard instruments. At 15, he was hired as a boy soprano in a Lutheran Church where he sang the finest choral music and acquired a deep religious belief.

After his voice changed, Bach was kept on at the church as an instrumentalist. When he was 18, he became organist at the Lutheran Church of St. Boniface in Arnstadt. At 20, he was granted a leave of absence to travel 300 miles north to the city of Lubeck to hear the great organist Dietrich Buxtehude, then near 70. He traveled most of the way on foot, but the visit proved to be a turning point in his life. Bach's own grand style of organ improvisation, his great organ works, and his cantatas and oratorios for voices and instruments grew from the seeds planted in Lubeck.

Most of Bach's great organ music was written during the period from 1708 to 1717 when he was organist for the Duke of Saxony-Weimar. His next position was at the court of young Prince Leopold at Cothen where he served as conductor of an orchestra of 18 players. It was here that he wrote most of his instrumental music. In 1723 at the age of 38, he was appointed choirmaster of the St. Thomas Church in Leipzig. During the more than 25 years he served at St. Thomas, Bach wrote more than 300 cantatas and many other works that are deeply expressive. His fugues are among the most skillful musical compositions ever created.

GEORGE FRIDERIC HANDEL

Born in Halle in central Germany in the same year as Bach, George Frideric Handel (1685-1759) received his early training in music as an organist. From the age of 7 to 10, he studied organ, harpsichord, oboe, violin, and musical composition. By the age of 11, he was already composing sonatas and church music. At 17, he was appointed organist of one of Halle's Calvinist churches. But unlike Bach, he did not choose to follow the old German musical traditions. Instead, he went to Hamburg as violinist in the opera orchestra. There and during three years that he lived in Florence, Rome, Venice, and Naples, he became familiar with the more melodious world of Italian opera.

Handel was soon writing Italian operas as well or better than the Italians. In 1710, he made his first trip to England for the performance of his opera *Rinaldo* in the Italian style. He fell in love with London and spent most of the rest of his life there. The craze in London for Italian opera was at a peak, and Handel took advantage of it. He made his living much as a Broadway composer does today. If his new opera was a hit, it played a long time. If it was a failure, he had to try again with a new work.

Handel's operas, which have little plot or action, are seldom staged today. These works were designed primarily to show off the voices. When the public grew tired of this style of opera, Handel turned his ability to writing oratorios. These lengthy works had many of the features of Italian opera, but they told the familiar and heartfelt stories of the Bible with soloists, chorus, and orchestra. In 1739, Handel produced *Saul* and later *Israel in Egypt*. Then, in just 21 days in 1741, he composed *Messiah*, perhaps his greatest vocal work. He wrote many other vocal works as well as harpsichord suites, organ concertos, and orchestral works such as his *Water Music* and *Fireworks Music*.

composition in several sections which is written for chorus, soloists, and instrumental accompaniment. Bach's cantatas usually end with a chorale. His melodies were very expressive of the words and the vocal parts were interwoven, like the colors in a great tapestry. Some of Bach's longer cantatas were written for special occasions. These are often performed in churches and concert halls today.

Bach wrote longer works for voices as well. His *B Minor Mass* and the *St. John* and *St. Matthew "Passions"* are works of a deeply religious nature that are widely performed today. Bach was, indeed, a giant in the history of music. Despite his greatness, most of his pieces were not published until 100 years after he died. Since that time, his genius has been widely recognized, and his compositions are now heard in every part of the world. It is easy to associate this period of music with Johann Sebastian Bach because historians have come to mark the end of the Baroque period with his death in 1750.

The music of the Baroque is full of energy, and basic emotions are expressed with exaggeration and drama. There is majesty, ceremony, and religious fervor. Because the music speaks so directly, it is not difficult for us to feel, to understand, and to enjoy this music today.

◀ Interior of a Baroque church, showing the heavy use of ornamentation.

VOCABULARY

aria	hymn	oratorio
bel canto	improvisation	passion
camerata	mass	recitative
cantata	opera	virtuoso

Chapter 11

The Classical Period c. 1750-1825

Much of the concert music that we hear today was written by three master composers who lived during the Classical period— Haydn, Mozart, and Beethoven. This was the Age of Reason, and composers, like their counterparts in other fields, sought to give clarity, balance, and order to their creations. They expressed emotion, but not as boldly as in the Baroque. There was a lightness, an elegance, and a simplicity to their music. Their art was more personal.

This early plan for the United States Capitol Building by the architect William Thornton, rendered in 1793, shows the classical symmetry of the design.

Political and Social Life

During this period, people became interested in their individual rights as citizens. They began to resist the political power and authority of their kings and queens (monarchs). One of the persons who wrote about this new way of thinking was Jean Jacques Rousseau (1712-1778), a French philosopher, who said "Man is born free but everywhere is in chains." Because of such ideas, people began to feel that they could rule themselves and help their friends and neighbors improve their social conditions.

Two major events that resulted from this call for freedom were the American and the French revolutions. In 1776, America declared independence from England and proclaimed that all people are free in the eyes of their Creator. In 1787, the French people also revolted against their ruler.

Along with their desire for political freedom, people became more interested in education. They wanted to be able to enjoy the cultural dimensions of life such as art and music which had been the province only of the rich. Publishing houses grew in number, and they printed many more books for learning and for use in schools. Musical scores were also printed and became available to more people. As audiences grew, new concert halls and opera houses were built. All classes of people were now able to learn to sing, to play instruments, and to enjoy listening to music.

Until this time in music history, the popes and other church leaders had provided for the development of choral singing. Now they had less authority over composers. Consequently, religious vocal music did not change very much during the Classical period.

During the Baroque period, instrumental music had achieved an independence, a variety, and an expressive power that had not been known. Now independent instrumental music and non-religious (secular) vocal music began to flourish, building on these past developments. Audiences heard new and larger instrumental works—symphonies, sonatas, suites, and chamber music for many combinations of instruments. People also wanted new music to sing and to play in their homes. Dancing became more popular, and composers were ready to meet these needs with a variety of new musical forms.

Arts and Invention

Beginning in the 18th century, architects, sculptors, and painters were able to see the Greek and Roman art works that were being dug up (excavated) in Athens, Pompeii, and other ancient sites. They saw the simplicity and proportion in these works as an ideal of beauty that they then tried to copy in their own creations. We can see buildings in the classical style here in the United States. Monticello, Thomas Jefferson's home, is a good example. Jefferson (1743-1826) was an architect as well as the author of the Declaration of Independence and the third President of our country.

Because the artists of this period were inspired by the logic and the symmetry of the classic art of the "Golden Age" in ancient Greece, the name "Classical" has been given to this period as well. The

Thomas Jefferson, third President of the United States, designed Monticello, his home, giving attention to a classical sense of balance and proportion.

ancient classical ideal of beauty replaced the heavy, overly decorated, unbalanced, exaggerated expressions of the Baroque. The period was called "Classical" (capital "C") because of a type of style and manner of thought that characterized the life at that time. The term "classical" (small "c") is also used to distinguish the whole field of concert music from the field of popular music.

Other creative people, besides artists, brought progress to society. In this country, Isaac Watts invented the steam engine in 1765, Eli Whitney invented the cotton gin in 1793, and Robert Fulton invented the steamboat in 1808.

During this period, Robert Fulton (1765-1815), an American inventor and engineer, designed the first commercially successful steamboat.

WOLFGANG AMADEUS MOZART

Despite a life of poverty which spanned the short period of only 35 years, Wolfgang Amadeus Mozart (1756 - 1791) must be recognized as one of the greatest geniuses of all time. In that brief time, starting at a very early age, he composed a continuous flood of great works for voice, piano, orchestra, and chamber groups. From his pen flowed 15 masses and other church music, many songs and arias, 5 violin concertos, 21 piano concertos, 4 horn concertos as well as concertos for other instruments, 26 string quartets and many works for combinations of other instruments, 17 sonatas for piano and many other works for this instrument, 17 sonatas for organ, more than 20 works for the stage, 49 symphonies, and many other works for orchestra.

By the age of six, Mozart was a skilled performer on harpsichord, violin, and organ, having taught himself the latter two instruments. Between the ages of six and nine, he toured to Vienna, Paris, London, and other cities where he performed before royalty, astonishing them with his ability to improvise. He had an amazing ability to sight read. He wrote his first sonatas and symphonies at the age of eight and his first opera at 12. In Rome at the age of 14, after hearing a chorus sing a nine-part *Miserere*, he wrote out the entire score from memory without a mistake. Later the same year, he conducted 20 performances of his latest three-act opera in Milan.

With such musical talent, it is surprising, perhaps, that he did not succeed financially. In later years, his genius was not always recognized or appreciated by the nobility who could afford to hire his services and commission him to compose. Yet his operas such as *Don Giovanni* and *The Magic Flute*, reveal his masterful ability to write expressively for voices and to portray clear character through melody. It is the power and the beauty of his music that continue to draw listeners and performers to his works.

Mozart's last work, his *Requiem Mass*, was one of his greatest choral compositions. A requiem is a mass to be sung at funerals or to commemorate a death. It was still unfinished when he died. He was so poor that he was buried in an unmarked pauper's grave. To this day, the location of his grave remains unknown, a sad fact in light of the musical joy and wonder he left to the world.

1750	1760	1770	1780

MUSIC

Franz Joseph Haydn, German composer, 1732-1809

Wolfgang Amadeus Mozart, Austrian composer, 1756-1791

William Billings, American Music Educator, 1746-1800

First public performance on piano by C.P.E. Bach, 1768

Composer sons of Bach:
Wilhelm Friedemann, 1710-1784
Carl Philipp Emanuel, 1741-1788
Johann Christian, 1735-1782

Opera becomes very popular

Development of the symphony

Development of the sonata form

OTHER ARTS

Francisco Goya, Spanish painter, 1746-1828

First Edition of *Encyclopedia Britannica,* 1771

Thomas Chippendale, furniture maker, 1718-1779

Thomas Gainsborough (1727-1788) *The Blue Boy,* 1770

Immanuel Kant, philosopher, 1724-1804

Joshua Reynolds, English Painter, 1723-1792

William Blake, English artist/poet, 1757-1827

Sir Walter Scott, Scottish novelist, 1771-1832

OTHER HISTORY

Benjamin Franklin invents lightning rod 1752

American Revolution, 1775-1783

Isaac Watts invents steam engine, 1769

Declaration of Independence, 1776

French Revolution, 17

Haydn

While the movement to gain greater freedom was spreading through European society, composers still needed the help of royalty and other wealthy people to employ them and serve as their patrons. Many of the sovereigns who governed in those days were surrounded by courts—family, councilors, ministers, and attendants who worked for them. The sovereigns also sponsored and supported musicians so that their guests could enjoy dancing and listening to music in the evenings. Franz Joseph Haydn (1732-1809), one of the foremost composers of the period, was supported by a patron during most of his composing life.

Haydn was born in a small town in Austria to a poor family of 12 children. His father repaired wheels (a "wheelwright"), and his mother was a cook. He showed musical talent at a young age, and his cousin helped him with his training. At eight years of age, he began singing in a church choir in Vienna, and as a young man, he studied composing by reading books, one of which was written by Carl Philipp Emanuel Bach, a son of the great Bach. In addition to singing, he learned to play the violin and harpsichord.

Haydn felt fortunate when he was appointed to a position in the Court of Prince Esterhazy, an estate outside of Vienna. He worked there for the next 30 years, composing and performing. Each week Haydn presented two operas and two concerts, and each day he provided chamber music for the prince. He wrote most of the music himself.

Haydn did not invent the symphony, the sonata, or the string quartet, but his genius for musical construction brought such perfection to these forms that he is often called "the father of the symphony." In writing symphonies, Haydn divided the orchestra into the four sections that we still use today—strings, woodwinds, brass, and percussion. Haydn must have composed music all day long, because he turned out more pieces than any other composer of the Classical period. Music historians say that he wrote 104 symphonies, 82 string quartets, 30 concertos, 50 piano sonatas, 14 masses, 3 oratorios, and many other smaller works for instruments and for voices.

In vocal music, Haydn's best known oratorio is called *The Creation*, a work with a text based on the book of *Genesis* in the Bible. His oratorio *The Seasons* is based on a poem about nature. These works were composed later in his life, and parts or all of them are still performed by choral groups today.

1790	1800	1810	1820	1825

Ludwig Van Beethoven, German composer, 1770-1827

Lieder (songs) become popular

Franz Schubert, German composer, 1797-1828

Invention of the metronome 1815

Thomas Paine writes *The Rights of Man*,1791

George Byron, English poet, 1788-1824

Percy Bysshe Shelley, English poet, 1792-1822

Building of U.S. Capitol begins, 1793

Elgin Marbles to British Museum 1816

Buckingham Palace completed, 1825

First vaccination, 1796

Napoleon crowned Emperor, 1804

Napoleon abdicates, 1813

Eli Whitney invents the cotton gin 1793

Streets lit by gas in London, 1807

Monroe Doctrine 1823

George Washington, (1755-1828), first president of the United States

Braille invents reading system for blind, 1809

Napoleon crowns Josephine, his wife, Empress.

LUDWIG VAN BEETHOVEN

Although he was primarily a composer of instrumental music, Ludwig Van Beethoven (1770 - 1827) wrote a number of cantatas and other works for chorus, works for solo voice and orchestra, many songs, the great *Missa Solemnis*, the opera *Fidelio*, and his *Ninth Symphony* with its choral setting of Schiller's "Ode to Joy" in the final movement. The drama and emotion of Beethoven's music set the tone for the Romantic period of the 19th century. During his lifetime, the American and French revolutions had declared the importance of every man, not just the nobility. In place of the aristocratic elegance and grace that had been expressed by Haydn and other composers who preceded him, there were stormy passion, warm tenderness, and serious expressions about life.

Beethoven was strong-willed and had great fortitude, character traits that show in his music. His life from an early age was difficult. His father, a poorly paid musician, gave Beethoven his first music lessons on piano and violin and, from the age of four, made him practice many hours a day. His mother died when he was 17, and his father began to drink heavily. Before he was 19, Beethoven took over his family and attempted to support his brothers. Fortunately, his great talent was recognized, and he was rewarded with commissions from the nobility. He made a modest living by selling his compositions and by teaching piano.

Although he was born in Bonn, Germany, Beethoven spent most of his life in Vienna, Austria, which was the musical center of Europe in his day. By the time he was in his early 30's, he was well-known and highly in demand as a conductor and pianist. It was then that he discovered that he was going deaf. At first he hid the fact. Then he withdrew from the public, since he was no longer able to communicate. "If I had any other profession, it would be easier," he wrote a friend, "but in my profession it is a terrible handicap." Still, he continued to compose with his inner ear—the ability to hear music in one's head—which we now call "audiation." Many of his greatest works, including his *Fifth Symphony*, were written when he was completely deaf.

Mozart as he was depicted in the film *Amadeus*

Later Musical Developments

If Haydn set much of the musical style for the period, other composers carried it to even greater heights. Although he was Austrian, Wolfgang Amadeus Mozart (1756-1791) applied the Classical style to Italian Opera. Even though his native language was German, he wrote his operas *The Marriage of Figaro* and *Don Giovanni* in Italian. But more important, his stories were about real human beings, and he developed the story line logically. The action proceeded more quickly. He used the instrumental accompaniment to set the moods and to suggest character. These changes gave his operas great delight and dramatic impact—reasons they are still being performed today.

Later on, Mozart composed *The Magic Flute* in German. This new style was called "Singspiel." Essentially, this was a simplified form of Italian comic opera in which the recitatives were spoken, and these spoken parts were alternated with simple songs. In these works, Mozart balanced text, music, and drama in such a way that they meld into one statement. Opera was no longer a series of recitatives, arias, dances, comic interludes, and choruses, but a continuous flowing drama. He created expressive melodies that singers like to sing and that audiences enjoy hearing.

One of the greatest achievements of the Classical period was to give instrumental music new expressive power. In the Baroque period, instrumental music had been successfully separated from vocal music and permitted to speak on its own. Now it was given the range of expression that, before this time, had only been achieved in vocal forms.

The developments in instrumental music are largely due to one man, Ludwig Van Beethoven (1770-1827). In his early works, Beethoven wrote in the Classical style of Haydn and Mozart. Gradually he developed and expanded his musical ideas. His nine symphonies trace these musical changes. He made his louds louder and his softs softer. He used dissonance—sounds that suggest conflict—for expressive effect. With rhythm, he was able to create surprise and the exciting feeling that the music was driving forward. He repeated melodic and rhythmic motives—short patterns—to give order and unity to a movement. He developed and reshaped his melodic material extensively to create interest and intensity. Beethoven was the first to use trombones (*Symphony No. 5*) and the first to add voices to the orchestral language (*Symphony No. 9*). This last symphony contains the "Ode to Joy," a large choral section at the end that speaks triumphantly about the brotherhood of man.

Beethoven's expressive ability can be readily experienced in his great vocal work, the *Missa Solemnis*. One need only listen to the "Gloria in Excelsis Deo" to realize the power of Beethoven's message. The upward, rapid thrust of the melody, the vigorous shouts of "gloria" by the whole chorus, and the unexpected accents combine to create a joyous expression of praise. But it was Beethoven's remarkable ability to make instruments speak as expressively as voices that is his greatest achievement. With the new emotional fire that lights his orchestral music, Beethoven opened the Romantic period. For this reason, he is thought of as a transitional composer between the Classical and Romantic periods.

German composer, Ludwig van Beethoven at the piano.

In summary, music of the Classical period was carefully thought out. It is music that is finely detailed, witty, and personal. It was constructed according to plan, and the plan was a given musical form—the outline of a sonata, concerto, or symphony—that the composer filled with sound. Emotion was not permitted to burst the form nor to change it for dramatic effect. Composers of the period used these outlines to structure expression and to achieve unity, clarity, and balance. Because this music holds back (restrains) its emotional charge, its high points often achieve a powerful emotional impact.

VOCABULARY

audiation	patron	string quartet
chamber music	requiem	suite
dissonance	singspiel	symphony
motive	sonata	

Chapter 12

The Romantic Period c. 1825-1910

The ideal of personal freedom finally became reality during the 19th century. The newly acquired political freedom brought artistic freedom as well. Artists began to express their personal feelings and emotions through their art. Composers of vocal music expressed their experiences with nature, love, and loneliness. Their songs, choral compositions, and operas were an emotional outpouring. Because individual expression of this kind was a characteristic of this time, the period has been given the name "Romantic."

Political Life

During the Romantic period, the middle classes gained power and confidence, and the wealth of nations was better distributed through trade and marketing. The Industrial Revolution, which brought on large-scale industrial production, created ample new manufactured goods as well as jobs for more and more people.

In the United States, the yearning for individual freedom continued to grow as lower class workers and slaves on plantations longed to establish a decent life for themselves. This condition grew into a struggle between the northern and southern states that erupted into the Civil War in which the freeing of the slaves was one of the chief issues. President Abraham Lincoln guided the nation through this sorrowful four-year conflict that ended in 1865. Again, it was a time of strong feelings, and the wounds would take a long time to heal.

This was a time, too, when citizens around the world expressed a growing patriotic pride in their country. This spirit of "nationalism" was often ex-

During the Civil War in the United States, the Union forces won a major victory at Gettysburg, Pennsylvania, July 1-4, 1863.

Immigrants arrive in New York City in the late 1800s.

pressed in music by composers such as Peter Tchaikovsky in Russia, Antonin Dvorak in Czechoslovakia, and Edvard Grieg in Norway among others.

Exploration and Invention

Throughout this period, American explorers such as Meriwether Lewis (1774-1809) and William Clark (1770-1838) mapped the vast western wilderness and helped open it to settlement. By 1869, there was a Transcontinental Railway that connected the east and west coasts. This helped to further open the western frontier. The invention of the telegraph in 1832 by Samuel Morse permitted people to communicate over long distances. Then, in 1876, the telephone was invented by Alexander Graham Bell. And the next year, Thomas Edison invented a machine that greatly affected music—the phonograph.

The westward expansion of civilization and the modernization of living conditions were outstanding features of the Romantic period in this country. It is difficult to imagine what our lives might be like today without the new ground that was broken by the pioneering spirit of those times.

The Arts

Because of the rise of the middle class, more people were able to afford tickets to cultural events. Artists who had been supported by wealthy patrons began to have their works heard in public halls or seen in galleries. Usually these audiences did not understand very much about the fine and performing arts. For this reason, artists tried to create works they thought people would readily understand and enjoy. Often they turned to the themes of nature or to the human emotions, such as joy and sorrow, that were common to all people.

In our country, painters such as George Bingham (1811-1879), Albert Bierstadt (1830-1902), and Thomas Cole (1801-1848) romanticized the American landscape. At the same time, George Catlin (1796-1872), Frederic Remington (1861-1909), and others painted the western life of cowboys and Indians. In Europe, the French painter Vincent van Gogh (1853-1890) expressed the conditions of poor people and also painted beautiful scenes of nature. Art alone made his life worth living, van Gogh said.

	1825	1830	1840	1850	1860

MUSIC

Johannes Brahms, German composer, 1833-1897

Robert Schumann, German composer, 1810-1856

Franz Schubert, German composer, 1797-1828

Giuseppe Verdi, Italian composer of operas, 1813-1901

Richard Wagner, German composer of operas, 1813-1883

Stephen Foster, American songwriter, 1826-1864

Felix Mendelssohn, German composer, 1809-1847

First public school instruction in music, 1838

OTHER ARTS

Charles Dickens' *Oliver Twist*, 1838

Harriet Beecher Stowe writes *Uncle Tom's Cabin*, 1852

Herman Melville's *Moby Dick*, 1851

Auguste Rodin, French sculptor, 1840-1917

Claude Monet, French painter, 1840-1926

Development of ballet

OTHER HISTORY

First Railroad: England, 1825 U.S. 1829

California Gold Rush, 1848

First telegraph message, 1844

First photograph, 1838

Charles Darwin, English naturalist, 1809-1882

Victoria, Queen of England crowned, 1837

Independence of Texas, 1836

Susan B. Anthony organizes Women Suffrage Association 1869

U.S. Civil War 1860-1865

Austrian composer Franz Schubert performs for a group of friends at one of his frequent musical salons

During this period, artists often worked together and were inspired by each other's work. This was especially true in vocal music where composers used poetry as texts for their songs and literature as the basis for their opera stories. Singers developed great skill in performing difficult music. They presented solo recitals and other concerts with great artistry. Musical performers were virtuosos who demonstrated great technical skill.

Art Songs

The most important vocal form to develop during the period was the art song or what the Germans called "lieder." These were very expressive songs for solo voice with piano accompaniment. The greatest Romantic composer of art songs was the Austrian composer Franz Schubert (1797-1828). Second only to him was the German composer Robert Schumann (1810-1856). In their songs, the piano performs an equal role with the vocal line, conveying mood and character.

Johannes Brahms (1833-1899) also composed lieder. One that almost everyone would recognize by its melody has come to be known as "The Brahms Lullaby." This composer is sometimes referred to as one of the "three great B's" of music— Bach, Beethoven, and Brahms.

Opera

In the Romantic period, opera grew to be even more elaborate and grand. Romantic composers tended to prefer serious and tragic subjects rather than stories that were comic. The German composer Richard Wagner (1813-1883) composed his first opera at the age of 19. He spent his entire life writing, producing, and conducting his own operas which he preferred to call "music dramas." Among his great achievements is *The Ring of the Nibelungen*, a series of four operas based on ancient German legends. Wagner often called for a very large orchestra of upwards

1870 | 1880 | 1890 | 1900 | 1905

Claude Debussy, French composer, 1862-1918

Impressionism in music begins

Metropolitan Opera opens, 1883

Sir William Gilbert, English playwright, 1836-1911

Sir Arthur Sullivan, English composer of operettas, 1842-1900

Giacomo Puccini, Italian opera composer, 1858-1924

Whistler's *Mother*, 1872

Van Gogh's *Wheat Field and Cypress Trees*, 1889

Impressonism in French art

Robert Louis Stevenson's *Treasure Island*, 1883

Sir Arthur Conan Doyle's *Sherlock Holmes*, 1891

Thomas Edison invents phonograph 1877

Statue of Liberty, 1876

Alexander Graham Bell invents telephone, 1876

Motion pictures, 1894

Sigmund Freud, Austrian founder of psychology, 1858-1939

First magnetic recording, 1899

First airplane flight, 1903

Einstein's Theory of Relativity, 1905

San Francisco Earthquake, 1906

Model "T." Ford, 1908

A scene from the opera *Aida* by the Italian composer Giuseppe Verdi.

of 120 musicians. The singers had to have strong voices to be heard above the orchestra, and they had to be in very good physical condition because some of his operas require them to perform for several hours. Festivals of Wagner's operas are still performed today in the small German town of Bayreuth, where he built his own opera theater.

FRANZ SCHUBERT

It has been said of Franz Schubert (1797-1828) that he surpassed all previous composers in composing songs. His melodies and harmonies are highly memorable, and they express the meaning of the text in a way not known before. He knew the precise moment to use a colorful chord to achieve a perfect effect. We hear the wheel spinning in the piano accompaniment in the song "Gretchen at the Spinning Wheel" and the pounding hoofbeats in the accompaniment of "The Erlking." In his brief, often unhappy, 31-years of life, Schubert composed over 600 songs, many of them masterpieces. His music is basically simple, friendly, and heartfelt.

Schubert's early musical training consisted of lessons on the violin and organ along with some study of musical theory. He was accepted as a member of the choir of the imperial Court Chapel at the age of eleven and soon became assistant to the conductor of the school's orchestra. When he was 14, Schubert began studying composition with Antonio Salieri, composer and music director at the Austrian court. Since he was not a great performer, Schubert decided to become a schoolteacher and compose in his spare time.

In his 14 or 15 years of active life as a composer, Schubert wrote vast numbers of works—operas, masses, choral works, piano pieces, symphonies, and much chamber music. Sadly, however, this great Austrian composer was never widely appreciated while he lived, even among the general public in Vienna where he spent his entire life. Many of his greatest works had to wait many years for their first performances. His *Symphony in B Minor, the "Unfinished,"* was not performed until 1865, 37 years after his death. Schubert has been called the last of the Classical composers and the first of the Romantics. After many years of sickness and despair, he died in 1828, only one-and-one-half years after Beethoven.

"Wheat Field and Cypress Trees" With repeated brush strokes, the French painter Vincent Van Gogh (1853-1890) creates the feeling of windy turbulence.

At the same time that Wagner was composing his operas in Germany, another great opera composer, Giuseppe Verdi (1813-1901), was at work in Italy. While these two opera composers were born in the same year, they held little else in common. Verdi used dramatic stories (librettos) based on well-known plays. He wrote soaring melodies in his solo arias and grand choruses to create dramatic action and mood. He kept the action moving. In contrast, Wagner's operas move more slowly. Verdi's opera *Aida* was commissioned (ordered) for performance in Cairo, Egypt to celebrate the opening of the Suez Canal. In addition to solos, choruses, and ballet, it contains a triumphal procession.

This giant among operatic composers of the period wrote 27 operas of which at least 15 are still regularly performed all over the world. These include *Rigoletto*, *Il Trovatore*, and *La Traviata*. When Verdi was 74 years old, his opera *Otello* was premiered. Based on the play by Shakespeare, this may be the greatest tragic opera of all time. Besides operas, Verdi wrote a *Requiem* that is frequently sung today and hailed as a masterpiece.

Another important name to know in the field of opera is Giacomo Puccini (1858-1924). He could make people weep, so beautiful were his arias. One of Puccini's friends was Arturo Toscanini, a world famous conductor or "maestro." He liked Puccini's operas very much and conducted them at the La Scala Opera House in Milan, Italy. Among his best loved works are *La Boheme* and *Madame Butterfly*, and tickets for them are almost always sold out!

FELIX MENDELSSOHN

In Berlin, at a very early age, Felix Mendelssohn (1809-1847) was tutored by his parents in arithmetic, French, German, literature, and fine arts. He was soon studying piano, violin, and musical composition with the finest teachers. By the time he was 13, he had composed several solo and choral songs, two cantatas, works for organ and for piano, two comic operas, eight string symphonies, two concertos, and a number of chamber works. He had extraordinary talent. At a concert in April 1827, his most popular work, the overture to Shakespeare's *A Midsummer Night's Dream*, was given its first public performance. He composed it when he was 17.

In spite of the fact that he lived in the early 19th century, his music is more Classical than Romantic. Inspired by Handel, he composed a number of dramatic oratorios for orchestra, chorus, and solo voices. Chief among these is *Elijah*, a work which tells the story of the struggle between the followers of Jehovah and the followers of Baal. He also wrote festival choruses, solo songs, and church music. Mendelssohn is credited with reviving public interest in the music of Johann Sebastian Bach.

During his busy life as a composer, conductor, pianist, and teacher, he traveled widely throughout Europe and visited England ten times. His trips to Scotland inspired him to write his *Fingal's Cave Overture* and his *"Scotch" Symphony No. 3*. As conductor, he made the Gewandhaus Orchestra in Leipzig the outstanding orchestra of its day. He organized the Leipzig Conservatory in 1842. He also directed the male-voice cathedral choir in Berlin. In 1936, the persecution of the Jews in Fascist Germany under Hitler led to the destruction of the Mendelssohn memorial in Leipzig and the suppression of his music.

Folk and Popular Songs

The nationalism that developed during the Romantic period stirred an interest in the folk music of particular nations and regions. Scholars studied the folk music of their peoples seriously, and composers included folk melodies in their works. Arrangers wrote choral settings of sea chanteys, work songs, and spiritual songs that came from their homeland.

In the United States, folk songs were part of the day-to-day life of sailors, cowboys, and farm workers. These songs sprang from the pioneers moving West, the builders of the railroads, and the men who manned the sailing ships. In the south, the slaves invented songs about their oppressed lives and the hope of a better life to come, and the "Negro spiritual" was born.

In the 1870's, a group called the Fisk Jubilee Singers from Nashville, Tennessee toured Europe singing choral music and presenting their spirituals. On one of their visits to Great Britain, they sang for Queen Victoria who was very pleased with their performance. Because of these concerts, many people were introduced to the moving words and music that rose out of the black experience. Harry Burleigh (1866-

ROBERT SCHUMANN

Only a quirk of fate permitted Robert Schumann (1810-1856) to become a composer and music critic. The small town where he was born in Germany (Kwikau) offered little music to him, and there was little in his home. In spite of his rather bland music lessons, he improvised his own pieces and grew interested enough in music to think about studying it at the university. Then his father died, and his mother insisted that he study law. By chance, a piano teacher at the university revived his interest in music and he began to compose.

By another quirk he became a composer. In his determination to ready himself for a career as a pianist, Schumann crippled the ring finger of his right hand by using a mechanical device (a spring and cable attached to the ceiling) which was supposed to give the finger independence and strength. Thereafter he turned his attention to the study of musical composition. He also spent a decade writing musical criticism for a magazine that he and a few friends founded in 1834.

His marriage to Clara Wieck, gifted daughter of his piano teacher, inspired a flood of new music. He poured his feelings into more than a hundred songs and many piano works. A fine pianist, Clara became the foremost interpreter of his works, performing them throughout Europe. Schumann's music is full of youthful vitality, joy, and rhythmic excitement. His songs are among the greatest of German art songs.

A modern production of Gilbert and Sullivan's operetta, *The Pirates of Penzance.*

GILBERT and SULLIVAN

Sir William Gilbert (1836-1911), British playwright, and Sir Arthur Sullivan (1842-1900), English composer, met in 1871 and formed a partnership in producing comic operettas. Gilbert wrote the librettos (the story and the lyrics) and Sullivan composed the music. The witty stories and the antics of the characters made these works very popular even among the upper classes whom they often ridiculed. Sullivan's music was as delightfully humorous as Gilbert's verses. The tunes were easy to remember. After 20 years of collaboration, the two had a quarrel. After a reconciliation, they produced two more works of lesser popularity. Among their best known and most loved works are *H.M.S. Pinafore*, *The Pirates of Penzance*, and *The Mikado*. Sullivan was knighted by Queen Victoria in 1883; Gilbert was knighted in 1907, hence the "Sir" that precedes their names.

The Fisk Jubilee Singers

1949), an arranger of these spirituals who was born in Erie, Pennsylvania, had a deep understanding of these works from his own heritage. That is why his arrangements capture the spirit of these works. He arranged and published more than 50 spirituals which have been sung by choral groups ever since.

Stephen Foster (1826-1864) was an American composer who wrote songs in a popular Romantic style. Although he based his words on the themes of life in the south, he was actually born in Law-

JOHANNES BRAHMS

Johannes Brahms (1833-1897) was a German composer of the late Romantic period. His life centered around Vienna where he conducted orchestras and choruses. He spent many of his summers in the country where he did much of his composing. Many of his large works were planned during his long walks in the beautiful valley of the Rhine in sight of the Alps, and these works seem to evoke the spacious outdoors.

As a youngster, Brahms began studying piano at the age of seven. His father, who played double bass in a local theater orchestra, taught him to play dance music on the violin, cello, and horn and how to arrange music for brass band. Brahms helped his family financially by playing at taverns and theaters and by making arrangements of popular waltzes for a local publisher.

Much of his early music was for the piano. He was a virtuoso pianist. Upon the death of his mother, he was inspired to compose *A German Requiem* for solo voices, chorus, and orchestra, one of his finest works. It was so successful after its first performance in 1869 that Brahms felt confident enough to begin writing large symphonic works, among them four great symphonies. His songs are among his most delightful works. Many are based upon folk songs or have a folk-like quality and are full of feeling and delight.

renceville, Pennsylvania and lived in the north. Most people will start to hum along when they hear one of his famous melodies such as "Oh! Susanna," or "My Old Kentucky Home," or "Old Folks at Home." It is said that Stephen Foster was the first composer of American popular music.

When we think of the period between about 1825 and 1910, we should remember the many different kinds of vocal music that developed during this time. So much of the music that we now take for granted came from the minds and hearts of the creative musicians who were Romantic composers. In fact, many of your great grandparents were living toward the end of this period and, for them, these Romantic songs were the music that they knew and loved. That makes this vocal music even more a part of your own musical heritage!

VOCABULARY

arranger	libretto	nationalism
art song	lieder	premiere
commission	maestro	spiritual
folk song	music	drama

Chapter 13

The Twentieth Century c. 1910 to present

Our own 20th century has been a time of much variety and many changes. Even though some of the old forms and styles remain, many new ones have been created. Rapid change and development have been characteristics of 20th century politics, science, technology, and the arts.

Political and Social Life

During the early years of the century, America continued to be the destination for thousands of people who were searching for freedom and the promise of a better life. The Statue of Liberty welcomed the downtrodden from many European countries. This stream of refugees brought their culture in their baggage—their folk music, their instruments, and their love for music. This vast treasury of musical styles, including the music of the Africans and others who were already here, helped us create an American music of great variety and vitality, a rich musical heritage.

When the New York Stock Exchange collapsed in 1929, it caused worldwide financial panic. The Great Depression followed, and many people lost their jobs. During the 1930's, the federal government under the leadership of President Franklin D. Roosevelt led the way toward recovery. Gradually industry revived, and people regained their confidence in the future. Musical instruments were manufactured, and people enjoyed listening to music on the radio, on phonograph, and in the new "talking" films.

Edvard Munch (1863-1944), the Norwegian painter, portrays the anguish of modern times. The work is called "The Scream."

Science and Technology

The 20th century has been a time of great leaps in science and technology. By the 1930's, most American homes had telephones, radios and electric lights, and most American families had an automobile. Soon to follow were television sets, and now, computers. But the leaps in knowledge have also produced atomic and nuclear weapons making it possible that humans, for the first time, can destroy all life.

Astronomers are using more powerful telescopes, and rockets have enabled us to send probes to study our solar system and outer space. The Voyager II spacecraft is now on its three-billion-mile flight to reach Neptune and beyond. On board is information about our civilization, including a recording with samples of music from all over our planet. Is there life out there? If so, will other creatures understand us through our music?

The technology that has affected music the most, perhaps, was the invention of long playing records in 1948. This paved the way for the development of cassette players in the 1970's and compact disc players in the 1980's. These electronic tools have made it possible for people of all classes to have fine recorded sound in their homes, in their automobiles, in schools—wherever they want it. What will be next?

Visual Arts and Literature

There have been enormous changes in visual arts and literature as well. The New York Armory Show of 1913 introduced modern art to the public. Here was a new, abstract art—paintings that depicted

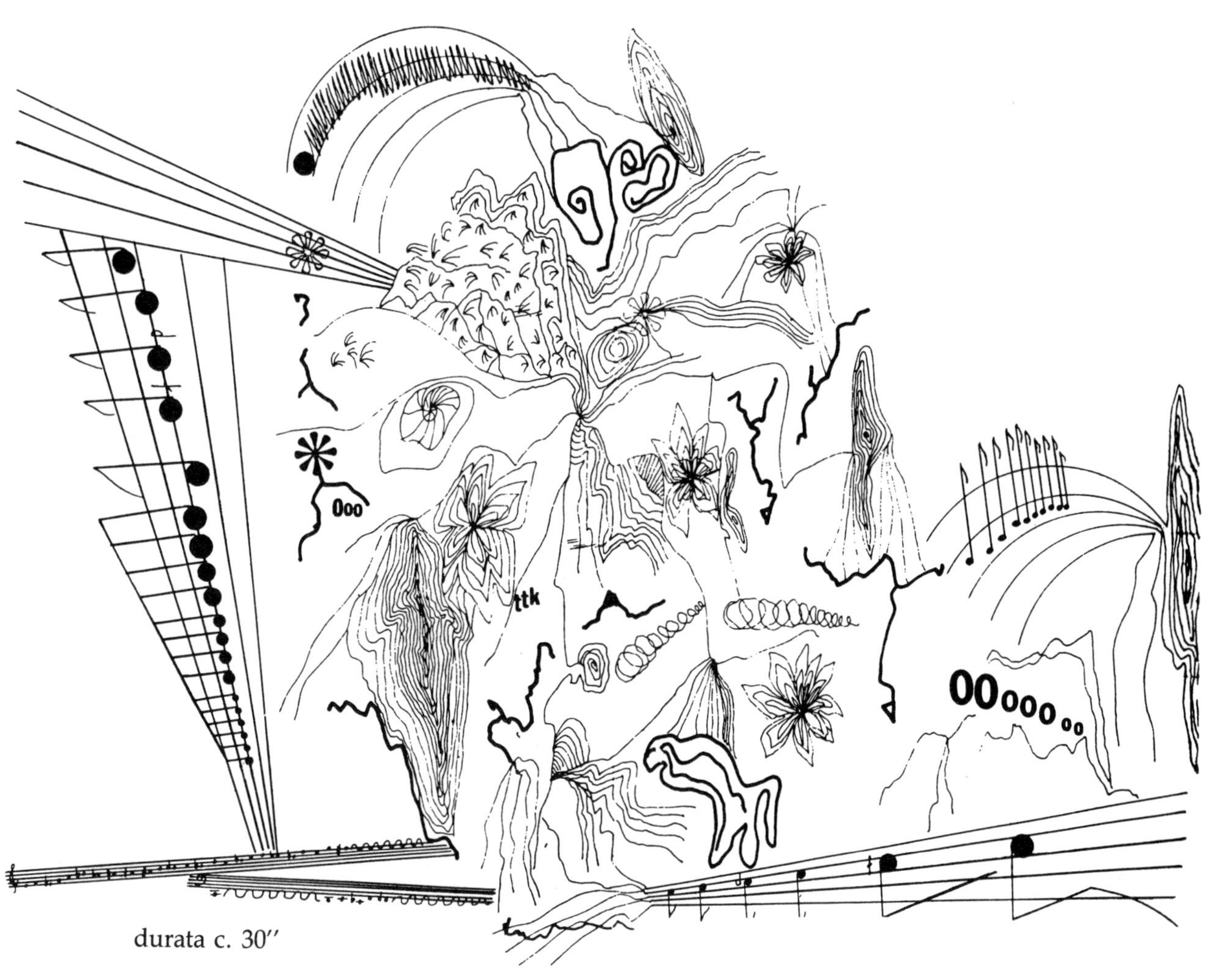

Lux, Lucet In Tenebris
by Cervetti

This page shows an example of modern musical notation. The composer's instructions for interpreting this notation are as follows:

Shout, clap hands, scream, talk about yourself, move your body, slap your body, stamp your feet on the floor, clear your throat, etc. Be creative! Singing at times but keeping one note at the time. Modulate this note through vibrato, shaking the lips, etc.
Avoid glissandi while singing. This 30 seconds should be a nightmare of sounds all fortissimo.
The conductor should do likewise.

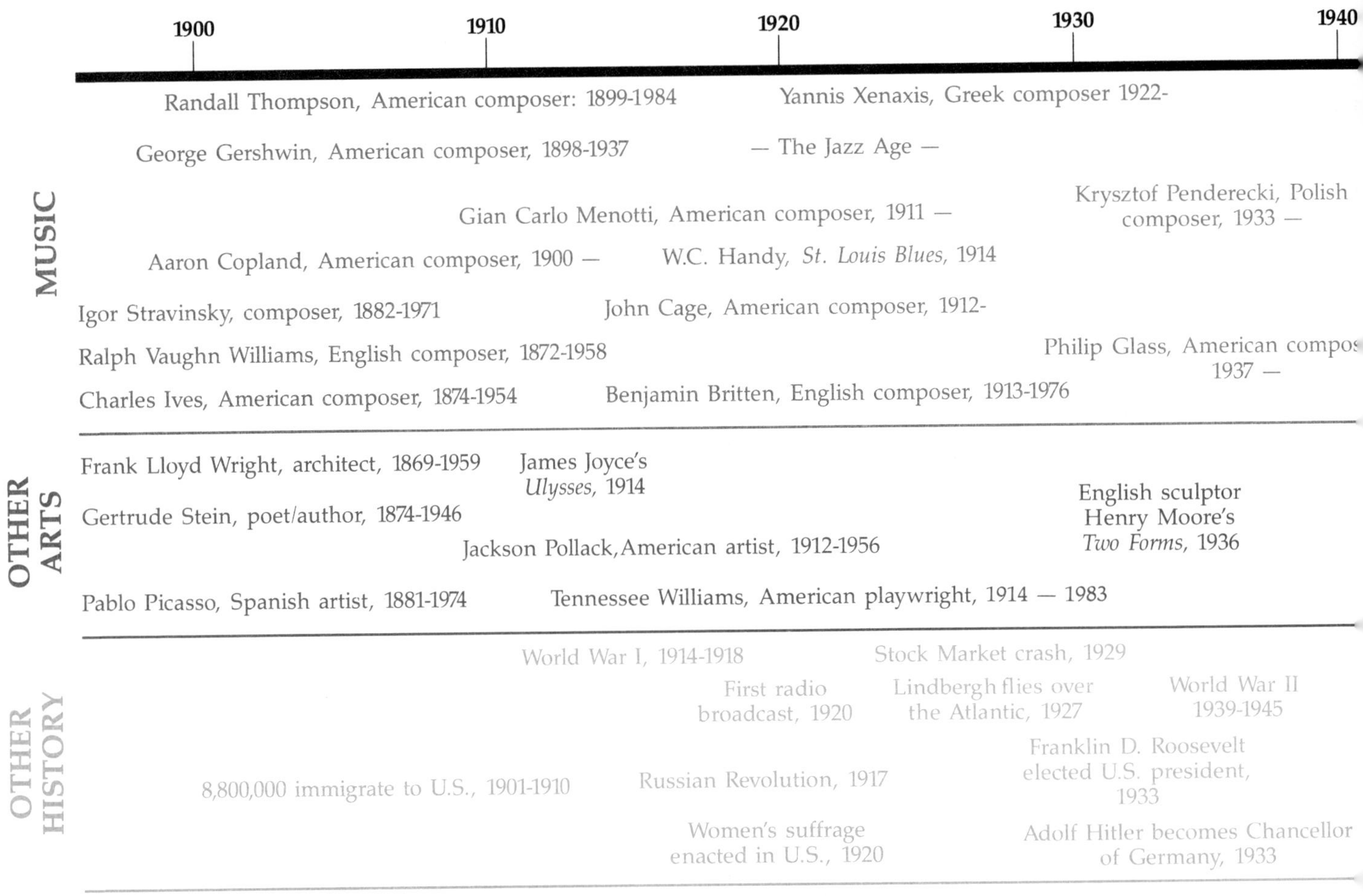

1900 1910 1920 1930 1940

MUSIC

Randall Thompson, American composer: 1899-1984

Yannis Xenaxis, Greek composer 1922-

George Gershwin, American composer, 1898-1937

— The Jazz Age —

Gian Carlo Menotti, American composer, 1911 —

Krysztof Penderecki, Polish composer, 1933 —

Aaron Copland, American composer, 1900 —

W.C. Handy, *St. Louis Blues*, 1914

Igor Stravinsky, composer, 1882-1971

John Cage, American composer, 1912-

Ralph Vaughn Williams, English composer, 1872-1958

Philip Glass, American compos 1937 —

Charles Ives, American composer, 1874-1954

Benjamin Britten, English composer, 1913-1976

OTHER ARTS

Frank Lloyd Wright, architect, 1869-1959

James Joyce's *Ulysses*, 1914

English sculptor Henry Moore's *Two Forms*, 1936

Gertrude Stein, poet/author, 1874-1946

Jackson Pollack, American artist, 1912-1956

Pablo Picasso, Spanish artist, 1881-1974

Tennessee Williams, American playwright, 1914 — 1983

OTHER HISTORY

World War I, 1914-1918

Stock Market crash, 1929

First radio broadcast, 1920

Lindbergh flies over the Atlantic, 1927

World War II 1939-1945

Franklin D. Roosevelt elected U.S. president, 1933

8,800,000 immigrate to U.S., 1901-1910

Russian Revolution, 1917

Women's suffrage enacted in U.S., 1920

Adolf Hitler becomes Chancellor of Germany, 1933

color, line, and shape but no recognizable subject matter. Here was cubism—nature represented by geometric forms.

Some American artists continued to paint pictures that were representational. Grant Wood (1892-1942), who lived his entire life in Iowa, painted the people and the landscapes of his own area. His painting "American Gothic" portrays a midwest farming couple. Other American artists experimented with new techniques. Jackson Pollock (1912-1956) dripped paint on canvas to create colorful abstract patterns. Alexander Calder (1898-1976) created huge metal mobiles of carefully balanced shapes.

In poetry, Robert Frost (1874-1963) wrote about his life in New England. Many of his poems have been set to music by choral composers. American composer Randall Thompson (1899-1984) set a series of Frost's poems to music in one work and called it *Frostiana*, a piece that is often performed by choruses today. On the occasion of the Statue of Liberty's 100th birthday in 1986, Pulitzer Prize winning poet Richard Wilbur wrote "On Freedom's Ground" as a text for composer William Schuman's (1910-) modern cantata of the same name. Unlike Frost's poetry, these verses do not rhyme, but they are powerful:

> Not that the graves of our dead are quiet,
> Nor justice done, nor our journey over.
> We are immigrants still, who travel in time,
> Bound where the thought of America beckons;
> But we hold our course, and the wind is with us.

In American architecture, there is one name that stands above all others—Frank Lloyd Wright (1865-1959). He designed houses so that they fit into their natural surroundings, and buildings that fit their function. If you want to see one of his buildings today, you can visit the house called "Falling Water" near Pittsburgh or the Guggenheim Museum of Art in New York City.

Trends in Musical Composition

America's most original contribution to the art of music may well be jazz, a unique form of popular music that has been enthusiastically received around the world. Jazz itself was an instrumental music that developed in New Orleans and spread around the country as black musicians moved to Chicago and other northern cities. From the same spirit came ragtime and syncopated dance music made popular by black musicians and stage performers. The jazz rhythms were complex, original, and infectious, and they rapidly became part of American musical style. The catchy rhythms and lively spirit of jazz soon invaded the music of Tin Pan Alley, the section of

1950 | 1960 | 1970 | 1980 | 1990

hn Rutter, English composer, 1945-

Compact disc recordings

Leonard Bernstein's *West Side Story*, 1957

New "popular" opera/theater

The Beatles 1960's

First performance of Menotti's *Amahl and the Night Visitors*, 1951

Ernest Hemingway, American author's *For Whom the Bell Tolls*, 1940

Rachel Carson's *Silent Spring*, 1963

"Pop Art" movement

Alvin Toffler's *Future Shock*, 1970

Japan bombs Pearl Harbor, 1941

Korean War, 1950-1953

Man lands on moon, 1969

First non-stop flight around world 1986

Vietnam War, 1962-1973

Nixon Resigns Presidency, 1974

omic bomb, 1945

President Kennedy assassinated, 1963

Challenger disaster, 1986

Hydrogen bomb, 1950

Martin Luther King assassinated, 1968

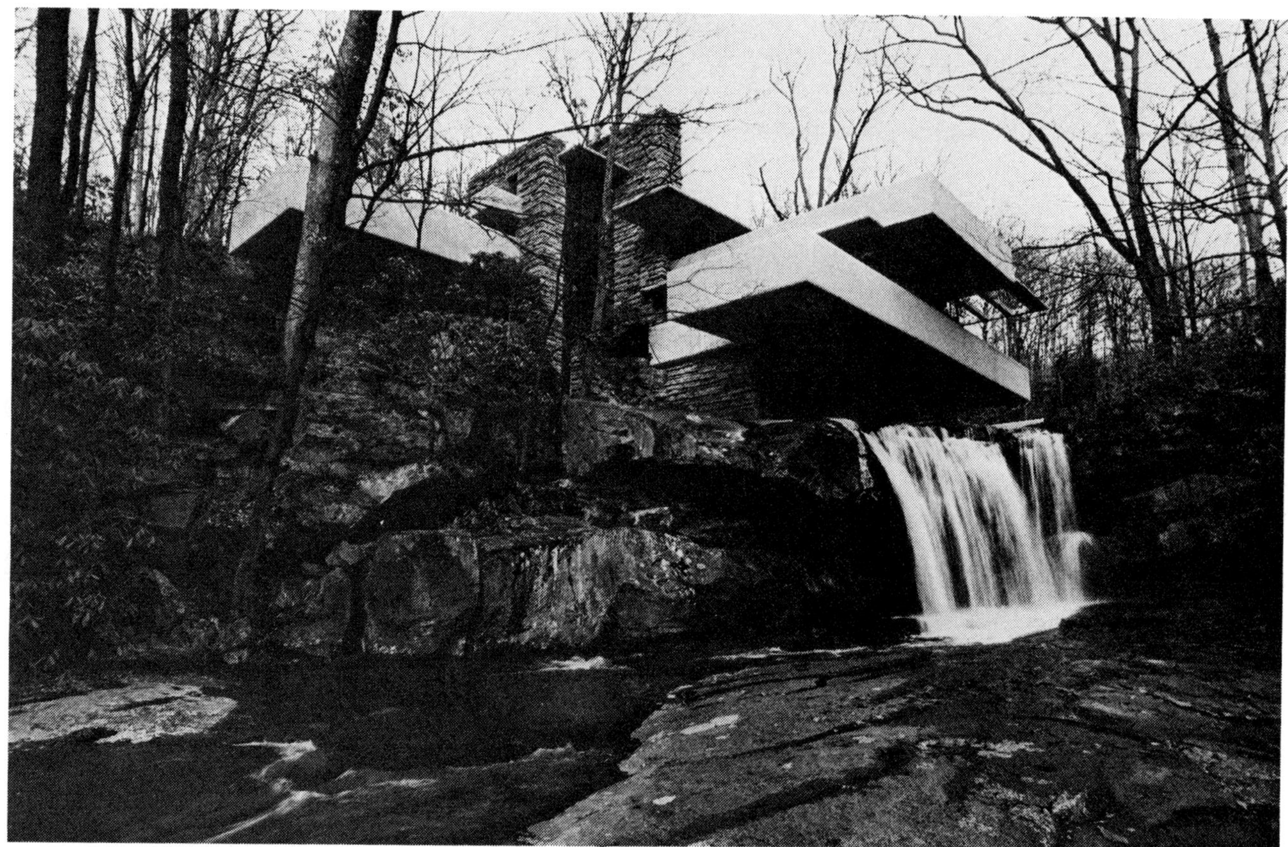

Frank Lloyd Wright's *Falling Water*.

IGOR STRAVINSKY

One of the musical giants of modern music was Igor Stravinsky (1882-1971), a composer who was born in Russia but lived most of his life in California. His father, a famous bass at the Imperial Opera, did not encourage Igor to become a musician. He wanted him to study law instead. But young Stravinsky was more interested in music and taught himself music theory. He also studied composition with Rimsky-Korsakov, a fine Russian composer and orchestrator. In 1925, Stravinsky toured America, and after World War II, he became an American citizen.

Stravinsky wrote music of many types and styles, both instrumental and vocal. One of his finest works is the *Symphony of Psalms* for chorus and orchestra. He also wrote a setting of the *Mass* and several other compositions for voice, including an opera, *The Rake's Progress*. His *Noah and the Flood* is a biblical spectacle that is narrated, mimed, sung, and danced.

His music, which includes ballets such as the *Firebird*, has grown more appealing to audiences as it has become more familiar. In fact, some people predict that Stravinsky will go down in the history of music as the greatest composer of the 20th century.

New York City that published tunes for the entertainment industry during the first three decades of the century. This original American musical form has made a deep imprint upon all American music, including choral music.

In the 20th century, performers and arrangers of songs have had many styles from which to choose. There are folk songs, art songs, opera arias, popular ballads, Broadway show tunes, jazz, and "pop" songs. Composers have used all these forms, and classical and popular composers have borrowed freely from each other's worlds. Classical composers have sometimes employed jazz rhythms, and popular composers have written Broadway musicals that used all the forms and techniques of opera.

In every field of the arts, the "language" has been stretched to say more. The American composer John Cage (1912-) played directly on the piano strings, made use of tone clusters (groups of close tones sounded together), and enlisted the performer in the creative process so that no two performances of a piece would be the same. To Cage, all sounds could be considered musical, depending upon how they were used. In this way he won new freedom for musical expression.

Another American, Philip Glass (1937-), wrote for electrically amplified wind instruments, used elements of rock music and the music of India, and incorporated theatrical techniques. In what is called "minimalism," he sometimes created near-hypnotic states in his listeners by repeating short rhythmic and melodic sections endlessly with very slight variations.

Other 20th century composers wrote songs without a tonal center or home tone. This atonal music often used combinations of the 12 tones of the chromatic scale—all the different tones within the octave set in a fixed order or "row." This twelve-tone music is called "serial" music. Rhythms became complicated with odd numbers of beats in a measure or measures that changed meters frequently. Singers found this music difficult to perform because of the wide leaps, the lack of a tonal center, and the inability to predict what the melody would do next.

Composers in the 20th century continue to explore new ways to express themselves. Some use percussion sounds borrowed from other cultures. Some use unusual combinations of instruments and voices. Others use electronically generated sounds made possible by the invention of the synthesizer and the computer. Among the most amazing of these new advances is the Synclavier, an instrument that records, notates, orchestrates, and prints the music that a composer plays upon it.

Pablo Picasso's *The Three Musicians*

Depression Lines in New York City in the 1930's.

RALPH VAUGHAN WILLIAMS

English composer Ralph Vaughan Williams (1872-1958) took great interest in the folk music of his country and wove many folk song themes into his music. He also borrowed the themes of some of the great English composers of the past, among them, Thomas Tallis. His music was nationalistic. After he served in the British army in World War I, he taught musical composition at the Royal College of Music in London and also conducted the London Bach Choir for a number of years. His first symphony which he called *A Sea Symphony* is scored for soprano, baritone, chorus, and orchestra. He wrote operas and works for orchestra and many other works for solo voices and for chorus, including arrangements of folk songs, hymns, and carols. He continued to compose well into his eighties, completing his *9th Symphony* at the age of 85.

Thomas Edison, American inventor, and his phonograph.

BENJAMIN BRITTEN

In England, Benjamin Britten (1913-1976) was an outstanding modern composer of vocal music. Britten began to write music when he was seven years old. He was so talented at musical composition that he earned his living as a composer from the time he was 18. Britten had a special gift for writing for voices, and he composed in a style that people easily enjoyed. His first opera was *Peter Grimes*, which was written after World War II to celebrate the reopening of a famous theater in London. The audience liked it so much that he went on to write 14 more. His opera *Noye's Fludde* is based on the biblical story of Noah's ark and is often performed in churches.

Musical Theater

Musical theater in the United States had its beginnings in the forms of entertainment called the minstrel show and vaudeville. These were variety shows much like our school talent shows today. There were singers, dancers, comedians, jugglers, animal acts, magicians, mimes, and other talent. Vaudeville began in the 1880's and was popular up to the beginning of the 1930's when talking pictures became popular. After the turn of the century, black and white performers played in vaudeville and minstrel shows, the first intermixture of these cultures.

During this time, the operetta also appeared. It was especially popular in Austria during the Romantic period, and it became equally popular in America during early decades of the 20th century. Operettas were like operas but were lighter in spirit and mood. The melodies were very singable—almost popular in style—and people left the theater humming them. The stories were simple and always had happy endings. These productions were fully staged with costumes, scenery, and an orchestra in the pit. Many have been made into films.

One of the first operetta composers was Franz Lehar (1870-1948), a composer from Vienna. He

The Houston Opera's production of the opera *Porgy and Bess* by American composer George Gershwin.

wrote his most celebrated operetta, *The Merry Widow* in 1905, and it was a great hit in many countries. Another musician in Vienna who eventually moved here was Victor Herbert (1859-1924). His more than 40 operettas include *The Red Mill, Naughty Marietta,* and *Babes in Toyland.* Another composer who emigrated to the United States was Sigmund Romberg (1887-1951). He composed over 70 operettas, including *The Student Prince,* and *The Desert Song.*

From the operetta, vaudeville, and the minstrel show, our own American style of musical developed. The Broadway musical or "musical comedy" has been popular in many parts of the world. In the 1920's and early 30's, George Gershwin (1898-1937) composed such shows as *Funny Face* (1927), *Girl Crazy* (1930), and *Of Thee I Sing* (1931). *Porgy and Bess,* Gershwin's American folk opera about the lives of Negroes in Charleston, South Carolina was premiered in 1935 and given its first Metropolitan Opera performance in 1985. Irving Berlin (1888-), who wrote such popular songs as "Alexander's Ragtime Band," "White Christmas," and "God Bless America," also wrote musicals: *Annie Get Your Gun* (1946) and *Call Me Madam* (1950), among others.

The development of the American musical comedy took another leap forward with the writing team of composer Richard Rodgers (1902-1979) and lyricist Oscar Hammerstein II (1895-1960). Their stories were more interesting, and the music became an important part in telling them. *Oklahoma* was a smash hit in 1943. Following this, they produced a whole string of hits, including *Carousel* (1945), *South Pacific* (1949), *The King and I,* (1951), and *The Sound of Music* (1959). These musicals have become "classics" or "standards" in American music.

Gradually, the Broadway musical became more serious. Leonard Bernstein (1918-), the gifted American conductor and composer, wrote *West Side Story* in 1957, a social drama about two street gangs, the Sharks and the Jets. American composer Stephen Sondheim (1930-) wrote in a more operatic style in *Sweeny Todd* (1979). Increasingly, composers began to adapt literary works and plays to the musical stage. Shakespeare was responsible for *West Side Story,* James Michener for *South Pacific,* Cervantes for *Man of La Mancha,* George Bernard Shaw for *My Fair Lady,* and Victor Hugo for *Les Miserables,* to name a few.

Popular Vocal Forms

In addition to musical theatre, many other forms of popular vocal music arose in the 20th century. One of the earliest was the Barbershop Quartet. Men gathered in the local barbershop to sing sentimental and humorous songs in four-part harmony. The tones were close together and often moved chromatically. The male quartet has two tenors, a baritone, and a

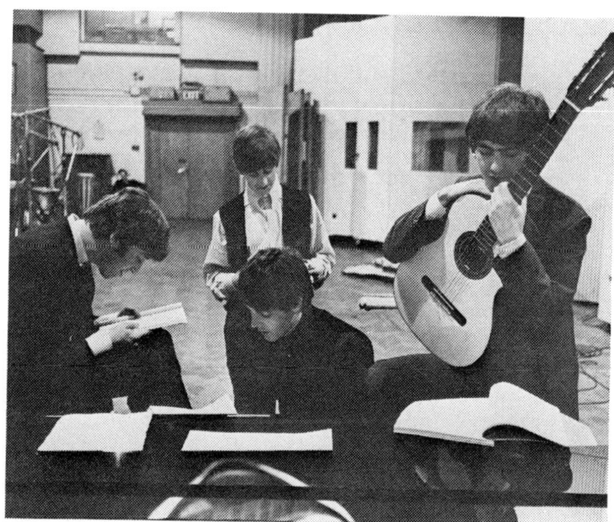

The Beatles, British rock group, took the world by storm in the 1960's.

GIAN CARLO MENOTTI

One of the outstanding opera composers in the United States is Gian Carlo Menotti (1911-). Born in Italy, Menotti began composing when he was only six years old, and he wrote his first opera when he was 11. As a young man, he moved to the United States where he has lived ever since.

The titles of Menotti's works are well known to opera lovers. Unlike many other opera composers, he wrote his own librettos (stories). Through his music and the dramatic action, he is effective in making an audience feel the emotions of his characters. His operas *The Medium* (about a person who communicates with the dead) and *The Consul* (about the red tape required to leave a Communist country) are gripping in suspense and grim in mood. In contrast *The Telephone* is light and humorous. *Amahl and the Night Visitors,* which tells a Christmas story, was the first opera written especially for television. It was first aired on Christmas Eve in 1951 and has been playing on our television sets at Christmas time ever since.

JOHN RUTTER

Born in London in 1945, John Rutter first attracted attention as a composer, conductor, and arranger of Christmas carols. He directed the choir at Clare College in Cambridge, England for several years and, in 1979, formed the Cambridge Singers, a choir of young mixed voices which has made a number of recordings and television appearances. *Bang!*, the first of two operas he has written for young people, was first performed in 1975. *The Piper of Hamelin* followed in 1980. He has written a number of other works for voices, including *Gloria* for choir and brass, *Canticles of America* for choir and orchestra, and *Five Childhood Lyrics* for unaccompanied choir, as well as church anthems and folk-song arrangements. His *Requiem* was completed in 1985. His first major orchestral work, *Partita*, was performed by the London Symphony Orchestra in 1976, and he has composed music for several television series.

bass. Women, too, sing this kind of close harmony and are called "Sweet Adelines." Such quartet singing is still popular today, and competitions are held each year at local, regional, and national levels to determine which quartets are the best.

From the 1930's onward, the number of popular singers has steadily increased. Many became box office stars. Names such as Bob Dylan (folk), Ella Fitzgerald (jazz), Billie Holiday (blues), Mahalia Jackson (gospel), Bill Monroe (bluegrass), Willie Nelson (country), Elvis Presley (rock), Diana Ross (soul), and Frank Sinatra (ballads) are connected with specific styles. Dozens of others could be mentioned, including your own favorites.

Groups of "pop" singers have also become common. By far the most celebrated of these were the Beatles. This group began in Liverpool, England in the 1960's with four musicians—John Lennon, Paul McCartney, George Harrison, and Ringo Starr. These musicians were inspired by a new form of American music made famous by Elvis Presley. They composed, arranged, sang, and played their own style of rock 'n' roll. This music had a strong rhythmic accent on the secondary beats. It was loud, it was honest, and it expressed strong feelings. The voices were equal partners with the instruments—guitars and drums.

Among the most creative and successful of the

Cats, the Broadway musical. The form has changed, but it is still popular around the world.

current popular stars are Stevie Wonder (1950-) and Lionel Richie (1950-), both inventive composers and effective performers. In some of his songs, Wonder has blended rock and traditional popular styles as in his 1973 hit, "You Are the Sunshine of My Life." Blind all his life, Wonder is admired for his talent and his character. Richie has written a great number of popular hits, including "We Are the World," the song that raised funds for the starving people in Africa.

We have come a long way since the Middle Ages when musical styles were few and could only be shared through live performance. Because we continue to alter music to suit our present tastes and needs, we know that it will continue to change in the future. What will vocal music be like in the 21st century? By your participation in the music of today, you are playing a part in creating the singing heritage of tomorrow.

Today, we are able to hear and see many styles and forms of pop music—from electronic sounds to music videos, soul to new wave rock, and heavy metal to punk. Our classical composers continue to produce choral music of many kinds as well as operas and solo songs. Through the vast communications network of radio, television, motion pictures, and recordings, such music is now accessible to people around the world.

VOCABULARY

atonal
barbershop quartet
Broadway musical
bluegrass
chromatic
classics
contemporary
country
gospel
heavy metal
jazz
lyricist
minimalism
minstrel show
musical comedy
new wave
operetta
orchestrator
punk
rock
serial composition
soul
standard
tonal center
tone cluster
twelve-tone music
vaudeville

Overleaf ▶

Crane Chorus of the Crane School of Music, State University of New York at Potsdam, performs at the Centennial Celebration of the Statue of Liberty, July 4, 1986.

Appendices

Appendices

This Appendix is divided into two sections: (1) Careers in Music, and a (2) Glossary of Musical Terms. *Careers in Music* contains a general overview of the wide variety of jobs in music and in fields closely related to music. These possibilities for professional employment are listed under three categories—Performance, Music Education, and Music Industry.

The *Glossary of Musical Terms* is an alphabetized "dictionary" of the musical terms used in this text. If you hear a term being used that you don't understand, look it up here.

Careers in Music

If someone said to you, "Quick, name all the careers you can think of in the field of music," you would probably spiel off a list that includes choral or band director, piano teacher, and "pop" performer. Actually, those three professions in music are only a few of the hundreds of music and music-related professions.

If you find this difficult to believe, think about one of your typical morning trips to school. If you pass a music store, you have already added one music-related profession to your original list. If you pass a theater where live performances of music occur, at least a dozen music-related professions are involved in that one enterprise!

Is your radio playing? Many music-related professions are required to get those sounds to your ears. Then there are record and tape stores, video stores, instrument sales stores, churches, colleges, and universities who hire musicians, and on and on.

Many thousands of people across the United States and around the world make their living through professions associated with music. These people aren't all musicians, nor need they be. You, too, may want to consider entering one of these fields. The following information may help you decide.

PERFORMANCE

Career opportunities in both the classical and popular music fields are extremely varied. Let's look at just a few examples in the world of performance.

Solo Artists

There are many solo artists, both singers and instrumentalists, who have very successful and rewarding careers. Some are the superstars among the current popular performers, others the virtuoso performers in the concert halls of the world. Success as a solo artist depends upon unusual talent, hard work, ambition, personality, and a bit of luck. Few solo artists reach the top, but many who achieve a lesser limelight enjoy their work and make an acceptable living.

Professional Ensembles

Many hundreds of singers and instrumentalists make their living performing together with other musicians. There are many different kinds of ensemble positions in music in both the popular and classical fields. From pop and rock groups to string quartets,

Singing in a professional choir

this area of performance is as diverse as music itself. Concert halls, auditoriums, arenas, restaurants, night clubs, and churches are filled with audiences enjoying a particular style of music. You may want to form your own group of singers or instrumentalists or join someone else's. A word of warning: This is a highly competitive enterprise. To become successful at it, you must develop both skills and determination. The following are some of the different types of musical positions you might consider in association with musical groups.

Orchestras. Professional orchestras recruit the finest players—those who have mastered the technical skills of their instrument and developed their musicianship to a very high level. The competition here is as keen as it is in sports. Knowledge of symphonic literature is essential. Of the more than 1500 orchestras in the United States, upwards of 500 pay their musicians. Related positions include orchestra manager and promoter, music librarian, educational director, and financial and promotional staff.

Choruses. In contrast to orchestras, only a few professional choral groups exist today. However, there are many symphony choruses and civic choral groups that demand the highest standards of vocal technique. Professional singers are often recruited for choral groups for special performances, recordings, and concert tours.

Opera and Musical Theater Companies. While leading operatic roles in the major opera houses are always sung by eminent solo artists, talented singers are required for many secondary roles and in the chorus. There are now upwards of 100 civic opera companies in the United States that offer opportunities for both professional and semi-professional singers.

Solo operatic performers

Performing in musical theater

The glamour of Broadway and other theaters in large and small cities, as well as dinner theaters in the suburbs, attracts many talented singers, dancers, and instrumentalists. Civic theaters, summer stock, and dinner theaters offer a wide range of employment for musicians.

Related positions include vocal coaches, accompanists, orchestral conductors, orchestral musicians, and hundreds of jobs outside music, such as lighting, costume, and scenic designers, choreographers, dancers, scenic carpenters and painters, wig makers, seamstresses, staging directors and managers, stage hands, promotional and box office personnel, advertising and financial staff, ushers, and other support staff.

Studio Musicians. Television, motion pictures, and recording studios require a wide variety of professional musicians as composers, arrangers, singers, and instrumentalists. To produce the huge volume of music that is used in these productions, exceptional skills are required, because most of the music is performed at sight, and time is a critical factor due to costs. An important related position is that of the sound engineer who does the recording.

Composer/conductor John Rutter (l.) discusses his score with producer Jillian White

Churches. Many churches employ a director of music as well as singers and instrumentalists, either full or part time. Churches hire organists and choir directors. Religious broadcasting provides numerous professional jobs for musicians of all kinds.

Armed Forces. Students who want to consider a career in the armed forces may not realize that there are many opportunities to use their musical skills. Each branch of the service has an entertainment division that organizes and supports both band and choral groups. Also, there are many church musicians who work with chaplains as organists and choir directors. The opportunities for travel, further musical training, and work in a top quality musical organization while serving in the military can be highly rewarding.

MUSIC EDUCATION

There are a surprising number of opportunities for careers in music education.

Public Schools

Most public school systems and private schools across the country hire music specialists to teach their general music, choral, band, and orchestral programs. Working with young people can provide many satisfactions, and most music teachers are usually well regarded in their schools and communities. These music teaching positions require a degree in music education, and teachers must meet state certification requirements.

Colleges and Universities

Teachers with special qualification in music are recruited by colleges and universities as instructors, professors, and administrators. Advanced degrees and teaching experience are usually required. Working with older students presents a different set of challenges. For many people who enter the teaching profession, college and university teaching presents another possibility to which they can aspire.

Private Teaching

A large number of musicians teach privately in their own homes or studios. One of the advantages is that these teachers can regulate their own schedules. Many people earn their living by teaching piano, voice, guitar, and other instruments.

Private music instruction

Specialized Teaching

A related, but very important career, is that of a music therapist. This growing field combines an interest in music and science in an effort to treat the emotionally disturbed and physically disabled.

Music Education in Other Settings

Many performing organizations such as symphony orchestras and opera companies have a director of education who organizes concerts and other educational activities, often connected with local schools. Another career closely related to education is that of music librarian in public and private libraries and with musical performing organizations.

THE MUSIC INDUSTRY

Most students think that the only careers in music open to them are in performance or education. Wrong! Music industry offers challenging and satisfying career opportunities. The business of music affects every aspect of both education and performance and, without its contribution, the music making process as we know it would not exist.

Careers in music industry are not for second-class musicians. Rather, these important people use the latest technology to translate the composer's creative ideas for an appreciative audience. Let us look at a few of these positions.

Music Publishing

In most publishing houses, there are editors, engravers, copyists, sales and promotional staff, and, obviously, management. While there are schools that offer degrees in the business of music, many of these careers are learned by on-the-job training. There are as many types of publishers as there are types of music. If you are interested in considering such a career, you will want to associate with a company that publishes the type of music that interests you most. A strong background in music education is a must, in any case.

Recording

Modern technology in both video and sound production has opened unlimited career opportunities to persons who want to combine musical interests with technical skills. These highly skilled technicians often contribute as much to the success of a record album, tape, or video as does the performer.

The remarkable applications of the computer to music, along with the high-tech development of synthesizers and other electronic instruments, offer unlimited challenges for musicians, engineers, and technicians in the music business.

Sound reinforcement is another whole area of expertise. Both outdoor and indoor performances often require elaborate systems to pick up and disperse the sound in vast and in intimate spaces. Commercial and home sound systems are another whole area that requires inventors, manufacturers, and sales personnel.

Selling musical instruments

Piano tuning

The Music Store

There are presently over 6,000 retail music stores in the United States, employing thousands of people as managers, salespersons, accountants, and support staff. Some stores sell everything related to music, while others specialize in a particular market such as instruments or sheet music. A knowledge of each specialty and a pleasing personality are the usual requirements for a position in one of these stores. Working in a music store is one of the very best ways to gain valuable experience that can open doors to other careers in the music industry.

Instrument repair

Instrument Manufacture and Repair

The manufacture of any musical instrument is an art and requires particular skills and craftsmanship. Young employees are usually trained by older employees who have devoted a lifetime to developing their craft. The popularity of electronic musical instruments and rapidly developing new technologies have combined to create a new and exciting world of musical instrument design and manufacture. Whether building the latest synthesizer or a fine concert grand piano, the individual who builds them has to maintain the highest standards of the craft.

Apart from the actual manufacture of instruments, companies require management, sales, and promotional personnel. The employee must have a thorough knowledge of the instrument and a good general musical background.

Once the instrument is made, it must be kept in repair. Instrument repair is an important service and a highly specialized skill. There are technical schools and colleges where such skills can be acquired. Many schools and colleges employ full-time repairmen such as a piano tuner. Other instrument repair specialists choose to operate a private business or work with a music store.

Management and Administration

Practically every performing group or soloist, from a symphony orchestra to the current "pop" superstar, has a manager and administrative staff to take care of their business affairs. This includes those who book concerts, handle financial matters and promotion, and protect their legal interests. Another aspect of management is the increasing numbers of fine arts centers and concert halls that require knowledgeable musicians on their administrative staffs.

Writing

The field of music criticism provides excellent opportunities for a musician to combine musical and literary skills. A music critic, for example, reports major musical events for newspapers, magazines, and very often, television. Another aspect might be writing articles for professional music magazines or books on music. To qualify for this type of work, one must have a vast knowledge of music literature and performance practices.

CONCLUSION

As you can see, music opens doors to hundreds of possible jobs. Your music teachers and guidance counselors can help you with more specific information about careers in music and related fields. Remember, it is most important that you develop your own musical skills in order to be qualified for whatever career you choose in the music profession. The more you know about music, the more apt you are to qualify for positions in this vast field.

Sound recording

Glossary of Musical Terms

A cappella. Designation for unaccompanied choral music.

Accelerando, accel. Becoming gradually faster.

Accent. Emphasis on a note or chord. Often indicated by > or ‾ placed above the note or chord.

Accidental. A sharp, flat, double sharp, double flat, or natural not included in the key signature.

Adagio. Slow tempo.

Ad libitum, ad lib. A term which gives a performer the freedom to vary a tempo and/or to include or omit a vocal or instrumental part.

Agitato. With excitement.

Al. To; used with other words such as *al Fine* (to the end).

Alla breve. A meter signature, ¢, indicating duple meter $\frac{2}{2}$.

Allargando, allarg. Slowing of tempo, usually with a crescendo; usually occurring near the end of a piece.

Allegretto. A tempo term, slower than allegro.

Allegro. A term which indicates a fast tempo; cheerful.

Alto, contralto. The lowest female voice.

Andante. A term which indicates a moderate walking tempo.

Andantino. As a tempo term, it is a modification of andante; in modern usage, it is slightly faster than andante.

Animato. Lively.

Anthem. A sacred choral composition with English text. It developed from the Latin motet.

Antiphon. A term for various types of Gregorian chant.

Antiphonal. A style of singing in alternating choirs.

A piacere. A term which gives a performer freedom, especially in rhythm and tempo. Synonymous with ad libitum.

Appoggiatura. A type of musical ornamentation which has been variously interpreted since it first appeared in the 17th century. Basically, it is a nonharmonic tone which is performed on the beat to form a dissonance and then resolved.

Aria. An accompanied song for solo voice (occasionally two solo voices); very important in cantatas, oratorios, and operas.

Arpeggio. A term which describes the playing or singing of the pitches in a chord one after the other, rather than simultaneously.

Arranger. A person who adapts a composition by adding or changing parts, as in a song, or by changing from the original medium to another.

Articulation. The term relates to clarity in vocal and instrumental performance. It involves phrasing, attack and release of pitches, and legato and staccato. In choral music it especially relates to the production of consonants.

Art song. A composed song for solo voice with accompaniment.

A tempo. A term which indicates a return to the previous tempo following tempo changes such as ritardando, etc.

Atonality. Lacking tonality or a tonal center.

Audiation. The process of hearing music inside the head, inner hearing.

Augmentation. The repetition of a melody in longer, often doubled, note values. The opposite of diminution.

Augmented. The term used to describe a major or perfect interval which has been enlarged by one half step.

Avant-garde. A term, meaning vanguard, used to describe new, experimental styles in music and the other arts.

Ballad. After moving from its origin as a dancing song through several stages, it is now a term for a popular song, usually a narrative.

Ballett, balletto. A Renaissance part song, characterized by a fa-la refrain.

Barbershop quartet. A colloquial term used for four singers (originally men) who practiced popular songs—usually in a barber shop. The songs were characterized by a type of harmony involving close position chords. The popularity of barbershop singing has been fostered by regional and national contests for both male and female quartets and choruses.

Baritone. The male singing voice in the range between tenor and bass.

Bar line. A vertical line drawn on the staff; it divides the music into measures.

Baroque music. The music of the period following the Renaissance, 1600–1750.

Bass. The male singing voice in the lowest range. Also, another name for the F clef.

Beam. The horizontal line which connects two or more eighth, sixteenth, or thirty-second notes. Ex.: ♫.

Bel canto. 18th-century Italian vocal technique which emphasized beautiful sound and virtuoso performance.

Binary form. A term used to describe a composition of two different, or contrasting sections, denoted by the letters AB. The sections may be repeated, AABB.

Bluegrass music. A style which emerged from the music of a group, the Blue Grass Boys, in the 1940s. It draws from dance rhythms, home entertainment, and religious folk music of Southeast America. A bluegrass band usually includes four to seven persons who sing and play acoustic string instruments such as guitar, double bass, fiddle, banjo, and mandolin.

Brio, con. With spirit.

Cadence. A melodic or chordal progression which gives a feeling of repose. It occurs at the end of a composition, a section, or a phrase.

Calmato, calmo. Calmly.

Cambiata. From the Italian word *cambiare*, meaning to change. Originally referring to nonharmonic tones, it was first used in the mid 1900's by Dr. Irvin Cooper, an American music educator, to describe the boy's changing voice.

Camerata. The name of a group of 16th century Italian writers, musicians, and amateurs who were responsible for the beginning of opera.

Canon. A strict form of imitation in which a melody is stated in one part and imitated in one or more other parts.

Cantabile. In singing style.

Cantata. A sacred or secular choral composition of several movements. It contains choruses, solos, and duets and has orchestral or keyboard accompaniment.

Cantor. A solo singer in Catholic and Jewish religious services. The term was also applied to the director of music in the early Protestant church.

Cantus firmus. A borrowed melody to which other voices or parts are added to make a polyphonic composition.

Carol. Originally from the medieval French word *carole*, a dance. In England it was first a pagan song of celebration and then became a song of praise, usually for Christmas.

Changing meter. The term which describes the use of two or more meters in a composition. Synonymous with shifting meter, multi-meter.

Chanson. Derived from the French word for song, the 16th century chanson was imitative in style. Later, in the 17th and 18th centuries, it was usually a short strophic song.

Chant. A synonym for plainsong, liturgical music which was monophonic, unaccompanied, and unmetrical.

Chantey, chanty, shanty. A song sung by early English and American sailors while working together on their ships.

Chorale. A German Protestant Church hymn tune, sometimes borrowed from secular folk songs. Four-part hymns are an example of chorale "style" today.

Chord. A combination of three or more tones sounded simultaneously.

Chordal. Derived from chord, the term describes a style of music which includes a series of chords. Church hymns are examples of chordal style, or texture.

Chorus. A large group of singers. Also, the music for such a group. Example: the choruses from Handel's *Messiah*.

Chromatic. A term used to describe half steps, both ascending and descending. An example: a chromatic scale or chromatic harmony.

Classicism, Classical. In music, the terms refer to the period 1750 (or c.1770) to 1825. With a small *c* the term *classical* is often used to distinguish the field of art music from that of popular music.

Clef. A sign placed at the beginning of the staff to indicate the pitch of the notes on the staff. Most commonly used in choral music are the G, or treble clef, 𝄞, the notes above middle C, and the F, or bass clef, 𝄢, the notes below middle C.

Coda. An added ending to a composition.

Commission. As applied to music, the word refers to the paying of a fee for the writing of a composition.

Common time. A meter signature, 𝄴, meaning $\frac{4}{4}$ meter.

Computer. The use of computers for musical purposes began in the mid-twentieth century. Along with their contribution to musical research, they are used by composers as a pseudo instrument for creating music.

Con. With; used with other words, as *con brio*.

Concerto. A composition for solo instrument (or instruments) with orchestra.

Conjunct. A term used to describe melodies characterized by stepwise intervals. The opposite of disjunct.

Consonance. A term associated with sounds of repose; as opposed to dissonance.

Consonant. A term used to describe: (1) intervals such as octave, perfect fourth and fifth, third, and sixth; and (2) chords which contain these intervals. Also, consonants are all the letters of the alphabet, excluding the vowels a, e, i, o, u.

Contemporary. In music, the term refers to music written by living composers or, in general terms, those having lived in recent years.

Contrapuntal. A term associated with counterpoint; descriptive of the texture in which two or more voices move independently.

Countermelody. A melody added to the original melody.

Counterpoint. A compositional technique in which single melodic lines of equal importance are combined.

Country music. A style of music which was first known as Hillbilly music. It came from the folk music of the rural South. At first the bands used fiddle, 5-string banjo, and guitar. After 1900 the mandolin, string bass, and steel guitar were added. By the 1970s the electric guitar was used, and the music became increasingly popular in the United States.

Crescendo, cresc. $<$ Gradually louder.

Cut time. A term which describes the meter signature, ¢, meaning $\frac{2}{2}$ meter.

Da capo, D. C. A direction in a musical score to repeat from the beginning.

Dal segno, D. S. A direction in a musical score to repeat from the sign, 𝄋 . It is frequently followed by *al fine*.

Decrescendo, decresc. $>$ Gradually softer.

Degree. One of the eight consecutive tones in a major or minor scale.

Descant. A countermelody, added to the original melody, sung by one or a few voices.

Diatonic. In modern usage the term describes a scale having both whole and half steps.

Diminished. A term used to describe an interval, a triad, or a seventh chord. A diminished interval is one which has been decreased: a major by two half steps (d-b♭♭ is a diminished sixth), or a perfect by one half step (d-a♭ is a diminished fifth). A diminished triad has a minor third and a diminished fifth (d-f-a♭). A diminished seventh chord has a minor third, a diminished fifth, and a minor seventh (d-f-a♭-c♭).

Diminuendo, dim. Gradually softer.

Diminution. The repetition of a melody in shorter, usually halved, note values; the opposite of augmentation.

Diphthong. The occurrence of two successive vowels on one syllable.

Disjunct. The term for intervals larger than a second; the opposite of conjunct.

Dissonance. The term associated with sounds of unrest; the opposite of consonance.

Divisi, div. A term for divided vocal parts. Ex.: T I and T II.

DO. The Italian solfège name of the first degree of the major scale.

Dolce. Sweetly.

Dominant. The fifth degree of the major or minor scale. Also, the name of the triad built on the fifth degree, labelled **V** in major and harmonic minor keys and **v** in natural minor keys.

Dorian. The first Medieval church mode.

Double bar. Two vertical lines drawn on the staff to show the end of a composition or a section. A repeat is indicated by placing two dots before the double bar.

Double flat. ♭♭ A musical symbol which indicates the lowering of pitch one whole step.

Double sharp. 𝄪 A musical symbol which indicates the raising of pitch one whole step.

Down beat. A term associated with the accented first beat of the measure and the downward direction of that beat in the conducting pattern.

Duple meter. Meter based on two beats, or a multiple of two, in a measure.

Duplet. A group of two notes performed in the time of three of the same kind.

Duration. Length of time as indicated by notes and rests.

Dynamics. Degrees of volume, from very soft to very loud.

Enharmonic. A term which describes notes of the

same pitch which have different names. Ex: a♯ and b♭; c♯ and d♭.

Enunciation. The manner of speaking and singing the words in a text to produce distinct vowels and consonants.

Espressivo, espress. Expressively.

FA. The Italian solfège name of the fourth degree of the major scale.

Falsetto. A method of singing used by male singers, especially tenors, to sing pitches higher than their normal range.

Fasola. A system of solmization in England and America in the 17th and 18th centuries. The syllables *fa, so,* and *la* were used for both c-d-e and f-g-a, while *mi* was used for the seventh degree of the major scale.

Fermata. 𝄐 An Italian term meaning pedal point. In American usage it indicates a hold, or a pause.

Fifth. The fifth degree of the scale; also, the interval formed by a tone and the fifth tone above or below it. Ex.: d up to a; d down to g. Fifths (intervals) may be perfect, corresponding to major, augmented, or diminished.

Fine. An Italian word for the end. Often used as *al Fine,* to the end.

First ending. One or more measures at the end of a stanza. It may be indicated as ⌈1.⌉ placed above the designated measure or measures.

Fixed *do*. The solmization system in which *do* is always c.

Flag. A short curved line added to a quarter note to form an eighth note ♪. Two flags produce the sixteenth note 𝅘𝅥𝅯 and three flags a thirty-second note 𝅘𝅥𝅰 .

Flat. ♭ A musical symbol which, when placed before a note, lowers the pitch one-half step.

Folk song. A song of the people, usually developed by tradition within a community or country and passed on to succeeding generations aurally.

Form. The structure of a musical composition.

Forte, *f*. Loud.

Fortissimo, *ff*. Very loud.

Forzando, forzato, *sfz*. An Italian term for forced or accented. Synonymous with *sforzando sf.*

Fourth. The fourth degree of the scale. Also, the interval formed by a tone and the fourth tone above or below it. Ex.: d up to g or down to a. Fourths (intervals) may be perfect, corresponding to major, augmented, or diminished.

Frequency. As related to music, the number of vibrations per unit of time, usually a second, used to generate sound.

Fugal. A descriptive term, derived from fugue, for a musical composition based on imitation. Also, contrapuntal.

Giocoso. Italian word for humorous.

Glee. An 18th century type of English choral music, unaccompanied, for men's voices in three or four parts.

Glissando, gliss. The rapid playing of scales by a sliding motion. It is most commonly used on the harp and piano.

Glottis. The opening between the vocal cords.

Gospel music. A large body of American religious songs having texts which reflect aspects of the religious experience of Protestant evangelical groups. They first appeared in 19th century religious revivals and are now included in many church hymnals. Today, gospel music is also a type of popular song with no religious association.

Grand staff, great staff. The G, or treble, and the F, or bass, clefs staves together form the grand staff.

Grazia, con grazia. Grace, or with grace.

Grazioso. Gracefully.

Gregorian chant, Roman chant. The liturgical chant of the Roman Catholic Church, perhaps named for Pope Gregory I. It is monophonic, unmetrical, sung by cantor and choir.

Half step. The interval from one pitch to the adjacent pitch, ascending or descending. It is the smallest interval on the keyboard.

Harmonic minor scale. Like the natural minor, the harmonic minor scale is taken from its relative major. Its pattern is: one whole step, one half, two whole, one half, one and one-half, and one half step.

Harmony. The singing or playing of two or more pitches simultaneously. The vertical aspect of music.

Harpsichord. A stringed keyboard instrument used from the 16th to the 18th centuries. Shaped like the modern grand piano, the harpsichord differed in that the tone was produced by the plucking of each string by a plectrum of crow quill. There has been a revival of interest in harpsichord music in the 20th century.

Hemiola. A rhythmic device commonly used in Renaissance and Baroque music, it is associated with time values in the ratio of 3:2. Ex.: three half notes in place of two dotted half notes.

Homophony, homophonic. The musical texture in which a prominent melodic line is supported by an accompaniment, either chordal or of some other type.

Hymn. A song of praise to God.

Imitation. A compositional technique in which a melodic line recurs in successive voices, or parts. Ex.: round and canon.

Impressionism. An artistic movement of the late 19th and early 20th centuries. In music the composers who were exponents of Impressionism were Debussy and Ravel.

Interval. The distance in pitch between two tones.

Intonation. A term which describes tuning: singing or playing pitches in tune.

Inversion. The term may be applied to both harmony and melody. It occurs in harmony when the root of a chord is in an upper voice rather than on the bottom. In melodic inversion the intervals are inverted.

Jazz. A type of twentieth century American music which grew out of several kinds of earlier American music, especially ragtime and blues. Its most important characteristic is its unique rhythmic beat, which emphasizes syncopation. Although shunned by early classical musicians, it gained respectability as it moved to the concert stage with the music of George Gershwin.

Key signature. The sharps or flats placed at the beginning of the staff to indicate the scale upon which the music is based.

Kinesthesia. A term associated with the involvement of movement in music learning.

LA. The Italian solfège name of the sixth degree of the major scale.

Larghetto. Slightly faster than largo.

Largo. Very slow tempo.

Larynx. The formation of muscle and cartilage at the upper end of the windpipe (trachea), containing the vocal cords.

Leading tone. The seventh degree of the major scale, so named because of its tendency to move upward to the tonic.

Lebhaft. Lively.

Ledger lines, lèger lines. Short lines added above and below the staff for pitches beyond the staff.

Legato. The Italian term for connecting pitches in both singing and playing music.

Leggiero. Italian term for lightly.

Lento. Slow tempo.

Libretto. The text of an opera or oratorio.

Lied. Pl., **lieder**. A song in the German language.

Linear. A term describing the horizontal, melodic aspect of music.

Lyricist. The writer of the words of a song.

Macro beat. In the Gordon counting system, the term given to the main beats and is named du.

Madrigal. Originating in Italy in the 14th century this vocal form reached its highest point of development in England in the Renaissance.

Maestoso. Majestically.

Maestro. A title given to show esteem for distinguished musicians, especially conductors.

Major. A term for scales, intervals, triads, and chords. The pattern for the major scale is two whole steps, one half step, three whole steps, one half step. Major intervals include seconds, thirds, sixths, and sevenths. A major triad is made up of a major third and a minor third. A major seventh chord includes a major third, a minor third, and a major third.

Marcato. Heavily accented.

Mass. A musical setting of the most solemn service of the Roman Catholic Church.

Measure. The group of beats between the bar lines on the staff.

Medieval period, Middle Ages. The period preceding the Renaissance, c.500–1450, including the music of the early Christian church.

Melisma, melismatic. A melodic passage, originating in Gregorian chant, in which one syllable is sung on several pitches. It contrasts with neumatic and syllabic.

Melodic minor. A minor scale seldom occurring in vocal music. Ascending, it is a major scale with a flatted third degree; descending, the flatted sixth and seventh degrees are added.

Melody. Representing the horizontal, linear aspect of music, a melody is an organized succession of musical pitches.

Meno. Less. Usually used with another term, as *meno mosso*, less motion.

Meter signature. The numbers placed at the beginning of a composition, immediately following the key signature. The upper number indicates the number of beats in a measure. The lower number tells what kind of a note will receive one beat.

Metrical. A term describing music which has a meter signature.

Metronome. Invented by Maelzel in 1816, an instrument used to indicate the tempo of a composition. When used, it appears at the beginning of the music, as M.M. ♩ = 80.

Mezzo. Meaning medium, the term is used with other terms, such as *mezzo forte*, medium loud; *mezzo piano*, medium soft.

Mezzo voce. In a half voice.

MI. The Italian solfège name of the third degree of the major scale.

Micro beat. In the Gordon counting system, the term given to the subdivisions of the beats.

Microtone. An interval of less than a half step.

Middle Ages. Synonymous with Medieval.

Minimalism. A term for a type of music created in New York and San Francisco from the early 1960s. It is associated with other art forms such as dance, theater, jazz, and minimalist art. It is based on an interest in the physical properties of sound and in the music of Africa and Asia.

Minor. A term for scales, intervals, and chords. The three kinds of minor scales are natural, harmonic, and melodic. Melodic is seldom used in choral music. The pattern for the natural minor scale is whole step, half, two whole, half, two whole steps. The pattern for the harmonic minor scale is whole step, half, two whole, half, one and one-half, and half step. Each minor scale is begun on the sixth degree, la, of a major scale. The two scales are called relative keys and have the same key signature. Minor intervals include seconds, thirds, sixths, and sevenths. A minor triad is composed of a minor third and a major third.

Minstrel show. A type of theatrical entertainment popular in the nineteenth and early twentieth centuries. It included songs, dances, and speech. At first it was performed by white actors impersonating blacks, later by black performers. By 1890 several black minstrel troupes had become very successful.

Minuet. A French country dance which originated at the court of Louis XIV about 1650. It was a popular dance in the early days of America.

Mixed meter. A term which describes the use of two or more meters in a composition. Synonymous with changing meter, shifting meter, multimeter.

Mixed voices. A combination of female and changed male voices.

Mode. A scalewise arrangement of pitches. The term usually refers to the Medieval type of scale which preceded the development of major/minor tonality.

Moderato. A tempo indication for a moderate speed.

Modulation. The process of moving from one key to another within a composition.

Molto. Very. Used with other terms, such as *molto rit*.

Monophony, monophonic. The texture of music which consists of a single unaccompanied melody.

Morendo. An Italian term indicating decreasing in volume, fading away.

Mosso. Moving tempo. *Meno mosso*, slower. *Più mosso*, faster.

Motet. The most important form of early polyphonic music, especially in the Medieval and Renaissance periods. Following many changes in its development, it is generally known as an unaccompanied sacred choral composition (there are also secular motets).

Motive, motif. A short melodic or rhythmic pattern which often recurs so as to serve as a unifying element in a composition.

Moto. Motion. It is often used with *con*. *Con moto*, with motion.

Movable DO. The system of solmization in which DO changes in each key, or scale. Ex: in the key of D major, DO is d; in B♭ major, DO is B♭; in the key of e minor, DO is g; in the key of d minor, DO is f.

Multimeter. The term which describes the use of two or more meters in a composition. Synonymous with changing meter, mixed meter, shifting meter.

Musical. A 20th century Broadway show type of light operetta which includes spoken dialogue, solo and chorus singing, and dancing.

Music drama. A name for Wagnerian type of opera.

Nationalism. Musically, a movement begun in the last part of the nineteenth century, which emphasizes national and ethnic traits. Music which represents this movement draws upon folk tunes and dances of the composer's native country.

Natural. ♮ A musical symbol which cancels a previous flat or sharp.

Natural minor scale. Like the harmonic minor, the natural minor scale is derived from its relative major. It begins on the sixth degree of its relative major scale and includes the identical pitches of that scale. The pattern of the natural minor scale is one whole step, one half step, two whole, one half, two whole steps.

Neumatic. A term which describes the style of Gregorian chant in which there is frequent use of groups of two to four notes on one syllable.

Neumes. Medieval notational signs used for writing the Gregorian chant of the Roman Catholic Church.

Nonharmonic tones. A term describing tones outside the structure of the chord which serve as melodic ornaments. Two of those most frequently occurring are the passing tone and the appoggiatura.

Non troppo. A term, meaning not too much, frequently used with other terms, such as *non troppo lento*, not too slow.

Notation. A system for writing music; it is designed to indicate pitch and duration.

Note. A musical symbol which, when placed on a staff with a clef, indicates pitch. With the addition of a meter signature it also indicates duration.

Nuance. Subtle variances in the elements of expressiveness such as phrasing, tempo, and dynamics, which refine a musical performance.

Obbligato. An added melodic line for either an instrument or one or a few solo voices.

Octave. The interval from a given pitch to the eighth tone above or below it.

Opera. A drama in which the dialogue is sung, rather than spoken, by soloists and choruses, with orchestral accompaniment.

Operetta. Light opera. It has both sung and spoken dialogue, solo voices, chorus, and dancers, with orchestral accompaniment.

Opus, Op.. The term, meaning work, shows the chronological order of a composer's musical works.

Oratorio. A large sacred musical work for solo voices, chorus, and orchestra. Unlike opera, the oratorio has no dramatic action; rather, it is performed in concert style.

Orchestrator. A person who arranges a composition as an orchestral piece, as in the *orchestration* of a piano piece.

Ordinary. In the Roman Catholic church, the part of the Mass which is included regardless of the day. The sections are Kyrie, Gloria, Credo, Sanctus, and Agnus Dei.

Organum. The name for the earliest polyphonic music—9th century. The first examples, based on plainsong melodies, were for two voices moving in parallel fourths and fifths. Later, more voice parts were added.

Ostinato. A repeated melodic or rhythmic pattern, often occurring in the bass part.

Palate. The roof of the mouth, the forward part called the hard palate, the back part called the soft palate, or velum.

Parallel motion. When two or more voice parts, at the same interval from each other, move in the same direction they are in parallel motion.

Parlando. A combination of speaking with singing, like "spoken music." It is most frequently used in fast tempo songs such as the patter song.

Passing tones. Rhythmically weak notes which move between chords to which they do not belong harmonically.

Passion. A musical setting of the Biblical text of the Passion. Like the oratorio, it usually includes choruses, solos—recitative and aria, and orchestra or organ.

Patschen. A thigh slap.

Patter song. A humorous song, in which many words are sung as rapidly as possible. The parlando style is often utilized.

Perfect. A term used for both intervals and cadences. Corresponding to major seconds, thirds, sixths, and sevenths, it is the name for fourth, fifth, and octave intervals. It is also used to label the cadence which includes the chordal progression dominant to tonic.

Phonation. A term which deals with the making of a voiced sound. In singing, it relates to the shaping of the vowel which is the basis of each word in a text.

Phrase. Somewhat comparable to a line or sentence in poetry and prose, a phrase is a division of a musical line. In choral music the length of the phrase depends upon the text and its punctuation.

Pianissimo, *pp*. Very soft.

Piano, *p*. Soft.

Picardy third. A compositional technique which originated in about 1500 and was widely used in the Baroque period. It consists of ending a minor key composition on a major triad, made by raising the third in that final chord.

Pitch. The highness or lowness of a tone. Its exact determination is made by frequency, the number of vibrations per second, of the sound.

Più. Italian term for more. Used with other terms, such as *più allegro*, more quickly.

Plagal cadence. Often called the "amen" cadence, it

is the chordal progression of sub-dominant to tonic.

Plainsong, plainchant. It is generally considered synonymous with Gregorian chant. However, it may also be used for the music of other liturgies—both Western and Eastern. It is characterized by the monophonic, unmetered, conjunct melodic line.

Poco. An Italian term for little. It is used with other terms such as *poco rall.*, a little slower.

Polychoral. A term used for a choral composition in which the chorus is divided into two or three groups which sing alternately together.

Polyphony, polyphonic. Music which includes two or more independent parts or voices.

Polyrhythm. The simultaneous use of two or more contrasting rhythms.

Polytonality. The simultaneous use of several tonalities.

Prestissimo. As quickly as possible.

Presto. Very quickly.

Proper. The part of the Mass in which the texts are varied to fit the special services of the Roman Catholic Church.

Pulse. The inner feeling for the beat of the music.

Quartal harmony. A 20th century compositional technique in which chords are based on intervals of fourths.

Quasi. Almost. Used with other terms such as *quasi recit.*, somewhat like a recitative.

Rallentando, rall. Gradually slower. Synonym for *ritardando.*.

Range. The full gamut of pitches, from the lowest to the highest, which a singer can perform.

RE. The Italian solfège name of the second degree of the major scale.

Recitative. A declamatory style of singing, characterized by freedom of rhythm and clarity of text. In oratorio and opera the recitative, often short, is usually followed by the longer aria.

Refrain. A relatively short section which is sung at the end of each stanza of a song.

Relative major and **minor**. The major and minor scales which have identical key signatures, such as C major and a minor; B♭ major and g minor.

Renaissance. The period between the Middle Ages and the Baroque period. There is a general lack of agreement on the dates of the Renaissance, especially as to the beginning. It is variously noted as c. 1400–1600, c. 1450–1600, etc. (The Harvard Dictionary of Music, second edition, suggests c. 1430–1650.)

Repeat. Several musical signs are used to indicate repeats.

:‖	Repeat from the beginning.
D.C.	Repeat from the beginning.
‖:: ‖	Repeat a section of the piece.
D. S.	Repeat from the sign 𝄋 .

Requiem Mass. A musical setting of the Mass for the Dead.

Responsorial singing. In Gregorian chant, the singing of the soloist, the cantor, in alternation with the choir.

Retrograde. A compositional technique in which a melodic line is performed in reverse.

Rhythm. The musical element associated with movement in time, the organization of sound in time.

Ritardando, rit. Gradually slower. Synonymous with *rallentando*.

Ritenuto. Immediately slower tempo.

Ritmico. Rhythmically.

Rock music. The dominant American popular music from about 1955, when it started as rock-and-roll, to the present. Its characteristics include amplified electric instruments, especially guitars and keyboard instruments, and strong rhythmic beat.

Romanticism. The Romantic movement, c. 1825–1900, or 1910, began in literature and spread to art and music.

Rondo. A musical form in which the first section, A, recurs after each of several contrasting sections, ABACA.

Root. The note upon which a triad or a chord is constructed.

Root position. The arrangement of a triad or chord in which the root is in the lowest voice, the third and fifth (seventh, also) are above the root.

Rote. The process of learning a song by ear—as opposed to reading the rhythm and pitch notation.

Round. Like the canon, a song in which two or more parts sing the same melody, starting at different points, often two measures apart.

Rubato. The term associated with flexibility of tempo, an important factor in achieving expressiveness. It was widely used in 19th century music.

Ruhig. Quietly.

Sacred music. Music composed especially for church services; it uses a religious text. Opposed to secular.

Scale. A succession of ascending and descending tones. The scales upon which Western music is based are the major and minor, the diatonic scales. Many other scales are used in non-Western music.

Schnell. German word for fast.

Second. The second degree of the scale. Also, an interval of a second, major, minor or augmented.

Second ending. A measure or measures which follow successive stanzas which may follow the first stanza. It may also follow the repeat of a section. It may be indicated thus: |2.

Section. A division of a composition.

Secular. A term for non-sacred music.

Semitone. A half step—the smallest interval on the keyboard.

Sempre. Always. It is used with other terms, such as *sempre legato*.

Sequence. A compositional technique in which a melodic pattern is repeated on another pitch, usually a second above or below the original tones.

Serial music. Twentieth century compositions based on the twelve tones of the chromatic scale arranged in non-traditional order. Music which has no tonal center.

Seventh. The seventh degree of the scale, ti. An interval of a seventh, which may be major, minor, augmented, or diminished. Also, a seventh chord, which contains a root, third, fifth, and seventh, such as c-e-g-b.

Sforzando, sforzato, *sf, sfz*. A sudden, forced accent on a note or a chord.

Sharp. ♯ A musical symbol which raises a pitch one-half step.

Shifting meter. A term which describes the use of two or more meters in a composition. Synonymous with changing meter, mixed meter, and multimeter.

Simile. A term which indicates continuing in the same manner.

Singspiel. In about 1700, the German term for serious and comic opera. By 1750, the term was applied to comic opera with spoken dialogue.

Six-four chord. The second inversion of a triad, with the fifth in the lowest voice and the root and third above it.

Sixth. The sixth degree of the major scale, LA. An interval of a sixth—major, minor, augmented, diminished. Also, a sixth chord, the first inversion of a triad, with the third in the lowest voice and the root and fifth above it.

Slur. A curved line above or below two or more notes of different pitch to indicate that they are performed legato.

SO. The Italian solfège name of the fifth degree of the major scale.

Solfège, solfeggio. Vocal exercises sung on the solmization syllables, DO, RE, MI, FA, SO, LA, TI, for music reading.

Solmization. A general term for the designation of syllables DO, RE, MI, FA, SO, LA, TI, for music reading.

Sonata. The general use of the word is a composition for solo instrument, in three or four sections called movements, and based on sonata form. (The term has been applied to various types of keyboard compositions through various periods of music history.).

Sonata form. The organization of musical material: (introduction), exposition, development, recapitulation. This form is used in many instrumental works, including sonata, symphony, string quartet, etc.

Song. The oldest musical form, a short composition for a voice or voices, accompanied or unaccompanied.

Song cycle. A group of related songs which form a musical entity.

Soprano. The highest female voice. Types of sopranos include: mezzo, lyric, dramatic, and coloratura.

Sostenuto. An Italian term for sustaining the tone which, in turn, causes a slight slowing of tempo.

Sotto voce. An Italian term for "under the voice"; in a very quiet whisper-like voice.

Sprechstimme. A 20th century compositional technique; speech-song.

Spirito, spiritoso. Spirited.

Spiritual. Folk songs, often sacred in character, of the American Negro.

Soul music. A type of popular music created, performed, and recorded chiefly by black American musicians from the early 1960s. Important characteristics are its portrayal of the performer's deepest emotions and the stylistic vocal devices, such as sighs, falsetto, chanting, used by the performer.

Staccato. Short, detached tones. It is usually indicated by *stacc.* or a dot over or under a note. The opposite of *legato*.

Staff. Pl., **staves**. The most commonly used staff has five horizontal lines, with four spaces, upon which clefs, notes, and other musical symbols are placed.

Stem. The vertical line attached to the note head. Ex: ♩ ♪ .

Step-wise. A term which describes a melodic progression of pitches ascending or descending with no skips. Ex.: C D E D C.

String quartet. A chamber music group made up of two violins, a viola, and a cello.

Strophic. The term which describes a song in which all stanzas of a song are sung to the same music, contrasted with through-composed.

Subdominant. The chord built on the fourth degree of the major or minor scale, labelled **IV** in major keys and **iv** in minor keys.

Subito. Suddenly.

Submediant. The chord built on the sixth degree of the major or minor scale, labelled **vi** in the major keys and **VI** in the minor keys.

Supertonic. The chord built on the second degree of the major or minor scale, labelled **ii** in major keys and **ii**° in minor keys.

Suspension. A nonharmonic tone used to delay the resolution of a chord, usually occurring in a cadence.

Syllabic. The term which describes the style of Gregorian chant in which each syllable is sung on one note (pitch).

Symphony. An orchestral composition in four movements, the first and fourth movements usually organized in sonata form.

Syncopation. Generally, any change in the normal pulse of meter, accent, and rhythm. A shift of accent to normally weak beats.

Synthesizer. Twentieth century electronic instrument used by musicians to perform traditional music and to create original compositions.

Technique. A procedure or method for developing skill (musically, in performance).

Tempo. The speed of a composition.

Tempo primo. A term indicating a return to the original tempo.

Tenor. In 13th and 14th century polyphony, the vocal part which sang the cantus firmus. It is generally known as the highest natural male voice.

Tenuto, ten. Held longer than the indicated duration.

Ternary form. A three part form in which the second section includes contrasting musical material. The return of the first section, A, may be exactly like the first section or slightly modified. Known as ABA.

Terraced dynamics. The Baroque period practice of using sudden contrasting dynamic levels rather than gradual changes in dynamics as practiced with crescendo and diminuendo.

Tertian harmony. A term for chords formed by intervals of thirds, as opposed to quartal harmony.

Tessitura. The general pitch range of a vocal part, excluding a few very high or low pitches which may occur.

Text painting. A style of writing in which the music perfectly describes or enhances words in the song text.

Texture. A term which describes the way in which the melodic and harmonic elements are combined. Types of texture commonly used in choral music are monophonic, homophonic, polyphonic, or contrapuntal.

Third. The third degree of the scale. Also, an interval of a third, which may be major, minor, augmented, or diminished.

Through-composed. A term which describes a song which has different music for each stanza. The opposite of strophic.

TI. The Italian solfège name of the seventh degree of the major scale.

Tie. A curved line connecting two or more notes of the same pitch. The first one is played or sung and then held for the duration of the other note or notes.

Timbre. A term which describes the unique quality of a voice or instrument.

Time signature. Synonymous with meter signature.

Tonal center. The home tone or key center. For example, in the key (or scale) of C major, c is the tonal center.

Tonality. A term which describes the way in which melodic and harmonic elements are organized around a tonal center. In general usage the term is associated with major and minor keys.

Tone cluster, tonal cluster. A group of neighboring pitches played or sung simultaneously.

Tone painting, text painting. A style of writing in which the music describes or enhances the words in the song text.

Tone row. The basis of the 12-tone system of composition originated by Schoenberg in the early twentieth century. An arrangement of the twelve tones of the chromatic scale in which no tone is repeated until the other eleven have been used. See **Serial music.**

Tonic. The first note in a scale, or key. Also, the name given to the chord built on the first degree of the scale.

Tranquillo. Quietly.

Treble. A term used to describe the highest voices in a composition for mixed voices. Also, another name for the G clef.

Triad. A chord of three tones, arranged in thirds.

Trill, *tr*. A type of musical ornamentation performed by the rapid alternation of a given pitch with one a half or whole step above.

Triphthong. Three successive vowels on one syllable.

Triple meter. Meter which uses three beats, or a multiple of three, in a measure.

Triplet. A group of three notes performed in the time of two of the same kind, indicated by a small number 3 above or below the group.

Troppo. An Italian term for too much. Used with other terms, such as *lento non troppo*, not too slow.

Troubadour. 12th and 13th century poet-musician of southern France.

Turn. ∾ A type of musical ornamentation in which a group of four or five notes which turn around a principal note. The exact performance of a turn varies according to the period in which the music was written.

Tutti. A direction for the entire ensemble—instrumental or choral to perform together.

Twelve-tone scale. Originally used by Arnold Schoenberg in the early 20th century, the scale uses the twelve tones of the chromatic scale in a non-traditional arrangement, a row or a series. Lacking a tonal center, the tone row has four forms: original, retrograde, inverted, and in the inversion of the retrograde. Synonymous with serial music.

Unison. The performance of the same pitches by all the players or singers. The pitches may be in the same or different octaves.

Upbeat. One or more notes occurring before the first full measure. They are usually necessitated by the rhythm of the text.

Variation. The restatement of a theme with changes in the melodic, rhythmic, and harmonic elements.

Vaudeville. In the late sixteenth century a French song, often with an amorous text, written in simple chordal style. In the eighteenth century it was the principal song of comic opera. In the nineteenth century the name was applied to short comedies which included popular songs. As used in early twentieth-century America, vaudeville was the name for music entertainments, including songs and skits, which were usually given in theaters, often as a co-feature with the silent movie.

Vernacular. In the native language.

Verse. A line of poetry. Sometimes used to denote a stanza of a poem.

Virginal. A type of harpsichord. The earliest (c. 1511) virginal was shaped like a small oblong box, placed upon a table or in a player's lap. By the end of the sixteenth century it was used to describe all types of harpsichords.

Virtuoso. A musical performer who excels in technical ability.

Vivace, vivo. Lively.

Vocalization. Derived from vocalise, a term describing a melody sung on a vowel or neutral syllable, used for vocal warm-ups as preparation for a choir rehearsal.

Voce. Voice.

Whole step. The interval formed by two half steps.

Whole-tone scale. A scale composed of whole tones, six in an octave